Prosperity Road

The FRED W. MORRISON
Series in Southern Studies

Prosperity Road

The New Deal, Tobacco, and North Carolina

by Anthony J. Badger

The University of North Carolina Press

Chapel Hill

© 1980 The University of North Carolina Press

Manufactured in the United States of America

ISBN 0-8078-1367-2

Library of Congress Catalog Card Number 79-310

Library of Congress Cataloging in Publication Data

Badger, Anthony J.
    Prosperity Road.

    (The Fred W. Morrison series in Southern Studies)

    Bibliography: p.
    Includes index.
    1. Tobacco manufacture and trade—North Carolina—
History.   2. United States—Economic Policy—1933–1945.
3. North Carolina—Economic policy.   I. Title.   II. Series:
Fred W. Morrison series in Southern studies.
HD9137.N8B32   338.1'7'37109756   79-310
ISBN 0-8078-1367-2

*To my Mother and
the memory of my Father*

Contents

Illustrations and Maps

Preface

It is a pleasant duty to acknowledge the financial assistance that has enabled me to undertake the research for this book. My first debt is to the Scholarships Committee of the University of Hull, which not only awarded me a three-year research scholarship but paid the travel expenses for my first trip to the United States in August 1969. That I was able in the next thirteen months to complete so much of my work in the primary sources was entirely due to the kindness of Professor Ralph W. Greenlaw, former chairman of the history department, North Carolina State University at Raleigh. The lucrative but undemanding instructorship which he provided allowed me to spend most of my time on research. Subsequent visits back to the United States have been made possible by generous grants from the American Council of Learned Societies, the Research Committee of the University of Newcastle upon Tyne, and the Margaret Gallagher Fund. Many friends by their hospitality increased in a very real sense the value of these awards. None suffered more from my importunate demands than Burton Elliott, Marilyn Dixon, and Sam and Sherri Wells, and without their generosity this book could not have been finished.

The staffs of libraries and archives in New York, North Carolina, and Washington treated me with unfailing courtesy and efficiency. I am particularly grateful for the help and friendly guidance given me in the early stages of my work by H. G. Jones, then Director of the North Carolina State Department of Archives and History, now curator of the North Carolina Collection, and by his former colleague, Fred Coker, who is now at the Library of Congress. I owe a special debt to the late Margaret Birdsong Price of the North Carolina State Library, who broke up the tedium of microfilm reading by acute and lively reminiscences of North Carolina politics and politicians of the 1930s.

Jonathan Daniels and the late Lindsay Warren kindly gave me permission to consult their papers at the Southern Historical Collection, and Mr. Daniels has confirmed and clarified for me a number of points about his role in the tobacco program. I am indebted to several agricultural officials who talked to me about the farm program of the 1930s and later, particularly James E. Thigpen. At various times I have received valuable assistance from David Brewster of the United States Department of Agriculture, professors Robert F. Hunter and George Tindall, John Cyrus and Tommy Bunn of the North Carolina Department of Agriculture, Jan Morris, and Alger Hiss. Joseph F. Steelman of East Carolina University, James Patterson of Brown University, and my colleagues John Cannon and Bill Speck read the entire manuscript with critical care and made many helpful suggestions. Jocelyn Palmer and Sheila Speck typed various drafts with exemplary patience, and the staff of the University of North Carolina Press, particularly Malcolm Call, have been models of tact and cooperation. To all these people I am extremely grateful.

My greatest academic debt remains, however, to my former supervisor, Philip Taylor of the University of Hull, who has consistently asked the right questions about this project and been immensely tolerant of my repeated inability to answer them. It is because of his and my other friends' enthusiasm and encouragement that this book has been completed. It is despite their efforts that so many errors remain. The responsibility for these is mine alone.

My father was tragically killed as this book was being prepared for the press. Only I know the full extent of my debt to him, to my mother, and to Ruth.

Introduction

In recent years the picture painted by historians of the New Deal has markedly altered. Attention has shifted away from Franklin D. Roosevelt and his advisers to particular New Deal agencies and away from Washington to state and local levels. In the process there has been an increasing emphasis on the essentially limited nature of the changes wrought by the New Deal. This book attempts to assess the impact of the New Deal in a particular locality, to study an individual New Deal program in operation from 1933 to 1940, and, in doing so, to examine the nature of the New Deal's limitations.

The New Deal could scarcely fail to have an impact on North Carolina. The federal government provided relief for the state's unemployed and gave jobs to over two hundred thousand people. It instituted a system of social security. It told tobacco growers what they could and could not grow and regulated the wages of textile workers. The results of its public works program can still be seen in almost every community in the state. Whether it was building a scenic highway through the Blue Ridge Mountains, establishing a self-help fishing cooperative, or setting up a symphony orchestra, the New Deal brought the federal government into new areas of North Carolina life. For many in the state, the federal government became for the first time an institution that was directly experienced.

At the same time, however, the New Deal always had to adapt to local conditions. Despite charges by conservatives that the New Deal meant regimentation and dictatorship, the New Deal rarely imposed its policies directly on the country. Policies were not dictated in Washington and then implemented by an army of federal officials loyal only to their New Deal employers. On the contrary, the New Deal depended to a large extent on decisions taken at the local level. Some programs like relief and social security were run by state government agencies. Some, like public works, rural electrification, and public housing, often depended on local communities to initiate and sponsor projects. Others, like the program for agricultural recovery, were administered by the participants themselves. All relied on administrators who might defer more to local sentiment than to directives from Washington. To what extent therefore was the New Deal able to impose its will from above, to break free from these local shackles and change the existing local conditions? To what extent, on the other hand, did these local constraints bind the New Deal and alter the policy and operation of programs as they had been conceived in Washington?

In answering these questions in North Carolina an assessment of the tobacco program of the Agricultural Adjustment Administration is crucial. Tobacco was central to the economy of the state. It was the most valuable crop in a predominantly rural state, and the manufacture of cigarettes was the state's most lucrative industry. No single New Deal activity had more significance for the state than the efforts to revive the fortunes of the tobacco farmers. Despite a growing literature on the New Deal and North Carolina, there has not been any full-scale attempt to study this particular aspect.[1]

Because North Carolina was the leading producer of cigarette tobacco in the nation, it is also possible to ask wider questions about the making and implementation of agricultural policy. The state produced 70 percent of the country's flue-cured tobacco crop and therefore offers a unique opportunity to study a New Deal program in operation at the local level and at the same time to study a national program almost in its entirety. There have not yet been any studies of a single commodity program in operation from 1933 to 1940. This reflects a certain imbalance in the historiography of the New Deal and agriculture. The paramount aim of New Deal agricultural policy was to secure agricultural recovery. Other aims of reforming agriculture by planning and regional adjustment and of securing social justice by eliminating hard-core poverty within agriculture were long-term and secondary. Yet the bulk of recent writing has concentrated on the efforts to implement these latter aims and has tended to ignore the primary aim of the New Deal—to raise farm incomes. Thus, there is no study of the Agricultural Adjustment Administration as a recovery agency after 1933 and no study of the farm legislation of 1936 and 1938, which provided the statutory base for the postwar American farm program. This historiographical trend is exemplified by the treatment of southern sharecroppers. They may have been the ''Forgotten Farmers'' of the New Deal, but any neglect by contemporaries has been amply offset by the attention of historians. Yet the cotton program of the Agricultural Adjustment Administration, which contributed to the sharecroppers' plight, but was also a major effort to raise the income of two million farmers in the South, still awaits its historian. This book on the tobacco program is an effort in part to redress that balance.[2]

The mechanics of such a program are worth studying in their own right. Crop control involved unprecedented and detailed government intervention in the daily lives of thousands of individual farmers. Could production control actually be put into practice, and would it work? What was the growers' response, the effect on their income, and the impact on other interests, like the auction warehousemen and the manufacturers?

There is also a wider interest in looking at the interaction of local and national pressures. The Agricultural Adjustment Administration proudly proclaimed that it practiced economic democracy. Policy was formulated only after elaborate consultation with the growers' representatives. Policy decisions were then usually sanctioned by the growers in referenda. The program was administered at the local level by committees made up of the growers themselves. How democratic were these procedures in reality, and what were their consequences? Was policy made by the farmers themselves, or was it dictated by Agricultural Adjustment Administration officials in Washington? What was the effect of such a policy-making procedure on interests that were not represented, like the consumers, and on the less powerful members of the rural community, like the sharecroppers and small farmers?

The inadequacies of the New Deal's efforts to help the rural poor have naturally contributed to the increasing emphasis that historians have placed on the New Deal's limitations. Agreement on the extent of these limitations has not, however, been accompanied by agreement on the reasons for the New Deal's shortcomings. Some have stressed the ideological conservatism of the New Deal itself. Others have stressed the conservative political, intellectual, and constitutional environment in which the New Deal had to operate. This book attempts to delineate the limitations of the tobacco program and tries to assess the options available to the policy makers in the 1930s. Were the New Dealers limited by forces beyond their control or were the constraints on them self-imposed?

Prosperity Road

Chapter 1

The Problems of Cigarette Tobacco

" 'Backer all the time,
pretty near all the year round"

By the 1930s, bright flue-cured tobacco was the most important type of tobacco in the United States. Used on its own in Britain, or blended with other types of leaf in the United States, its distinctive taste had made it an essential ingredient of cigarettes, for which demand had increased dramatically in the years after World War I. By 1929 bright flue-cured tobacco accounted for over half the nation's tobacco acreage.[1]

It had first been grown in the Piedmont areas of Virginia and North Carolina, where the poor soil starved the leaf and gave it its characteristic yellow color. In the 1890s production spread to the coastal plain of eastern North Carolina and South Carolina, and then in the 1920s to Georgia and Florida. The center of flue-cured production was, however, firmly established by the 1930s in North Carolina, which was the largest producer of any type of tobacco and produced almost 70 percent of the flue-cured crop. The eastern counties of the state were the heart of the tobacco region. This "New Belt," centered on a triangle of market towns—Wilson, Kinston, and Greenville—alone grew 40 percent of the crop.[2]

If North Carolina was crucial to American tobacco production, tobacco in turn underpinned the farm structure of the state. Four out of ten workers in North Carolina were still on the farm in 1930, and flue-cured tobacco was the most valuable crop. It was true that more farms grew cotton—tobacco was grown on little more than a third of the state's 280,000 farms—but by 1932 cotton was neither as valuable as tobacco nor of comparable national importance. The state cultivated less than 4 percent of the nation's cotton acreage, and it was falling steadily behind states like Texas and Oklahoma, whose large-scale farms could take advantage of mechanization. The two staple cash crops between them nevertheless brought in 56 percent of North Carolina's farm income in 1932.[3]

Few crops required as much labor to produce as these two, but even cotton did not demand the time and effort that was devoted to tobacco. "By God," complained sharecropper Clint Shaw in Guy Owen's novel *Journey for Joedel*, "it takes thirteen months to the year to raise that infernal crop." From the time the seed bed was prepared to the time the crop was marketed, tobacco needed constant attention. The work was both hard and skilled. Almost every task had to be carried out by hand, and at every stage decisions had to be made that might drastically affect the quality of the leaf. Such decisions had financial implications at market time, since good-quality leaf might fetch ten times the price of poor-quality tobacco.[4]

As early as December, the farmer's first task was to prepare and plant a seed bed. He had to choose the right site, since the tobacco had no reserve food and had to supply itself immediately from the soil. He sowed the seeds only after burning the prospective bed in order to sterilize it and prevent the growth of weeds. Then the bed was covered with a cloth to protect the seeds from insects and the cold. In the spring, eight to twelve weeks later, the tobacco could be transplanted. In South Carolina this could be as early as 1 April; further north, in the western part of the Virginia–North Carolina Old Belt, this might be as late as 15 June.

Conventional wisdom suggested that half the battle to produce a good-quality leaf lay in the preparation of the soil before transplanting. In the previous fall the farmer had to cut the stalks of his past crop and plow the fields in order to give all forms of vegetation a chance to decay and to freeze off harmful disease organisms during the winter. Four or six weeks before he actually transplanted his tobacco, the grower had to plow the soil again and apply as much as two thousand pounds of fertilizer per acre. The fields were laid out in a series of ridges about three and a half feet apart, so that a sled could travel between the rows at harvesting. The farmer finally set out the plants two feet apart on each ridge. The space between plants and between ridges allowed adequate sunlight, drainage, and soil aeration. Later research and the stimulus of acreage reduction moved the plants closer together and produced a thinner-textured leaf.

Ten days after transplanting, the farmer loosened the soil around the plants with a hoe and did the first weeding. Until the crop was ready to be laid by, eight or nine weeks after transplanting, he might have to weed as many as six times. When the flower cluster began to appear the farmer had to top the plant, breaking off the terminal bud so that the plant could mature and ripen more uniformly. Skilled topping needed experience. If it was too low the plant produced fewer leaves, and these were coarse and rough. If it was too high the leaves were small and immature.

Once the terminal bud had been removed, suckers began to sprout in the axils of the leaves, sapping their nourishment. If these were not removed before they grew five inches long, the crop would lose weight and quality. Each had to be removed by hand. Since the suckers reappeared at once, the grower had to cover the crop five or six times at intervals of a week to cut them off. At the same time the farmer had to watch out for, and destroy, the hornworms, which could devour the best leaves despite his closest attention. At any time the crop could also be damaged by the weather. Storms, especially late hailstorms, easily bruised or broke the leaves, while too much rain could prevent the leaves' ripening. Clint Shaw's crop was flattened by hailstones "the size of bantam eggs" that struck the earth "with such force they bounced a foot off the ground." Tobacco was also susceptible to disease. In the 1930s little could be done to combat such diseases as black shank, blue mold, and Granville wilt.[5]

The farmer then had to harvest and cure his tobacco—lengthy tasks which in the 1930s took up 40 percent of his time. Harvesting might start at any time from the end of June, depending on the weather and how far south the farm was situated. Once again it was precise work. Although an acre produced between one hundred and one hundred and fifty thousand leaves, each leaf had to be harvested individually. It was cut off as it ripened and handed to a stringer, who would tie two or three leaves into a hand and then loop the hands on sticks ready to be hung in the curing barn. Harvesting took from five to eight weeks.[6]

Topping tobacco

(From Howard W. Odum, Subregional Photographic Study 3167-B, photograph no. 140, Southern Historical Collection, The University of North Carolina at Chapel Hill)

Tobacco ready for curing

(From Howard W. Odum, Subregional Photographic Study 3167-B, photograph no. 160, Southern Historical Collection, The University of North Carolina at Chapel Hill)

After harvesting, the tobacco had to be cured to starve the leaf of any surplus food and then to dry it out. Most tobacco in the world was air-cured by simply hanging out the leaves to dry naturally. Some was fire-cured. There, the smoke from the fire came into direct contact with the leaf. The flue-curing of tobacco avoided this by forcing hot air from a furnace into the curing barn through pipes or flues. An average barn held between sixty and eighty thousand leaves, still containing probably seven thousand pounds of water, and needing three or four days to cure. First, a moderate heat yellowed the leaf. Then the temperature was slowly raised to fix the color and finally dry the leaf out. The curing had to be supervised all the time. If the temperature was raised or the humidity lowered too quickly, the leaf could scald or sponge and be discolored. It was part of the annual ritual of the tobacco belt for growers to invite their friends around to stay up overnight with them—"watching the tobacco"—to control the temperature and to make sure the barn did not catch fire. When the tobacco had dried out, the barn was cooled and the doors opened to allow some moisture back into the leaf so that it could be handled without breaking.

Even after curing, the farmer still faced a considerable amount of work before the tobacco was ready for market. He had to sort the tobacco into approximate grades according to the position of the leaf on the stalk, its quality, color, and texture. Each leaf had to be examined individually and then tied into hands with six or seven leaves of similar quality, except on the Georgia-Florida belt, where the growers left their leaves loose. These were gathered into lots to be taken to the market. If the grower sorted his tobacco poorly he was unlikely to receive the price he deserved for his best tobacco. He would also be at the mercy of speculators or pinhookers who, spotting a poorly graded lot, would buy it, re-sort it, and resell it at a profit. Even determining the size of the lot was important. If the lot was too large the buyer might suspect that poorer-quality tobacco was being hidden. If it was too small the baskets took up more space on the warehouse floor and increased the grower's handling costs. All this sorting took over a quarter of the man-hours producing tobacco.

The transplanting, weeding, topping, suckering, worming, and harvesting had all to be done by hand. There were some minor mechanical advances during and immediately after the 1930s: transplanters became more common, seed beds were sometimes steamed

Tobacco in the curing barn

(From Howard W. Odum, Subregional Photographic Study 3167-B, photograph no. 184, Southern Historical Collection, The University of North Carolina at Chapel Hill)

Sorting tobacco for market
(From Howard W. Odum, Subregional Photographic Study 3167-B, photograph no. 167, Southern Historical Collection, The University of North Carolina at Chapel Hill)

rather than burnt, and curing barns became more sophisticated, usually with oil-burning furnaces; but by and large the production of flue-cured tobacco has remained unmechanized almost to the present day. It is only in the 1970s that a tobacco harvester has been developed and put into limited commercial use. It is estimated that it reduces the need for harvest labor by 85 percent, and in 1978 the harvesters could not be manufactured fast enough to meet demand. The only other major labor-saving device has been the development of bulk-curing, which, rather than hanging the leaves on sticks, packs them on racks and forces the air through them. This is calculated to reduce the labor in curing by half, since it dispenses with the need for handers and stringers. The farmers now also sell tobacco in loose piles on the floor, claiming that too much labor was involved in sorting the leaves. As a result, the preparation of tobacco for market now takes a matter of hours on an average farm, rather than a couple of weeks.[7]

These heavy labor requirements and the high investment costs per acre, because of the need for fertilizer and curing barns, dictated the size of land holdings in the tobacco belt. Since the value of the crop per acre was also relatively high, especially compared with cotton, flue-cured tobacco was always cultivated in small land units, often of no more than four or five acres. A survey in 1928 in the New Belt of North Carolina showed an average cultivated acreage on 230 farms of twenty-seven acres, of which seven were planted in tobacco. A survey in Pitt County a year later found acreages of tobacco varying from two to twenty-five acres with slightly less than half of the farms cultivating between four and six acres of tobacco. In the Old and Middle belts of the North Carolina Piedmont such small farms were usually operated by their owners, but in the Eastern Belt tenants usually operated the farms. The customary arrangement in the east was for the sharecropper to receive half the proceeds of the crop when the landlord provided the land, seed, wood, and fertilizer, although sometimes, as in the farms surveyed in 1928, the cropper also shared the cost of the fertilizer. It was estimated in that survey that the average cropper received $313 for his share of the cotton crop and $593 for his share of the tobacco, which left him, after paying his share of the farm expenses, with a cash farm income of $766. Four years later that would probably have fallen to $350—if the cropper was lucky enough still to be on his farm. Even that calculation is probably generous. Other surveys have suggested a net cash income for sharecroppers as low as $134 in 1932.[8]

The first opportunity the farmer had to market his tobacco was at the end of July, on the markets of the Georgia-Florida belt, but only about 8 percent of the flue-cured crop was sold there. The tobacco-selling season really started in earnest with the opening of the Border Belt markets in the second week of August. About 20 percent of the crop was sold on these markets in South Carolina and southeastern North Carolina. The most important markets, however, which accounted for as much as 40 percent of the flue-cured sales, were those of the New or Eastern Belt in eastern North Carolina, which opened in the third or fourth week of August. They were followed in September by the Middle Belt markets in the central part of the state and finally at the end of the month by the Old Belt markets of piedmont North Carolina and Virginia. These last two belts had long since lost their leading position to the New Belt, but they nevertheless marketed 32 percent of the crop between them.[9]

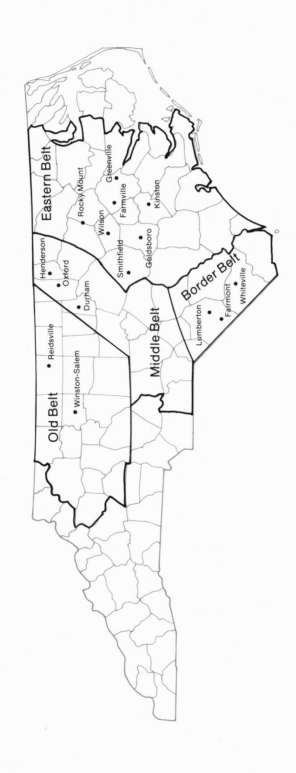

Major flue-cured tobacco belts and market towns in the 1930s

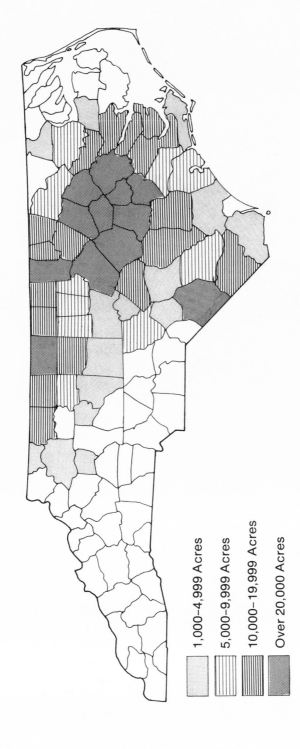

1,000–4,999 Acres

5,000–9,999 Acres

10,000–19,999 Acres

Over 20,000 Acres

Distribution of tobacco acreage in 1929

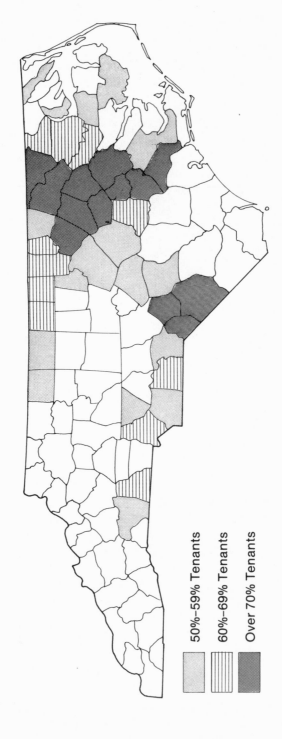

50%–59% Tenants

60%–69% Tenants

Over 70% Tenants

Selling tobacco on the auction warehouse floor

(From Howard W. Odum, Subregional Photographic Study 3167-B, photograph no. 410, Southern Historical Collection, The University of North Carolina at Chapel Hill)

In the market towns tobacco was sold by auction in the warehouses. The warehouseman acted as middleman between the grower and the buyer, receiving from the grower a weighing fee, an auction fee, and a commission on the final selling price. In each town their operations were regulated by a tobacco board of trade, an organization of warehousemen and buyers. In turn these local boards combined to form a national organization, the United States Tobacco Association, whose sales committee set the opening dates for each belt.

Most of the markets were small, handling between one and twenty million pounds of tobacco annually. The large market towns were in North Carolina in the Eastern Belt. There, Wilson and Greenville each handled over seventy million pounds a year and vied with each other for the title of the largest tobacco market in the world. Kinston and Rocky Mount both sold over forty million pounds, as did

Winston-Salem in the Old Belt. No matter what the size of the market, however, the warehousemen were always competing with neighboring markets to attract growers to their particular town. Newspaper advertisements and billboards on the highways all promised the grower more sets of buyers and higher prices if he came to one market rather than another. It was not just the warehousemen whose prosperity depended on the success of these campaigns: the whole business community in each of these eastern Carolina market towns was geared to tobacco production and sales. Banks, retail merchants, and car dealers were all aware that the tobacco farmer received a cash payment just once every year, and the local stores held their annual sales in the three months the markets were open.

Most growers were in debt from January onward and they needed year-long credit, with their crop as their only security. Banks were reluctant to make such short-term credit available to farmers, who had instead to turn to one of the standard institutions of the tobacco belt—the time merchant. He provided the growers with general supplies and fertilizer on credit, charging not only high rates of interest but also credit prices, which were considerably higher than prices for cash payment. This meant that for the growers the cost of short-term credit, which the banks would not provide, was extremely high. An Agricultural Experiment Station survey in North Carolina in 1926 suggested that merchants charged an interest rate of 25 percent per annum, while fertilizer manufacturers charged an even higher rate. About three-quarters of the tenants' annual cash gain had to be used to pay back cash advances from landlords and settle accounts with the time merchants. In the 1930s banks came to play an increasingly important role in rural areas, but it was still a secondary one. As late as 1942, a survey in Pitt showed that federal land banks, production credit associations, and commercial banks were between them responsible for less in crop-lien loans than the time merchants and the fertilizer companies.[10]

At the warehouse the grower found that his tobacco was being examined by buyers from three main groups: the domestic manufacturers, the major export companies, and the independent leaf dealers.

Before 1911 domestic tobacco manufacturing had been dominated by the so-called Tobacco Trust—the American Tobacco Company under James Buchanan Duke. It had been the largest single purchaser of flue-cured tobacco, but in those days cigarettes were a relatively small part of tobacco manufacturing. In 1910, for example, only one-twentieth of the tobacco leaf purchased in the United States was used for cigarettes. After the dissolution of the Tobacco Trust in 1911 the successor companies developed their own standard brands of cigarettes in which they increased the amount of flue-cured tobacco and replaced Turkish leaf with Burley and a small amount of Maryland tobacco. R. J. Reynolds with Camels, American Tobacco with Lucky Strikes, and Liggett and Myers with Chesterfields were therefore ready to cater to the boom in cigarette smoking after World War I. The war had itself made Turkish leaf rare and expensive, virtually forcing changes in consumer preference. The government had helped by buying domestic blended cigarettes for the troops, and small cigarettes were ideally suited to the postwar advent of women smokers. As a result, the production of small cigarettes increased by over 1300 percent between 1910 and 1930. By 1929 cigarettes accounted for 53.6 percent of the value of tobacco products, compared with 16.6 percent fifteen years earlier.

Relying on their standard brands, which they heavily advertised, the Big Three companies dominated the market so that by the early 1930s they were manufacturing over 90 percent of the nation's cigarettes. They had successfully survived two main challenges to their dominance. Lorrilard, which had been handicapped at the dissolution of the trust by being allocated the Turkish brands, was slow to develop a standard brand. When they finally marketed Old Golds in the 1920s they never succeeded in capturing more than 7 percent of the market. They were eventually overtaken by Philip Morris. In the early 1930s the Big Three faced a greater potential threat from small independent companies producing cheap cigarettes. When the Big Three raised their cigarette prices in 1931 the cheaper independents like Brown and Williamson and Axton-Fisher made such inroads into the market that for a time they captured 20 percent of it. In order to fight off this challenge the Big Three had to reduce their own prices at the start of 1933.[11]

The Big Three were important to North Carolina. American Tobacco had plants at Reidsville and Durham, Liggett and Myers at Durham, and R. J. Reynolds at Winston-Salem. Although they employed less than one-tenth of the state's industrial labor force in 1929 they produced over one-third of the value of the state's manufactures. The plants in North Carolina produced almost 57 percent of the value of the nation's cigarette production. Naturally, the Big Three were the largest domestic purchasers of flue-cured leaf, each purchasing over 10 percent of the crop.[12]

About 60 percent of the flue-cured crop, however, was exported. Of this, about half went to the United Kingdom and a quarter to China. There were two main purchasers for these markets: the Export Leaf Company, a subsidiary of the British-American Tobacco Company, and the Imperial Tobacco Company of Great Britain. Both these companies had been founded in the early 1900s as a result of American Tobacco's efforts to fight its way into the British market. Imperial had been founded by British manufacturers to meet that threat and in 1902 had reached an agreement with American whereby the British market was left to Imperial and the United States market was left to American. A new company, British-American, was formed in which both Imperial and American had an interest and which was responsible for the rest of the world. It was this company which had built up the China trade.[13]

A final 10 to 20 percent of the flue-cured crop was purchased by the independent leaf dealers. These dealers did not manufacture cigarettes themselves. Instead they redried and processed the tobacco and resold it. Occasionally the Big Three domestic manufacturers bought leaf from them that had been picked up at the smaller markets where the Big Three had not sent buyers. In the main, however, the dealers sold to those export outlets that had been left untouched by Imperial and British-American. There was some consolidation of these dealers in the 1930s. One company, Universal, gained control of enough companies to become a major leaf buyer in its own right by 1940, when it purchased as much leaf as any of the domestic manufacturers.[14]

"The farmers were starvin' to death"

The nature of the crop, the structure of the manufacturing industry, and the system of marketing meant that before 1933 flue-cured tobacco growers were in a weak marketing position.[15]

Tobacco was a perishable crop that needed redrying and storing within weeks of being cured. Since no individual grower could afford the cost of this redrying, he had to sell his tobacco immediately. He could not hold it off the market if the market was glutted and prices were low. Even a decision to hold off the crop until later in the same marketing season could damage the leaf and lower prices. There was a further stimulus to ignore the market situation and sell at once: tobacco was often the grower's only source of income, and he needed ready cash to pay off the debts incurred during the year.

The prices the buyers paid for the tobacco depended on how they graded it. These grades were secret and varied from company to company, so that the farmer had no means of knowing whether he was receiving a fair price for his tobacco, nor could he concentrate on growing the most profitable grades. Government grading was one solution to this. The Warehouse Act of 1916 authorized the government to provide an inspection service that would grade the farmer's tobacco according to standard grades. It was not until 1929 that such a service was introduced, and then it only covered four markets, one of which—Smithfield—was in North Carolina. In the next three years it was extended to seven more markets in the state, but even then only six million pounds were graded. There was little incentive for the growers to use the service, since they had to pay for it themselves and there was no guarantee that the buyers would take any notice of the government grades.[16]

The buyers' position was strengthened further by the fact that the manufacturers carried stocks-in-hand of two to three years' supply of tobacco, in order to achieve the right blending of grades and the correct aging of the leaf. If in any year the crop was short, pushing prices up, the manufacturers did not have to buy at that higher price. They could afford to wait. The grower could not.

The growers' lack of knowledge and their inability to hold their crops off the markets were compounded by the absence of competition among the buyers. Many in the tobacco belts would have echoed the complaint of Richard Russell, governor of Georgia, that the price paid for tobacco in his state in 1932 forced him to conclude that the manufacturers of tobacco ''have as complete a monopoly and combine as this Nation has ever seen.'' Josephus Daniels, whose hostility to the manufacturers dated back to the days of Duke and the Tobacco Trust, was equally emphatic the following year, in explaining the situation to the Secretary of Agriculture. The tobacco industry, he said, which had once been a monopoly, was still dominated by three American and two foreign companies. ''Of course, they do not meet and fix the prices. That would invite prosecution. But there has been no real competition for many years. They have been paying the farmers just enough to encourage them to grow the weed.''[17]

These were familiar charges. Economists, however, have failed to prove or disprove the accusations of a price-fixing monopoly, even when they have been able to use the evidence assembled in the antitrust action brought against the domestic companies in 1940. What their studies have shown is that it made little difference to the prices the growers received whether there was a price-fixing arrangement or not. Prices under the conditions of monopoly would have differed little from prices in a freely competitive situation. The existence of a monopoly would have made little difference to what was already a fundamentally weak marketing position for the growers.[18]

It is unlikely, as Daniels admitted, that there was outright collusion among the Big Three, but there was little in their buying policies that seemed likely to lead to higher prices to the growers. What seemed to determine their prices were, first, the need to pay enough to ensure that the farmers produced tobacco again the following year; second, a determination to see that the other manufacturers were not buying their tobacco more cheaply; and third, a concern to see that no manufacturer was attempting to buy more leaf than he needed for his share of the cigarette market. Since the Big Three had no intention of competing in the pricing of cigarettes, it was unlikely that any of them would make an aggressive attempt to capture a larger share of the leaf market.

It might have been expected that the independent dealers and the export companies might upset this arrangement by competing with the domestic manufacturers in leaf buying, but they tended to buy different grades from the ones that attracted the domestic companies. Imperial bought higher-priced, higher-quality leaf, and Export bought lower-grade tobacco for the China trade. Most independent dealers were assumed to take the low-priced, low-grade leaf that nobody else wanted.

Given the structure of the manufacturing industry, therefore, the growers could not look to competition between buyers of their leaf for their salvation from a weak marketing position. The marketing of tobacco by the auction warehouse system also handicapped them. It did have some advantages: it provided a rapid method of sales that gave the growers cash payments immediately, but it also was expensive, duplicated buyers, and was open to abuse. There was no doubt, for example, that the speed of selling led to many mistakes by the buyers. The buyers could average these mistakes out during the day, but for the grower, whose entire year's income might be dependent on the price he received, one such mistake could be disastrous. The grower could reject a bid, turn his tag, and offer his tobacco again, but he had to pay another auction fee with no guarantee of securing a better price.[19]

All these weaknesses—the perishability of the crop, the lack of competition in leaf purchases, the secret grades, the companies' carry-over, and the auction warehouse system—contributed to the growers' basic inability to adjust supply to demand. There was always a chronic tendency to overproduce. Good prices always led to increased production the following year. When prices fell, however, there was not necessarily an equivalent cutback in production. Growers tended to respond to a fall in prices with either a slight curtailment of acreage or even an increase of production in an effort to minimize total losses. The situation was aggravated when poor cotton prices tempted growers to turn to tobacco. Occasionally, as in 1920 and 1931, prices went so low that growers could not finance a large crop the following year. There were then drastic reductions, but they were only temporary. Production leapt again the following year.[20]

Because so much of the flue-cured crop was exported, growers were also affected by the difficulties facing American exports after 1929. With the virtual cessation of United States' lending abroad and the existence of high Republican tariffs, it was difficult for foreign nations to buy American goods. Tobacco exports held up better than most. The importance of tobacco as a source of government revenue in Britain, the resistance of consumers to changes in taste or decreases in tobacco use, and the failure of governments to stimulate domestic or colonial tobacco production meant that the United States was still the only source of substantial tobacco exports. Flue-cured exports nevertheless fell by almost 40 percent between 1930 and 1932.[21]

The perennial tendency to overproduce, the decline in foreign markets, and the onset of a general depression had catastrophic consequences for both the tobacco growers and North Carolina between 1929 and 1932. Flue-cured prices, which never fell below 20¢ a pound from 1920 to 1927, dropped to 17.3¢ in 1928, to 12¢ in 1930, and plummeted to 8.4¢ in 1931. There was a slight rise to 11.6¢ in 1932, but this was offset by a sharp reduction in acreage that year. Total receipts for the 1932 crop were one-third of those for 1930. In North Carolina flue-cured growers received only $34.9 million in 1932 compared with $93.4 million in 1928. Growers in the east felt the pinch dramatically. New Belt growers who had collected over $91 million in 1919 and $50 million as recently as 1928 now had to survive on $18.9 million.[22]

Tobacco farmers could not turn to other crops for solace, since the collapse in tobacco prices was paralleled in cotton. North Carolina cotton growers had averaged 17.0¢ a pound from 1925 to 1929, but this had fallen to an appalling 6.0¢ in 1931. The total income from cotton and cottonseed fell from $91.2 million in 1928 to a mere $27 million in 1932. The total value of all North Carolina crops fell from $280.3 million in 1928 to $122.4 million in 1932. As early as January 1930, there were reports of farmers facing starvation. Leading bankers and supply merchants in eastern North Carolina confirmed these reports and, anxious to maintain their customers' purchasing power, attempted to launch local community relief schemes. The collapse in cotton and tobacco was accompanied by heavy unemployment in the state's manufacturing industries, particularly textiles. In November 1930 the state's governor, O. Max Gardner, reported that "the whole structure of industry is in a desperate state and agriculture is beyond description." By February 1933 an estimated 25 percent of the state's population was on relief.[23]

One immediate consequence of the crisis, particularly the plunge in farm income, was the pressure on landowners who were unable to pay their property taxes or keep up their mortgage repayments. By the end of 1930 $7.5 million were owed in delinquent property taxes, and over 150,000 pieces of property were on sale for nonpayment of taxes. Nash County in the tobacco belt with 5,280 farms had 3,500 foreclosures in that year alone. One result of this was intense pressure from the rural east in the 1931 General Assembly for lower property taxes. This pressure proved irresistible, although there were bitter sectional quarrels over the alternative sources of revenue.[24]

Worse was to follow with the collapse of credit facilities in the rural areas. In 1930 a record total of ninety-three banks over the whole state collapsed. The closing of three banks in one month in Kinston in 1931 left that major tobacco center with no bank, while in Wayne County in February 1932 the county agent reported that as far as the farmers were concerned there were no banking facilities available. The chain banks that had remained open were not interested in loans to farmers. Because of the bank failures in Pitt and Lenoir counties, the state director of the Governor's Council on Unemployment and Relief found that credit would be available only to one-third of the normal number of farmers. As the banks collapsed, so, he reported, "the time-merchant system is cracking further every day." The culmination of this came in eastern North Carolina in early 1932, when it became clear that landlords and time merchants just could not finance their usual tobacco crop and that tenants would have to be displaced. Two Kinston time merchants summed it up bluntly: there was "no money or credit available. Worthless farmers and tenants cannot be carried and the more worthy must go without financial aid." These worthy farmers could not put down seed beds, because they had no money for seed or fertilizer. The North Carolina Agricultural Extension Service feared that landlords were reducing their number of tenants by as much as 25 percent and that between fifteen and twenty thousand tenants would not be retained for the 1932 crop.[25]

While tobacco leaf prices fell, however, and depression enveloped North Carolina, the tobacco manufacturers demonstrated that tobacco was virtually a depression-proof industry. Manufacturers' profits rose from $115 million in 1927 to $145 million in 1930 and remained at that level through 1932. American Tobacco was able to raise its special compensation to its president, George Washington Hill, from $191,000 in 1926 to $892,000 in 1931. In 1931 the Big Three had enough confidence to raise cigarette prices not only in the middle of a depression, but also at a time when they were paying record low prices for their leaf. In fact, the depression did affect the industry. Cigarette consumption did not fall, but it failed to rise as fast as it had in the 1920s. The price rise in 1931 did allow the cheaper independents a chance to cut into the Big Three's markets, and that price rise had to be rescinded in order to deal with the threat. Nevertheless, at the start of 1933 President S. Clay Williams of R. J. Reynolds Tobacco Company was able to assure stockholders that the company was in the "strongest financial condition of its history."[26]

"Farmers never have worked together long at a time"

Between the end of the war and the advent of the New Deal there were four main attempts to improve the marketing position of the tobacco growers and to raise leaf prices: the Tri-State Growers'

Cooperative, Governor Gardner's "Live at Home" campaign, an attempt to form a cooperative under the auspices of the Federal Farm Board, and an attempt to restrict production by interstate agreement or individual state legislation.

The intention of the Tri-State Growers' Cooperative, organized in 1921 and 1922, was to remedy the growers' plight by better marketing. Better marketing, however, was not meant simply to help the grower by reducing his marketing costs. The cooperative had a far more ambitious aim that reflected the philosophy of Aaron Sapiro and his followers. The organizers believed that the tobacco growers could, through cooperative action, attain monopoly power and thus set the prices for their leaf. Growers handed their tobacco over to the cooperative, which then graded, redried, and stored the tobacco, which would be pooled according to grade. The crop would then be held off the market until a favorable time for selling. The growers received an advance payment when they delivered their crop and a second payment, depending on the amount of tobacco they held in any particular grade, when the tobacco was sold. They were bound to hand over their entire crop to the cooperative for five years under a legally enforceable "ironclad" contract.

The Tri-State failed and by 1926 was in the hands of receivers. It had to contend with the opposition of powerful vested interests—the manufacturers and the warehousemen. Of the manufacturers only Reynolds and Liggett and Myers bought substantial amounts of leaf from the cooperative. American and Imperial bought virtually nothing after 1922. There was no evidence, however, of a concerted effort by the manufacturers to break the cooperative.

There was much more determined opposition from the warehousemen. Advocates of the cooperative had adopted a particularly belligerent attitude toward the warehousemen. Some had threatened to "make the grass grow in the streets of Wilson." As a result warehousemen saw the cooperative as an attempt to destroy the whole auction warehouse system of buying and selling tobacco. Their fears were shared by merchants, businessmen, and bankers in the leading marketing centers, who thought that the use of cooperative warehouses in the smaller markets would hit their own trade. They also realized that the successful operation of a cooperative would lessen the farmers' dependence on them for credit. A vigorous propaganda campaign was launched against the cooperative led by the trade paper, the *Southern Tobacco Journal*, and the Wilson *Daily Times*.

There was therefore tremendous pressure on growers either not to sign up with the cooperative or to break their contracts. Because of the sympathies of the time merchants with the warehousemen and the links between bankers and the tobacco trade, the growers' creditors pressed them to desert the cooperative. Warehousemen refused to lease sales houses to the cooperative, but kept their own sales open even at a temporary loss. Local buyers were often prepared to offer a better price to nonmembers of the cooperative. Warehousemen could also pay the growers immediately, whereas for full payment from the cooperative growers had to wait for it to sell off their tobacco. This was not always a profitable wait. The advantage the cooperative gained by being able to hold surpluses off the market in order to wait for better prices was nullified when prices did not improve. Redried cooperative leaf frequently had to sell for less than green leaf.

The cooperative could do little to keep the growers in the face of these incentives to leave. Legally enforceable contracts were only satisfactory if they were not broken. The resort to the courts in the event of widespread contract breaking was too slow to be effective, yet effective enough to build up massive resentment against the cooperative. There were also errors of management. The leaf-drying operations were expensive, and the growers' confidence in the organization could not be helped by revelations that some officials had financial interests in the leaf dealers who were engaged to do the redrying. Critics exaggerated the mismanagement of the cooperative, but the damage was done.

In any case, whatever the attitude of the warehousemen and the mistakes of management, the basic reason for the cooperative's failure lay in its faulty premise: the belief that farmers could achieve monopoly power through cooperatives and thereby set prices. Such monopoly power was impossible to attain by voluntary methods, even if there were ironclad contracts to support them. This was especially so when powerful vested interests like the manufacturers and the warehousemen had been unnecessarily antagonized. Simply not enough tobacco growers were prepared to participate in the cooperative on an all-or-nothing basis. Thirty-five percent of the flue-cured growers never became members. Growers in the important New Belt of North Carolina, where the influence of the warehousemen was so strong, were particularly reluctant to join. Since the cooperative never controlled enough of the crop it could never guarantee its members a higher price for their tobacco than nonmembers received. This, in turn, led to more contract breaking and even less control of the crop by the cooperative. To succeed a cooperative would have to have more limited aims and concentrate on slowly building up an informed and enthusiastic membership. The Tri-State Growers' Cooperative failed in the final analysis because in the mid 1920s North Carolina tobacco growers were not yet ready to cooperate.[27]

Governor O. Max Gardner, a successful textile manu-facturer, came into office in 1929 with the intention of capitalizing on a prosperous economy to promote reform. He epitomized "business progressivism" in his desire to expand the services provided by the state government and to make them more efficient. It was natural that an interest in the fullest possible exploitation of the state's economic resources should lead him to look at the problems of agriculture, particularly the wasteful dependence on the two staple cash crops of cotton and tobacco. Agricultural economists, extension service work-ers, and farm editors had, for many years, preached the virtues of crop diversification to North Carolina farmers, but with little success. The relative absence of livestock and poultry on the state's farms meant that the state had to rely heavily on other states for food and feed. In 1930, for example, the state produced less than one-sixth of the beef and one-third of the milk and butter that it needed.[28]

In order to lessen this dependence on the staple cash crops Gardner launched a "Live at Home" promotional and propaganda campaign. This had two main aims. First, by growing their own food and feed North Carolina farmers would have a subsistence living standard that was not dependent on the fortunes of cotton and tobacco; this program would also cut down the $250 million spent each year outside the state on foodstuffs and feed. Second, it was hoped that by reducing the acreage devoted to staple crops, the price of cotton and tobacco would rise. What started out in prosperity as a campaign for the more efficient use of resources soon became a desperate struggle to alleviate the effects of depression.[29]

Gardner himself never lost an opportunity to put over the virtues of living at home. He was supported enthusiastically by the Extension Service, since he was preaching a traditional Extension Service mes-sage of better farming practices. The campaign succeeded to some extent. Gardner recalled that "the power of suggestion is tremendous . . . by appeal and persistent persuasion we persuaded the cotton farmers in North Carolina to reduce their acreage planted in cotton 535,000 acres.'' One extension official calculated that the acreage in the state in cash crops had been reduced in 1930 and 1931 by 575,342 acres, while the acreage in food and feed crops had been increased by 837,841 acres. There can be no calculation of how many farmers may have been able to survive the depression by producing their own food.[30]

Unfortunately, this had no significant effect on the prices of cotton and tobacco. Gardner's wider aim of increasing prices by reducing acreage through diversification could only fail. Subsistence farming appealed only to a small farmer. It had no appeal to the large commercial farmer and landlord, and if they did not cut back their production there could be no effective acreage reduction. Cotton was not reduced in other states, and there was little reduction in North Carolina's tobacco acreage until 1932. The acreage cut in that year had less to do with Gardner's persuasive powers than with the inability of landlords to finance a large crop, along with bad weather in the planting season.

Gardner's remedies for the plight of the tobacco grower were essentially long-term. The low prices in the years before 1933 led the growers to search for more immediate solutions to their problems. Discontent with prices in the 1929 marketing season led to protest meetings of growers, time merchants, and bankers in the Eastern Belt and conferences of farm leaders in Raleigh. A delegation of growers' representatives led by the governor went to Washington to meet the North Carolina congressmen and senators. Nothing came of the visit. For all the talk of ''heartbreaking prices'' below the cost of production, warnings of imminent bankruptcies, and threats of revived agrarian radicalism, no one had very much in the way of specific proposals to make. Suggestions of a reduction in the federal cigarette tax, with a refund going to the grower, and of a congressional investigation of low prices were familiar proposals that had little hope of implementation. The delegation did meet representatives of the tobacco companies. Predictably, that was futile.[31]

A more promising approach seemed to be the formation of another growers' marketing cooperative under the auspices this time of the Federal Farm Board, which had been established by the Agricultural Marketing Act of 1929. The Board's vice-chairman visited

Raleigh in September 1929 and repeatedly stressed that the government could not provide financial assistance to the growers until they
organized themselves into a cooperative. His suggestion was enthusiastically endorsed by Clarence Poe, a champion and organizer of the
old cooperative and editor of the state's leading farm journal, the
Progressive Farmer, and Josephus Daniels, editor of the most important newspaper in the tobacco belt, the Raleigh *News and Observer*. It
seemed that with the help of the government the growers could avoid
the mistakes of the old Tri-State cooperative. Government supervision
would control the activities of the organization's officials, while government loans would enable the cooperative to make a much more
attractive advance payment to the grower when he delivered his crop.
The ironclad contract would be discarded. Growers could simply
withdraw from the cooperative at a stated time each year. The cooperative would also be organized on a more compact state- or belt-wide
basis, rather than attempt to straddle the whole flue-cured area.[32]

In December 1929, five hundred tobacco growers met at North
Carolina State College in Raleigh and elected an organizational committee to set up the new cooperative. Very little was achieved, however. When the organizing committee met the following February, its
members had to report that the majority of growers in their districts
were not yet ready to join another cooperative. In March therefore
another committee, the Interstate Flue-Cured Tobacco Committee, was
formed under the chairmanship of Dean I. O. Schaub, Director of the
North Carolina Agricultural Extension Service. Its role was to undertake the long-term task of educating the farmers so that they would be
ready to join a cooperative.[33]

This educational work was scarcely under way by the time of the
1930 marketing season. Indeed, as the New Belt markets opened, the
Extension Service and the Farm Board were just starting a county-by-
county educational campaign about cooperatives. The growers had
to face the new season without either having reduced their acreage
or having organized. Once again prices were low. Once again there
were protest meetings and once again proposals to launch an acreage-
reduction campaign, to investigate the tobacco companies, and to form
a cooperative. This time the Eastern Carolina Chamber of Commerce
based at Kinston channeled the discontent into a mass meeting of
growers and businessmen at Raleigh on 11 September. Three thousand
people attended and resolved that the governor should appoint a to-

bacco relief commission that would launch an intensive campaign for a 25 percent acreage cut, secure proper grading of tobacco, find out from the tobacco companies the sort of leaf they wanted, and organize a cooperative.[34]

The governor quickly endorsed these proposals, and the Farm Board emphasized once more that it could only aid a cooperative. County mass meetings immediately elected members of the new commission, which aimed to have a cooperative functioning by the end of the current marketing season. The commission hoped to sign up 100,000 pounds and keep that off the existing market. Failing that, it would sign up growers so that the cooperative would be in operation for the 1931 season. An executive committee drew up a contract for county agents to discuss with the growers at mass meetings in the counties and decided to seek the cooperation of the warehousemen to avoid the opposition that had so harmed the old cooperative.[35]

An impressive start had been made, but once more the movement to form a new cooperative failed. Gardner had hoped that the immediate appointment of leading banker Frank Page would inspire the necessary business confidence, but Page refused the offer, and it was not until 15 October that his brother, Robert N. Page, was persuaded to take the job. By this time the small attendance at county mass meetings had made it clear that not enough growers could be signed up to keep any of the 1930 crop off the market. In February 1931 the organization still had no headquarters and had yet to start a sign-up campaign for the 1931 crop. In May the organization committee had to admit that they had only managed to sign up fifteen million pounds and that the cooperative would not be in operation in 1931. Despite expressions of confidence that enough growers would be signed up by 1932, the failure in May 1931 marked the end of the attempts to form a cooperative under the Federal Farm Board.[36]

The reasons for failure were not hard to find. Despite the conciliatory efforts of supporters of the cooperative, warehousemen and time merchants were still basically hostile. As they controlled the growers' sources of credit, this opposition was bound to be influential. More important was the residual distrust felt by the growers themselves for cooperative marketing. They were simply unwilling to submit to the discipline involved in membership in a cooperative. Although the new contract was much more liberal than the old ironclad contract, the Craven County agent explained that farmers in his district were refusing to sign it because it was still too much like the old one. There was still a penalty for noncompliance, whereas his growers wanted a completely optional contract. Harold Cooley, a Nashville lawyer, argued at the relief commission that the growers should only be required to hand over half of their crop to the cooperative. When the commission insisted on delivery of the whole crop, Cooley rightly predicted that growers in Nash and adjoining counties would not sign up. Following the failure of the Tri-State, promoters of a new cooperative faced an insoluble dilemma. A new cooperative could not work and show that it could bring improved prices unless it controlled a large portion of the crop; but growers were unwilling to sign over that large portion of the crop until they could see that cooperative marketing worked.[37]

If the growers looked at the experience of the one tobacco cooperative that functioned at this time they would have found little to change their minds. South Carolina growers had formed a cooperative in 1929 at the instigation of the Farm Board. In 1930 it handled seven million pounds of flue-cured leaf from five thousand members, but by 1931 it had still been unable to sell three-quarters of that tobacco. Members were therefore unwilling to deliver their new crop to the cooperative, and operations were suspended. Clarence Poe might argue that the cooperative had handled the crop efficiently and that the buyers had failed to give it a square deal, but its example was scarcely an incentive to North Carolina growers interested in better leaf prices.[38]

In September 1930 first district Congressman Lindsay C. Warren complained to one of the sponsors of the resolutions at the Raleigh mass meeting that "acreage curtailment will help and is about the only practical thing which can be suggested . . . you and I know that the farmers of eastern Carolina are not going to join a cooperative marketing association, so why strangle a movement in the very beginning by adding that to it." Both those who shared Warren's pessimism about a cooperative and those who still regarded it as a feasible proposition seemed increasingly to realize that cooperative marketing in itself would not bring about higher leaf prices. Whatever else might happen, there would have to be a substantial cutback in production.[39]

Such an emphasis on acreage reduction was bound to attract warehousemen, who saw it as a way to deflect the growers' interest in cooperatives at the same time as it raised tobacco prices—which was in everybody's interest. In September 1930, for example, Bill Fenner, a Rocky Mount warehouseman, had called a meeting of a thousand growers in Nash County and presented detailed proposals for a "crusade" to persuade farmers to sign a "morally bound" contract to reduce their acreage by 20 percent. He thought that a cooperative would merely encourage increased production. The Tobacco Relief Commission had combined its call for a cooperative with a plea for a 25 percent acreage cut. In March 1931 a committee of leading warehousemen planned a propaganda campaign to secure a 25 to 35 percent cutback in the 1931 crop, and Governor Gardner spoke on the radio in support of their plea. As always, such exhortations failed. As long as an individual grower could finance his crop, he would not voluntarily reduce his own acreage unless he had some guarantee that the other growers would do likewise. As a result, the 1931 crop was not significantly reduced, and when the markets opened, prices reached an all-time low.[40]

On this occasion the growers seemed initially to accept the situation with sullen resignation. It was true that Nash County farmers asked the governor to use the militia to close down the markets until better prices were paid. The Eastern Carolina Chamber of Commerce also discussed launching an acreage-reduction drive for 1932 in the hope of raising 1931 prices, but there were not the same urgent protest meetings and conferences in Raleigh that had taken place in the previous two years.[41]

There was, however, considerable interest in the cotton situation. In August the Federal Farm Board had suggested that the solution to cotton overproduction was for the growers to plow under every third row of cotton. Huey Long, governor and senator-elect of Louisiana, had reacted by calling a special session of his legislature to prohibit totally the production of cotton in his state in 1932, provided that states representing three-quarters of the nation's cotton acreage passed similar legislation. Governor Gardner's response was that he would not call a special session in North Carolina to enact the Long plan, but he did suggest a conference of southern governors to formulate a uniform plan and indicated that he would follow any initiative taken by Texas, which planted half the country's cotton acreage.[42]

It was soon clear that Governor Ross Sterling of Texas had no intention of enacting the Long moratorium, but he did call his legislature into session where it was prepared to pass legislation reducing the 1932 cotton acreage by one-third. Mass meetings of cotton growers in North Carolina now called on Gardner to call a special session to enact a similar law. In the tobacco belt the meetings also called for North Carolina to take the lead and legislate to reduce tobacco acreage. The tobacco growers were supported by Josephus Daniels of the *News and Observer*, who constantly called on Gardner to follow Texas as far as cotton was concerned, but to take the initiative for tobacco, since North Carolina was far and away the largest producer. There was, the *News and Observer* said, "only one thing that will secure better prices for tobacco—drastic reduction by law." The government could justify such unprecedented action, since the tobacco growers faced a "condition not a theory," an emergency in which "conditions [were] worse than war."[43]

Gardner was concerned by the agitation, but he refused to be moved by the mass meetings, the growers' delegations, and the editorials. His one concession was to call a conference of the governors of the flue-cured tobacco states, but he used that meeting at Charlotte merely to state his total opposition to the idea of trying to reduce tobacco acreage by law. He was also able to show that the governors of Virginia, South Carolina, and Georgia had no intention of acting, even if North Carolina had been prepared to take the lead.[44]

Gardner refused to act, because he was opposed in principle to the idea of compulsory crop control and also because he doubted its practicality. Government had no right to interfere in such areas. He would not "foster any law which will take a North Carolina farmer and make him a criminal to grow anything on his land which he wants to grow." There was no knowing where the power of the state would stop if it controlled planting, for he regarded it as "fundamental that if the State passes a law making it a crime to work that the next and inevitable thing that the State will have to do is to feed the man it denies the right to work." Senator Josiah W. Bailey, who would be in a position of some power when Congress eventually considered crop control legislation, agreed: "If we control production, we must also control consumption: we might as well go to the logical conclusion and control the number of children in a family." The Constitution had to protect "the unfettered right to sow, to plant, to work, to produce, and to enjoy the fruits of one's labor." Gardner's successor, J. C. Blucher Ehringhaus, who was to play a crucial role in the tobacco growers' later fight for better prices, also agreed with the governor at this time that there was "no power in the State itself to control production."[45]

Apart from the constitutional objections, Gardner also could not see how control legislation could be enforced. He remembered the attempts to control production in Kentucky that had resulted in "night riders, murders, feuds, and total destruction of orderly government." He was satisfied that any crop control law "would require a million dollars for enforcement and result in infinitely worse conditions than we are now trying to prevent." This problem of enforcement was an intractable one for the advocates of acreage reduction. Nash County farmers had envisaged local committees that would just go around and cut down excess tobacco acreage, and an agricultural economist at North Carolina State College argued that "there are too many farmers to be regulated. Any attempt to regulate cotton planting by several million farmers would require a regiment of marines or soldiers in each community." Voluntary acreage reduction did not work, but there seemed to be no way of enforcing compulsory crop control that was practical and did not infringe on individual liberties in an unacceptable manner.[46]

The merits or difficulties of crop control were not, however, the only considerations in Gardner's refusal to call a special session. The controversy also fueled the traditional sectional conflict that characterized North Carolina politics and had been revived by the depression and the 1931 General Assembly.

Liberals in North Carolina complained that the oligarchy that dominated the economic life of the state also dominated its political life through a conservative political machine. They portrayed first Senator Furnifold Simmons and then Governor Gardner as bosses of an organization that drew its electoral strength within the Democratic party from the industrial Piedmont and the west and was opposed by liberals from the agrarian east. The liberals' picture was oversimplified. Both Simmons and Gardner had to deal with independent local politicians throughout the state who had their own power bases. Simmons and many of his supporters came from the east, and Gardner also had many links with ambitious young politicians there. Nor did Gardner simply inherit Simmons's organization when the senator forefeited the loyalty of party regulars in 1928 by renouncing the candidacy of Al Smith. Gardner won the governorship with little assistance from Simmons, whose friends were rapidly losing influence in the state.

Nevertheless, both men had close links with the business community in the state and candidates inimical to the business interests of the Piedmont were rarely elected to statewide office. Gardner was clearly the dominant political figure in the state when he took office in 1929, able to exploit an effective personal following of young politicians, control over the patronage of the state government, and the support of the business community.[47]

As a reform governor who had been unopposed in the 1928 primary, Gardner seemed unlikely to provoke the hostility of a liberal opposition faction. The 1929 General Assembly revealed no hard-and-fast Gardner or anti-Gardner factions. With the advent of the depression, however, Gardner had to turn from ideas of reform and spending to retrenchment and a desperate search for revenue to meet existing commitments. In the 1931 legislature there was a consistent anti-administration bloc of legislators from the agrarian east who opposed Gardner's policies of centralization and wanted to reform the state's tax structure. At issue was not only the necessity of lowering property taxes, but also of raising the revenue to finance the state's commitment to take over from the counties the responsibility of maintaining a six-month school term. Three alternative sources of revenue were suggested: increased taxation of out-of-state corporations by radically altering the base of taxation, a luxury tax on tobacco and cars, or a general sales tax. Gardner joined the agrarian liberals to defeat the sales tax, but deserted them in favor of the powerful lobbyists of the tobacco manufacturers and the power companies to defeat the luxury tax as well. There was an increase in corporation taxes, but not the fundamental change in the assessment of out-of-state corporations that the liberals wanted.[48]

Gardner did not want to fight again battles that he had already won in the General Assembly and thus risk jeopardizing the fiscal soundness of the state, and so he was reluctant to call a special session in the fall of 1931 to satisfy the tobacco farmers' demands. He feared that once in session the legislature might not content itself with crop control legislation, but move once again to the question of taxation. He had no veto power, and he was afraid that an uncontrollable legislature might lead North Carolina to the "slaughterhouse" by irresponsible financial legislation. He was joined in his fear by representatives of the industrial section of the state who feared that this time the rural representatives might succeed in introducing a luxury tax or reforming corporate taxation. Business leaders in the state praised Gardner for standing firm. As he admitted, his opposition to the special session "renewed my strength with the best people of the state."[49]

What worried Gardner and other organization politicians was that the special session controversy would be exploited by that inveterate foe of special privilege, Josephus Daniels. The editor of the Raleigh *News and Observer*, a devotee of Bryan and Secretary of the Navy under Wilson, had long been the most important national political figure in North Carolina. Within the state, however, he was not the leader of any organized faction, as he had never run for public office. His hostility to corporate interests ensured that at some point every state administration would come under his editorial fire. During the Gardner administration the *News and Observer* had articulated the antimachine sentiment of the eastern legislators and had demanded that the state should "get the money where the money is," namely from the tobacco and power companies. Daniels powerfully championed the later demands of the farmers for a special session and was bitterly disappointed at Gardner's refusal to act. Predictably, he saw behind that refusal the hand of the power companies and the tobacco manufacturers.[50]

Even before this special session controversy conservatives had feared that Daniels, whom they regarded as a demagogue, was capitalizing on the discontents of the 1931 General Assembly and exploiting "all the agencies of unrest in the state," in order to organize and take over the party. These fears were heightened when the political temperature was raised by the special session agitation, and it looked as if Daniels was launching a campaign for the governorship, based on his advocacy of the farmers' cause. Gardner and Daniels both spoke at a farmers' rally at Faison on 6 November 1931. Daniels's speech was greeted with shouts of "the next governor of North Carolina" as he launched a bitter attack on the tobacco companies and Gardner's tax policies. Gardner later told Daniels that at this point the governorship would have been his for the taking, but Daniels's age, a serious car crash in January 1932, personal money problems, and the prospect of a well-financed opposition candidacy led him to announce in February that he would not run, a decision that brought ill-concealed relief to his family.[51]

Rural discontent did not die down with the withdrawal of Daniels from the 1932 race. The support of the Gardner organization had been given to the Elizabeth City lawyer J. C. B. Ehringhaus, who led comfortably by 47,000 votes after the first gubernatorial primary. In the second primary, however, he found himself in a desperately close race with Lieutenant Governor Richard T. Fountain from Rocky Mount, in the heart of the tobacco belt. Fountain had earlier fallen out with Gardner over government reorganization and taxation, and in the second primary he sharpened his rhetoric and denounced Ehringhaus as a tool of the corporations in general, and of R. J. Reynolds Tobacco Company in particular. These interests, he argued, favored a sales tax, even though Ehringhaus and Gardner claimed to oppose one. Fountain's campaign seemed to catch fire in the rural east, where Ehringhaus found himself to be an object of hatred and suspicion to a degree that was profoundly embarrassing to his political allies there. He lost eastern counties to Fountain in the second primary and only scraped home to victory by 13,000 votes in a total vote of over 350,000. There were other issues in the campaign besides rural discontent and the state administration's alleged closeness to the tobacco manufacturers, but when Ehringhaus did later become the leader of the tobacco growers' fight for better prices in 1933, it gave him special pleasure, precisely because he could then answer some of "the outrageous and unjustified accusations of the primary campaign."[52]

Agrarian dissatisfaction with the political status quo was also strongly revealed in the senatorial primary when a political neophyte, Robert R. Reynolds, overwhelmed one of the shining lights of the North Carolina political establishment, Cameron Morrison. Morrison's political credentials were impeccable: a leading figure in the campaign to disfranchise Negroes, a former governor, and a resolute "dry." He was defeated by a much-married, much-traveled, "wet" Asheville lawyer. Reynolds clowned his way around the state, feigning poverty, attacking the corporate interests and Wall Street bankers, and ridiculing Morrison's wealth and social pretensions. This struck a responsive chord in the east, just as Fountain's charges did. Reynolds, who ran poorly in the Piedmont, piled up votes in the tobacco counties to provide a winning margin of more than 100,000 votes. Conservatives were horrified. A former governor concluded that the people were in a "state of revolution" succumbing to what Governor Gardner described as a doctrine "so strange and radical that it had never been heard before by this generation in North Carolina."[53]

The tobacco growers may have been prepared to vent their spleen in the primaries of 1932, but they endured the continued low leaf prices of that summer with remarkable equanimity. Conservatives may have feared revolution, but resigned acquiescence seemed to characterize the farmers' attitude during the hardships of the marketing season and the winter that followed. There was, in any case, very little the tobacco growers could do about their plight, for two main conclusions had emerged from the failure of their various efforts before 1933 to improve their marketing position. First, there had to be some form of acreage reduction to adjust supply to demand; second, voluntary and local methods of achieving this had failed. The attempts at cooperative marketing had failed, because not enough growers could be persuaded to join; the cooperatives could never control enough of the crop to raise prices. Growers and their leaders therefore appeared by 1933 to have accepted the theoretical necessity of acreage reduction. This was no small advance, since Gilbert Fite has shown that by no means all farmers had accepted this principle before the New Deal.[54]

All efforts to translate this principle into practice had failed. Appeals to growers to reduce their tobacco acreage had failed, because no grower would voluntarily cut back his own crop unless he had some assurance that other growers would reduce as well. Although the tobacco growers did reduce their acreage in 1932 when they could not finance a larger crop, they still produced as large an acreage as ever in 1933. Compulsory acreage reduction by law clearly did not appeal to key politicians. In any case, no one knew how to enforce such legislation without either vigilante activity or massive and impractical police action. Such action by one state would have been simply quixotic if other states had taken the opportunity to expand their own production. Interstate agreement to avoid this had been impossible to secure. In 1933 therefore the tobacco growers of North Carolina had little option but to wait for Washington and Franklin Roosevelt's New Deal.

Chapter 2

The 1933 Crisis:
A New Deal for the Growers

In the early summer of 1933 it seemed unlikely that
the frantic activity of the New Deal would bring much joy to the
tobacco growers of North Carolina. Tobacco played an insignificant
role in the formulation and passage of the Agricultural Adjustment
Act. When individual crop programs were planned, flue-cured tobacco
received a low priority. The plan that did emerge was a long-term
program of acreage reduction that would have had little effect on leaf
prices in 1933. Only after protests from the growers themselves, which
culminated in the closing of the tobacco markets, did the Agricultural
Adjustment Administration (AAA) take steps to secure a marketing
agreement with the manufacturers that guaranteed prices for the 1933
crop. The results exceeded the most optimistic hopes, for in this
haphazard way one of the most successful crop programs of the AAA
was launched.

"To increase agricultural
purchasing power"

The Farm Relief bill that Roosevelt sent to Congress
on 16 March 1933 was essentially an enabling act that outlined alternative plans for agricultural relief to be used at the discretion of the
Secretary of Agriculture. The core of the measure, however, was the
provision for production control, the so-called Voluntary Domestic

Allotment Plan. The secretary was given power to enter agreements with producers of basic commodities, who would contract to reduce their acreage. In return the producers would receive rental and benefit payments. A producer was free not to sign a contract, but he would then receive no payments. The scheme would be self-financing from a processing tax levied on the first processing of the commodity.[1]

The plan appeared to offer a solution to those problems that had plagued the tobacco growers' previous attempts at crop control. It was a voluntary program and thus might avoid the constitutional scruples of men like Governor Gardner. At the same time, where earlier voluntary schemes had foundered because not enough growers cooperated, there were now positive incentives for the farmers to participate. In the past, the uncertain prospect of a price rise was not enough to win over farmers, who had no guarantee that their neighbors would cooperate. Now the tangible inducement of government payments was held out in front of the grower. Finally, the plan suggested a remedy to the hitherto intractable problem of compliance and enforcement by allowing the Secretary of Agriculture to appoint state and local committees of the producers themselves to administer the program.[2]

Tobacco, however, had not played an important part either in the drafting of the bill or in the consideration of its effects. It had not figured prominently in earlier farm relief proposals. It had not, for example, been one of the basic commodities in the original McNary-Haugen bills, although it was added in 1927 to broaden the political appeal of the legislation. The initial concerns of the advocates of the domestic allotment plan had been concentrated on wheat and cotton, but by the summer of 1932 tobacco was included in the first legislative trial run of the plan, the Hope-Norbeck bill. It remained as one of the basic commodities in both the bill that the chairman of the House Agriculture Committee introduced in the lame-duck session of Congress and the final bill that was drafted after the March meeting of farm leaders.[3]

It was not immediately clear why tobacco was included in the first place, nor why it survived. None of the farm leaders and politicians who were involved in the drafting of the bill had any special interest in tobacco with the exception of Senator Ellison D. ''Cotton Ed'' Smith of South Carolina, who did not approve of the domestic allotment plan in any case. It was true that tobacco fulfilled some of the criteria used in designating basic commodities. It was exported in large quantities, and exported crops were relatively worse off than those consumed only in the domestic market. It was processed before reaching the consumer and thus could more easily be regulated and taxed. As the Master of the National Grange later complained, however, tobacco was "not a basic crop in the whole relationship to agriculture." In this fundamental sense tobacco had little claim on special consideration. The crop was simply not grown in large enough quantitites for changes in its price to influence strongly the price of other commodities.[4]

Tobacco's designation as a basic commodity was therefore an early demonstration of the political power of a small group of congressmen representing tobacco-growing constituencies. These representatives had expressed little interest in and shown scant understanding of the domestic allotment plan. They had no precise idea how it might benefit tobacco, but they were determined that tobacco should at least be in a position to benefit from any advantage that might accrue from the Agricultural Adjustment bill. They made sure that tobacco remained in the bill as a basic commodity, displaying the power as a pressure group that they were to display on many occasions in the future.[5]

The tobacco representatives also secured one important change in the bill. The goal of the domestic allotment plan was to raise farm prices to parity, a fair exchange value for the farmer that would establish for him the same relationship between the prices he paid and the prices he received that had existed between August 1909 and July 1914. It was pointed out to members of the House Agriculture Committee that this base period would lead to a parity price for tobacco that was less than the price growers received in 1932. It was not possible to amend the bill under the closed rule that governed the debate in the House, but, with the agreement of an informal committee already at work in the Department of Agriculture and the Senate Agriculture Committee, it was amended in the Senate. The base period for tobacco was changed to August 1919 to July 1929, which allowed for the striking new trends in marketing and consumption and promised a much higher price. Attempts by the representatives of other commodities to alter the base periods for their own crops failed.[6]

All the North Carolina members of the House, with the exception of John H. Kerr who was absent, voted for the bill. Its impact on tobacco seemed to arouse little concern among their constituents. Farm leaders in the state endorsed the bill, but indicated no specific interest in the bill's provision for tobacco. The tobacco industry itself seemed unconcerned. The tobacco manufacturers made no public complaint about the processing tax. There was some opposition from leaf dealers. The president of the United States Tobacco Association was opposed to any action on tobacco that might interfere with the laws of supply and demand, and he was supported by the *Southern Tobacco Journal*, which saw no reason why tobacco should be included in the bill at all, but no one else expressed such views publicly.[7]

The fate of cotton was of more immediate interest to North Carolina, since there was already a large carry-over of cotton and a further large crop in prospect. The textile manufacturers were bitterly and vocally opposed to a processing tax, and they found a sympathetic listener in Senator Josiah W. Bailey. He soon made it clear that he was opposed to virtually every aspect of the domestic allotment plan. The processing tax was objectionable on two grounds: it relinquished taxing and appropriating powers to the secretary of a bureau, and it would not bring any benefit to the farmer. Since the tax was only to be levied on the portion of the crop consumed domestically, he argued that it would do little to benefit export crops like tobacco and cotton. There was also no guarantee that the tax collected on tobacco would necessarily ever find its way to the tobacco growers.[8]

Bailey admitted that the only hope for the North Carolina grower was a small cotton and tobacco crop, but he thought that legislation to that end was unconstitutional; "I think this one [the farm bill] vitally strikes at the character of our Republic." He also thought that statutory crop control attempted to achieve the impossible. Secretary of Agriculture Henry A. Wallace's economic adviser, Mordecai Ezekiel, was, Bailey maintained, no Joshua. Ezekiel might just as well have ordered that "this old world should reverse her course and turn backward 365 days in the year on her axis from east to west, and then reverse her course upon her great orbit and go the other way for 20 years" as legislate for acreage reduction. In any case, he argued, it was too late to put any such plan into operation for the 1933 cotton or tobacco crops.[9]

The idea of the base period was also misguided, since "it attempts with the 1914 parity to establish something in the nature of an income for the farmer and . . . omits the primary and overwhelming factors of the farmer's debt, the farmer's taxes and the farmer's wages." His conclusion was that the bill was like a sandwich with an excellent top—the Smith Cotton Option Plan—and an excellent bottom—the mortgage refinancing program—yet "in between there is supposed to be the meat, but it [the domestic allotment plan] is the worst concoction of legislative confusion I have ever seen." The argument that nevertheless the bill was supported by the farm organizations left him unimpressed, because "the farm organizations have proposed about ten different measures in the last ten years in the name of the farmers. Each one has been adopted and each has done more harm than good." After contributing to the lengthy Senate debate Bailey therefore voted against the Farm Act on April 28. He was the only southerner apart from Senator Smith to do so.[10]

This, and other anti-administration votes by Bailey during the Hundred Days, contrasted strongly with the loyal support given to the New Deal by fellow Senator Reynolds and the North Carolina congressmen. They suppressed whatever doubts they had about the wisdom of the emergency legislation, because they perceived that their constituents expected them to support the President. Bailey's more independent line prompted sufficient criticism in the state for him to prepare a lengthy defense in the newspapers. He took refuge in the fact that the President had admitted that the Farm Bill was experimental and had not recommended the whole bill. Indeed, Bailey claimed, the President was not "in favor of many of the features of the Farm Bill . . . I think it will be found out in due time that I supported the ideas that were agreeable to the President."[11]

It was embarrassing to Bailey to vote against his party and President, because it had been on the very issue of party regularity that he had challenged and defeated his old mentor, Senator Simmons, in 1930. Many leading North Carolina Democrats had deserted Simmons for Bailey in that primary, because Simmons had refused to support his party's nominee, Al Smith, in the 1928 presidential election. As the *News and Observer* noted, the right to take a stand of conscience, which Bailey claimed now, was precisely the right he had denied to Simmons earlier.[12]

Once the Agricultural Adjustment Act had passed, the immediate problem facing the newly established AAA and the farmers in North Carolina and the South was what to do about cotton. The decision to plow up ten million acres that had already been planted in cotton in turn dictated the local administrative forms and procedures within which the tobacco program would later operate. Over one million cotton farmers had to be reached and persuaded to sign individual contracts in a matter of weeks. This necessity for prompt action merely confirmed a decision that Secretary of Agriculture Wallace had intended to make in any case to use the Extension Service to administer the Agricultural Adjustment programs at the local level.[13]

The Extension Service was the obvious choice, since it was the only organization with the necessary field staff available for immediate action throughout the rural areas. Most rural counties had a county agent—an extension employee sponsored by the county government or local private organization. The role envisaged by Wallace for these agents was, however, a new one. Although they had helped in the distribution of seed loans, their main function was to make available to farmers the benefits of the education and research carried out at the colleges of agriculture. State directors of Extension in the north and east feared that their role as impartial educators might be compromised by the tasks of enforcement and regulation that would be involved in the implementation of the new farm program. They were therefore reluctant to cooperate with the AAA.[14]

No such qualms worried Dean Ira O. Schaub, North Carolina director of Extension. On the contrary, like most directors in the South, he saw the AAA as an agency that could strengthen his own organization. The North Carolina Extension Service was not protected by a powerful farm organization like the Farm Bureau, and during the depression county commissioners, anxious to economize, often considered dispensing with their county agents. Overall, North Carolina had been fortunate with a net loss of only one agent, but those that remained had had their salaries slashed, sometimes by as much as 50 percent. The situation was so dire at one point that Schaub believed that the only way for the county agents to survive was to suspend the offset provision requiring local contributions and temporarily maintain the agents out of federal funds. It was against this background that Schaub saw the virtues of cooperation with the AAA. He foresaw that the clamor for aid under the cotton and tobacco programs would convince county commissioners of the wisdom of financing the agents. He was proved right, because the emergency agents, funded by the AAA to run programs in 1933 in counties where there were no agents, were soon funded by the counties themselves. Schaub, however, not only saw administering the farm program as a means of protecting his organization from outside attack, but also saw that a much-needed boost might be given to the traditional educational work of the Extension Service. In the next eighteen months county agents in fulfilling their AAA duties would see more farmers than they had ever seen before and would have an ideal opportunity to put over to them the extension message.[15]

Extension officials were immediately plunged into the job of signing up the state's more than 150,000 cotton growers. The pattern of the sign-up—the use of emergency agents, the full mobilization of all extension personnel, the community programs to explain the government's offer to the farmers, and the propaganda barrage from the press, businessmen, farm leaders, and politicians exhorting the farmers to accept the offer—was one that would be repeated in the tobacco program. As elsewhere in the South, progress was slower than expected because of the speculative rise in cotton prices that followed the announcement of the plow-up. In retrospect, however, it is far more impressive that the farmers were signed up in just over a fortnight, given the unprecedented nature of what they were being asked to do. Inevitably, local administrative problems occurred, and some farmers remained reluctant or obstinate, but on the whole it was surprising, as Schaub commented, how well the farmers understood the government's proposition. In fact, the major administrative headaches and complaints in the cotton program in the state were to come later when the benefit checks from Washington were so slow to arrive.[16]

The law had been passed, the administrative machinery set up, and a program launched for cotton. North Carolina farmers could now examine what was in store for the tobacco growers.

"Don't expect us to devise a plan and say here it is"

Even before the Agricultural Adjustment Act had passed, a small committee of officials in the Department of Agriculture interested in tobacco had met to discuss the problems facing a possible tobacco program. Two basic decisions were taken: that the circumstances of production and marketing for each type of tobacco were so different that separate plans would have to be made for each, and that, of the six types of tobacco, the situation for cigar-leaf tobacco was so critical as to demand immediate attention.[17]

When the act was passed and the AAA was established, John B. Hutson of the Office of Foreign Agricultural Relations was appointed to head its tobacco section. Hutson had grown up on a tobacco farm in Kentucky and had vivid memories of the violence of the night riders in 1908. A graduate of Kentucky State University, he had come to Washington in the 1920s to work for the Bureau of Agricultural Economics. Since 1929 he had been in Europe studying the tobacco industry, and he returned to Washington to find himself plunged into the conferences that accompanied passage of the Farm Act.[18]

Hutson was the only career official in the Department of Agriculture to be appointed to run a commodity section in the new agency. He proved an excellent choice. Not only was he a sharp and decisive administrator, who built up an extremely proficient technical staff underneath him, but he also had essential political skills. He was able to work with, and gain the respect of, the growers, cantankerous politicians like "Cotton Ed" Smith, and smooth urban lawyers like Alger Hiss. This revealed a breadth of vision that was often absent among the agrarian fundamentalists who ran some of the commodity programs, and it explains why the tobacco program escaped the conflicts between the liberals of the legal division of the AAA and the commodity specialists, conflicts that plagued the cotton section.[19]

Some crops, like cotton, had two sections in the AAA: one in the production division headed by Chester Davis and one in the processing and marketing division under W. I. Westervelt. Hutson's tobacco section was, however, responsible both for production and for processing and marketing. Since Hutson's own experience lay in production and the study of the long-term fluctuations of supply and demand, he looked for an assistant with experience in the practical marketing side of tobacco. He chose J. Con Lanier, a lawyer from Greenville, who was a former mayor of that major marketing town and owned several large tobacco farms in the area. It was a shrewd political move, since Lanier was endorsed by two of the North Carolina congressmen who later took a close interest in the running of the tobacco program—Lindsay Warren, who represented Lanier's district and was a close personal friend, and John H. Kerr, whose second district was the largest tobacco-growing district in the country.[20]

Hutson's first responsibility was to supervise the drawing up of a program for cigar-leaf tobacco. Because it was grown by a small number of growers, much of whose crop had not yet been planted, it was possible to instigate a 50 percent reduction in acreage for 1933. Growers were paid to restrict their plantings or to destroy tobacco already planted. A processing tax was imposed to finance the scheme. The plan worked. Seventy-five percent of the growers cooperated. The acreage harvested was 43 percent less than in 1932. The leaf price rose, and the farmers received over $2 million in benefit payments.[21]

Of the remaining types of tobacco, the situation of Burley was considered the most urgent. As for flue-cured, Hutson believed that it was "comparatively favorably situated," given the size of the crop, the carry-over, and the exchange situation. The government's main emphasis was therefore placed on developing a long-term plan for acreage reduction in 1934 rather than on raising the price of the 1933 crop. G. W. Forster, head of the Department of Agricultural Economics at North Carolina State College, was coopted to work out the details of a plan to remove one hundred thousand acres from production in 1934. Hutson hoped to implement the plan in the fall of 1933, when the processing tax of three or four cents a pound would be levied and contracts would be offered to the growers. Such a plan would have no direct effect on 1933 prices, although the AAA hoped that the knowledge of a reduced crop in the future would prod the manufacturers into paying higher leaf prices in 1933. With the Georgia markets due to open on 1 August this appeared to be the limit of the AAA's immediate plans.[22]

However, from the start the AAA had emphasized that programs would only be implemented after consultation with the interested parties: the producers, the manufacturers, and the distributors. The rationale adopted by the AAA that summer was that in launching striking new measures of crop destruction and acreage control, the New Deal was merely carrying out the wishes of the farmers themselves. As Secretary Wallace told a leading farmer in the corn belt, "he was not going to impose any program on any group. The wheat program had been asked for by the wheat growers—if the corn and hog farmers wanted a corn program they would have to ask for it." Securing consent by some form of economic democracy made actual implementation of control programs much easier and disarmed conservative critics. It also allowed for the possibility that the farmers might positively contribute to a two-way process of policy making. Before final decisions were taken on the plans for flue-cured tobacco for 1933 and 1934 the tobacco growers were therefore to have the chance to be heard.[23]

As early as 19 July a former North Carolina State Department of Agriculture specialist in marketing and rural organization, L. V. Morrill, Jr., had gone to Washington on his own initiative with two of the largest farmers in Greene County to meet Hutson and Chester Davis and try to convince them that something should be done to protect the 1933 crop. The AAA agreed to meet selected tobacco growers in Raleigh on 28 July, and leading government officials went to the tobacco belt during the week of 24 July. Their theme was consistent: if the growers wanted something done for the 1933 crop they should make proposals of their own. On 24 July Henry Wallace opened the Extension Service's annual Farm and Home Week in Raleigh, and the *News and Observer* interpreted his speech to mean that if the farmers wanted government action on either the 1933 or 1934 crops they only had to say so. Hutson and Chester Davis delivered the same message at the American Institute of Cooperation meeting in Raleigh. As Hutson warned the farmers, "Don't expect us to sit in Washington, devise a plan and say here it is. . . . If any of you feel that you have a very definite suggestion as to how this [removing the 1933 surplus from the market] may be made applicable to any particular type of tobacco we shall be glad to get the proposal and study it." Davis drove the point home, "We think we are going to go further safely if we do not go too far in front of the army and get shot from behind."[24]

The growers who were invited to the 28 July conference took up this government challenge. They made it clear that they expected early action from the government to ensure favorable prices for the 1933 crop, in addition to the long-term acreage reduction program. Exactly what sort of action they expected was not so clear. It seems that they thought that the immediate levying of a processing tax would yield funds to supplement 1933 prices. They had no more specific proposals.[25]

They left the meeting determined to keep the pressure on the government. They wanted, in the words of the *News and Observer*, to show "the Secretary of Agriculture that the farmers do want help." The man who took the lead was once again L. V. Morrill, Jr., of Snow Hill, whom Jonathan Daniels has described as the "forgotten evangel" of the movement to win better flue-cured prices. Morrill toured eastern North Carolina buttonholing the large farmers with local political influence: members of the county boards of agriculture or the General Assembly and growers who had been at the 28 July meeting. With their help, he organized and coordinated a series of mass meetings in the tobacco counties for the week of 3 August. He paid out of his own pocket for circulars advertising the meetings and then drove around the tobacco belt whipping up support. He was helped by the low prices paid on the Georgia-Florida markets when they opened on 1 August. These led Governor Eugene Talmadge to denounce the tobacco manufacturers for playing "the biggest skin game on the face of the earth," and mass meetings of growers in Georgia asked for the markets to be closed. North Carolina growers watched anxiously, concerned about the likely prices when the Border markets opened on 10 August and the New Belt markets on 29 August.[26]

The mass meetings therefore captured this disquiet. Each meeting passed similar resolutions expressing three main ideas: that the government should take action to secure parity prices for the current crop, that the growers were willing to reduce their acreage in 1934, and that a flue-cured division should be set up with its headquarters in Raleigh. To underline the willingness of growers to cooperate in 1934 in return for help with the present crop, the Goldsboro *News Argus* printed slips that were to be signed, collected, and sent to Secretary Wallace. The farmers who signed promised to reduce their tobacco acreage for the next two years, in return for a speedy payment from the proceeds of a processing tax.[27]

Officials at North Carolina State College were skeptical, even scornful, of the efficacy of this haphazard and unofficial activity, although their county agents had cooperated with the mass meetings. Dean Schaub did, however, hope to capitalize on the growers' discontent to form the statewide organization of tobacco growers that the farmers had for so long been unable to achieve. He asked his agents to arrange county mass meetings to elect delegates to a 6 September meeting in Raleigh, but he disassociated his plan from the " 'hot-air' speech making" of the earlier protest meetings. But his aim, in fact, was very much the same as the growers'. He explained that organization was necessary because the tobacco section of the AAA expected the growers to show some interest if a commodity program was to be launched. He was deliberately creating a means of communication between the AAA and the growers by which the growers could put pressure on the AAA. Both Schaub and the growers were responding to the challenge thrown down by Hutson, Davis, and Wallace to let them know if they wanted government help.[28]

One common feature of the growers' meetings had been, as one set of resolutions said, that they "have no stock in the promises of tobacco companies." It became clear, however, that it was through negotiations with the tobacco companies that the AAA hoped to meet the growers' demands for action and secure better prices for the 1933 crop. An informal conference with the tobacco manufacturers had been held on 27 July at which Hutson had outlined three alternative proposals: that the manufacturers pay a specified price by grade with no restriction on the growers' production, that they pay such a specified price if the growers agreed to reduce their acreage, or that a processing tax be levied, part of which could be used as a benefit payment to growers who agreed to reduce their crops or who even removed surplus tobacco already produced. The manufacturers flatly rejected all three proposals on four grounds: first, they would not be able to construct a formula for specified prices, because they used different grading systems; second, if there was no production control, increased prices would merely stimulate even greater production the following year; third, if the government tried to control production it would not actually be able to make the growers reduce their acreage; and fourth, they simply did not want a processing tax imposed. This left little room for negotiations, and the manufacturers came up with virtually nothing in the way of counterproposals. They confessed that they knew no way of controlling production. They suggested instead only a reduction in the cigarette tax, which, S. Clay Williams of R. J. Reynolds argued, would increase consumption and leaf purchases. Although Williams's concern was supposedly solely for the grower, the manufacturers did not offer any guarantee that a tax reduction would be passed on to the consumer in lower cigarette prices. Far from raising farmers' income, the reduction might simply increase manufacturers' profits.[29]

The AAA did not seem unduly worried by the lack of progress made in these talks nor by the meetings and protests in the tobacco belt. The stock response to protests from North Carolina was that if prices on the Georgia and South Carolina markets were maintained, the average price would be near the parity level. The AAA admitted that prices for the better grades seemed slightly lower than the previous season, but this was offset by a material improvement in the prices for lower grades. The government stated that its negotiations with the manufacturers to improve prices for the current crop would continue, as would the plans for production control in 1934.[30]

The AAA nevertheless recognized that the growers' unrest could be utilized as a weapon against the manufacturers. The AAA discussed its plans with an advisory committee of flue-cured growers, which recommended the levying of a processing tax, to be used to fund an acreage-reduction campaign, and a continuation of the efforts to reach agreement with the buyers on prices for the current crop. These recommendations gave added credence to the likelihood of acreage reduction in 1934 and strengthened the AAA's bargaining position with the manufacturers.[31]

This proposal by the growers for a processing tax was clearly going to be used by the AAA as a threat to bring the manufacturers into line at a conference on 30 August. By the time of the conference the AAA had accepted the growers' argument that, in the case of flue-cured tobacco, prices appeared to be well below parity despite the good quality of the crop. Nor was the tobacco section under any illusions about the attitude of the manufacturers. Inviting Wallace to address the conference with the buyers, Hutson wrote that "the men who will be here today have been in the past perhaps as arrogant as any group of industrial leaders in the United States." The manufacturers were no less arrogant on this occasion. They would come to no agreement on their own to raise leaf prices. There was a proposal to take a surcharge on their Internal Revenue Stamp as an alternative to the processing tax, but the independent makers of cheaper ten-cent cigarettes argued that this was simply an effort by the Big Three to drive them out of business. The companies blandly talked instead of the long-term need of the farmer to reduce his crop and diversify. There was little, they argued, that they could do to help him.[32]

Faced with this intransigence, the AAA gave up the attempt to negotiate higher leaf prices with the buying interests. On 1 September it announced that a processing tax would be levied in any case, effective from 1 October, and that plans would be put into effect for production control in 1934. As for the 1933 crop, the AAA could only hope that the prospect of a small crop in 1934 would induce the tobacco companies to pay higher prices in 1933.[33]

Closing the Markets

Events in the tobacco belt itself, however, had overtaken both the AAA and the manufacturers. A hint of this came at their meeting, when Con Lanier and Hutson read out telegrams from some of the "best citizens" in the New Belt expressing the farmers' disappointment at the opening prices on the eastern markets. Prices on the first two days of these markets averaged between ten and twelve cents a pound.[34]

Even before the markets had opened, forty leading businessmen and farmers from the Eastern Belt had arranged a mass meeting of growers in the Memorial Auditorium in Raleigh for 31 August. Once again the man responsible was L. V. Morrill. Disappointed by the AAA's lack of reaction to the earlier protest meetings, he then thought of a central mass meeting of growers in Raleigh. He took the idea to Jonathan Daniels, editor of the *News and Observer*, who agreed to support the meeting and publicize it. Once more Morrill drove around the New Belt enlisting the endorsement of the time merchants and large farmers. The meeting was the first of the mass meetings in Raleigh that were to become a regular feature of the tobacco program under the New Deal. As was also to be common practice, the *News and Observer* put a special editorial on its front page urging anyone who was interested in securing better tobacco prices to come to Raleigh for the meeting.[35]

Two thousand growers attended the meeting. They were an angry, excited crowd. There were vague general threats of violence, and one speaker specifically advocated the use of force to keep tobacco off the markets, but most speakers wanted to give the government a chance to act first. Two sets of resolutions were passed. The first called on AAA administrator George Peek to take immediate action to ensure parity prices for the 1933 crop, to reduce acreage in 1934, and to arrange for the orderly marketing and government grading of tobacco. The growers promised their cooperation and appointed a delegation to go to Washington. The key second resolution demanded that North Carolina governor J. C. B. Ehringhaus "close every tobacco warehouse in North Carolina, under his exercise of martial law, and that he keep them closed until the federal government has time to put into effect measures that will raise the price of tobacco to a level of 20 cents average or more, or until the tobacco companies agree of their own accord to raise prices to that level." Another delegation was appointed to present these resolutions to the governor, who was on holiday.[36]

Growers had held mass meetings before. They had "been as mad, stomped as loudly, resoluted as vigorously and ordered tobacco holidays as earnestly'' as they did in Raleigh that day. Usually nothing followed. What was different on this occasion was the unexpected speed with which the governor reacted. One reporter at the meeting detected a distinct feeling of skepticism and hostility toward the man so many growers had voted against the year before. They clearly expected him to follow the examples of earlier North Carolina governors and turn down their request. Instead, before any delegation could reach him, Ehringhaus issued a proclamation declaring a voluntary marketing holiday that would provide a reasonable opportunity for action by the federal government. To make this voluntary holiday effective he persuaded the governor of South Carolina to issue a similar proclamation and secured the cooperation of the warehousemen, without whose support no holiday could be successful. After a day to clear the tobacco already on the warehouse floors, the markets closed on 2 September. Ehringhaus also announced his intention of accompanying the growers' delegation to Washington. With one act he had put himself at the head of the movement to secure better tobacco prices. It was a leadership he would not willingly relinquish.[37]

In the tobacco belt there was almost unanimous approval of Ehringhaus's action. He was deluged with hundreds of congratulatory telegrams. The reaction of Washington, however, was less favorable. The 1 September announcement of a processing tax and a plan for acreage reduction in 1934 indicated that the AAA had given up any hope of improving the 1933 price. There were some who therefore thought that the closing of the markets was irrelevant and that there was no point in coming to Washington now that a policy had been decided upon. Ehringhaus, however, was adamant that the 1 September announcement was beside the point. "This will not cause us to change our plans. Of course, we are interested in the 1934 prices, but our main concern now is 1933 prices." He found it difficult to convince anyone in Washington of this. The growers' delegation was due in the capital on 4 September, Labor Day, but, despite Ehringhaus's plea that the "very economic life of the people of three states is involved," he found it difficult to persuade anybody in the AAA to meet them. It required considerable persistence eventually to arrange an appointment with Hutson and Davis.[38]

The original intention at the mass meeting had been for the delegation to the AAA to consist simply of growers. Almost immediately the warehousemen decided to send representatives as well, and by the time the delegation actually reached Washington for the 4 and 5 September conference the politicians had arrived in force to demonstrate their devotion to the tobacco growers' cause. Both Senator Reynolds and Senator Bailey sent their secretaries, and almost all the North Carolina congressmen from tobacco-growing districts attended. Edward W. Pou, chairman of the Rules Committee, and Robert L. Doughton, chairman of the Ways and Means Committee, lent the delegation considerable political weight, although neither veteran politician would play a prominent role in the tobacco program. The New and Middle Belt growers around Raleigh were the most important group in Pou's fourth district, but Pou was already a sick man and would be dead within the year. Doughton was seemingly indestructible, but the Old Belt growers in his ninth district were not a major force. The younger members at the conference, however, would all be conspicuous in the tobacco politics of the 1930s. Tobacco growing was the single most important interest both in Lindsay C. Warren's first district, centered on the leading market town of Greenville, and in J. Bayard Clark's seventh district in the Border Belt. Frank W. Hancock (fifth) and William B. Umstead (sixth) not only represented Middle and Old Belt growers, they also had the manufacturing centers of Reidsville, Durham, and Winston-Salem in their districts.[39]

The conference reached two key decisions: first, that the AAA would launch an immediate sign-up campaign in which growers would sign contracts agreeing to reduce their crops in 1934; second, for the first time the government pledged itself to secure parity prices for the 1933 crop. Hutson's original plan was that final contracts would be drafted and that only when these had been signed would the markets reopen. He thought this would take about thirty days. Lindsay Warren and the eastern Carolina warehousemen were appalled at the thought of the markets being shut that long. They argued that it would be disastrous both for business and the growers, since the growers would have no cash and their tobacco would be deteriorating all the time. Frank Hancock and the growers, on the other hand, were equally appalled at the prospect of the markets reopening before the sign-up was complete. The compromise solution was suggested by Warren and Con Lanier. The growers would only have to sign a tentative contract, the details of which—the size of reduction, the amount of payments, and so on—could be worked out later. This would enable the sign-up to start almost at once and the markets to reopen shortly after.

What was not decided, and was left to the AAA to work out for itself, was how the government was going to make good its pledge to bring about parity prices for the current crop. Possibilities discussed by both the government and the warehousemen included government purchase of surplus tobacco that did not sell for parity and government price-fixing by licensing the manufacturers. For the time being Ehringhaus, as the growers' spokesman, was not concerned. He had a touching faith in the power of exhortation, "if the President of the United States himself, or speaking through someone authorized to speak for him, shall say that a certain price is a fair price to be paid for tobacco, that price will then be paid by the buyers without argument." It was not to be so simple.[40]

The Sign-Up

Hutson and Ehringhaus left at once for North Carolina to launch the sign-up campaign on 6 September in Raleigh. Here the growers' protest movement and the Extension Service's organizational drive at last linked up, because Hutson and Ehringhaus had a ready-made audience for the start of their campaign—the meeting of growers' delegates from the tobacco counties, which Dean Schaub had arranged before the marketing crisis. Hutson outlined to this meeting the terms of the tentative contract that the AAA had drawn up and submitted to the Washington conference. The growers were to agree to sign contracts reducing their acreage in 1934 by an amount specified by the Secretary of Agriculture, but by not more than 30 percent of their average acreage in 1930–33. They would receive rental and/or benefit payments, also at a rate which the secretary would decide. Hutson made the crucial promise in return that the plan would "make it so that the grower will receive more for his tobacco if he participates than if he does not."

The meeting unanimously approved the plan, and delegates vied with each other for the honor of being the first to sign a contract. At the same time they accomplished the purpose for which the meeting was originally intended: they organized the North Carolina Tobacco Growers' Association, electing Claude T. Hall of Woodale as chairman and Charles Sheffield, assistant director of Extension, as secretary. An executive committee was elected with three members to represent each belt. This committee was to confer with Hutson over any difficulties and help the Extension Service with the sign-up. Eventually this committee replaced the ad hoc growers' advisory committee that the AAA had used in August.[41]

Dean Schaub put E. Y. Floyd, extension tobacco specialist, in charge of the sign-up campaign, and Floyd retained that responsibility for AAA tobacco programs in the state throughout the 1930s. He was to be assisted by the county agents and the delegates elected from each county for the Raleigh meeting. In contrast to the cotton campaign, growers would not be sought out individually, they would have to come to designated centers to sign up. County meetings were to be held to explain the agreement on Saturday 9 September, and the growers would start signing on 11 September, when the contracts arrived from Washington. In fact, contracts arrived in time for some to sign on the Saturday.[42]

Governor Ehringhaus believed that, although the sign-up was purely voluntary, the force of public opinion would be so overwhelming that the sign-up would be completed in two days. It was certainly in everybody's interests, not just the farmers', to cooperate so that the economic life of eastern North Carolina could start moving again. County agents found that local businessmen and warehousemen enthusiastically offered the use of their premises and staff. Agents were able to muster a team of fifty or more volunteers to help in most counties. They were helped by the newspapers, who urged growers to sign and to sign early. Community sentiment also had its coercive side. The Greenville *Daily Reflector* reminded its readers that it would be easy to find out who had not signed, and they would be treated as ''slackers'' had been in World War I. The Rockingham County agent wrote to each farmer expressing the hope that there would be no ''shirkers'' in the county. There were other promises to ''deal with'' nonsigners in the spring—a scarcely veiled threat to destroy their crops.[43]

The growers responded enthusiastically. They turned up in thousands at the county mass meetings, which were often the largest gatherings in living memory. Eight thousand people, for example, attended at Kenansville, Duplin County, and four thousand went to Lumberton in Robeson County. They signed up quickly. Two hundred and fifty signed on the spot at the Granville County meeting. Sixteen hundred signed in one day at Whiteville. At Greenville five hundred growers signed in the first hour, and there were queues all day long at the twenty signing tables. In Wayne three hundred signed in the first hour. Nevertheless, the early predictions that the sign-up would be over in a couple of days proved optimistic. After three days only 60 percent of the growers had signed.[44]

One reason for the delay was that small growers who cultivated less than four acres of tobacco were reluctant to sign. Many of these argued that they had reduced their acreage during Governor Gardner's "Live at Home" campaign, and they did not think it fair that they should be asked to reduce their crops in the same proportion as those who had not previously cooperated. One grower complained that he had reduced his tobacco acreage by 40 percent in the last four years and could not sign a contract now to reduce by perhaps another 30 percent. Others felt, as the county agent in Lenoir observed, that a 30 percent reduction on three, four, or five acres did not leave the grower with very much. Hutson recognized the validity of these complaints, but insisted that the reduction had to be the same for all, although he also promised that "the interest of the small grower will be adequately protected" possibly in the calculation of the base acreage.[45]

Growers in the Old and Middle Belt were also slower to sign than farmers in the east. None of their tobacco had yet gone to market, and perhaps they still needed to be convinced of the seriousness of the price situation. Many were still busy on their farms curing and preparing their tobacco for market. The Granville County agent had to abandon the idea of getting these farmers to come in and sign their contracts. His team of volunteers, with the help of local businessmen who provided cars and drivers, had to go out to the farms and canvass farmers individually. The influence of the warehousemen in the Piedmont was also not as great as in the east, nor were they playing as prominent a part in the campaign. Finally, as the Yadkin County agent noted, it was the one- or two-acre farmers who failed to sign, and the Piedmont was the area that had the most small farmers.[46]

In the final stages of the campaign a rumor threatened to wreak havoc with the sign-up. It was alleged that Tucker C. Watkins, who had been intimately involved with the mismanagement of the old Tri-State Cooperative, was to be appointed to head a flue-cured division office in Raleigh. As one official of the newly formed Growers' Association said, "I am sure that fully ninety percent of the growers in this section would refuse to sign the acreage reduction contracts if they knew he had anything to do with it." Fortunately, most growers had signed by the time the rumor had gained prominence, but so many growers threatened to return their contracts that Dean Schaub had to telephone Washington to get a formal denial of the report. Despite these setbacks, when the sign-up officially ended on 20 September, 95 percent of the growers had signed up.[47]

Once the sign-up neared completion there was considerable pressure on Ehringhaus to allow the markets to reopen. The warehousemen themselves naturally wanted to open as soon as possible, particularly in South Carolina where they wanted to stop tobacco moving to other, later markets. Ehringhaus, however, wanted to wait until Washington expressed its satisfaction with the sign-up and the government had acted on its pledge to secure parity prices. As he explained to the AAA on 14 September, if the markets reopened and parity was not reached, the effect on the whole program would be disastrous. On 15 September the AAA gave Ehringhaus his chance when it presented its marketing agreement to the buyers. The governor could now announce that the markets would remain closed until 25 September, thus allowing time for the hearings on the marketing agreement to take place on 21 and 22 September. Warehousemen in the Middle Belt and in the Border areas where crops were deteriorating through storm damage greeted this news with alarm and protest, but Ehringhaus remained adamant. He repeated that he was striving "to accomplish a substantial increase in price realization and this, rather than the sign-up, which was incidental, is the purpose of the holiday declaration." His prestige in the tobacco areas was now so great that when the governor of South Carolina unilaterally ended the marketing holiday in his state, the Border markets in both North and South Carolina nevertheless remained shut.[48]

The Marketing Agreement

Once it was clear that the sign-up was succeeding, attention shifted from North Carolina back to Washington. It was now up to the AAA to find some way of increasing the 1933 leaf prices.

To do this the AAA turned to a marketing agreement. Previously the AAA had waited for the processors to put forward proposals for such agreements, but it seemed unlikely, given the attitude of the tobacco manufacturers in the earlier conferences, that the manufacturers in this case would come forward with any scheme. For the first time therefore the AAA submitted a marketing agreement on 15 September on its own initiative to serve as a basis for informal discussions with both growers and manufacturers before a public hearing on 21 September. Under it, the manufacturers would pay a minimum price for tobacco for the rest of the season, and possibly future years, which would be fixed each week by an executive committee chosen by the buyers and the Secretary of Agriculture. This committee would also decide whether the prices of manufactured tobacco products would be allowed to rise above their 15 September level. The manufacturers would be licensed by the secretary, who would have a veto power over all the executive committee's actions. In three respects the agreement presaged a potentially drastic amount of government intervention in, and control over, the tobacco industry. First, it was implicit that the government might have to enter the markets itself and buy tobacco that the buyers were not prepared to pay the minimum price for. Second, the secretary could forbid cigarette price increases. Third, the secretary had the right of access to all the tobacco companies' books and records.[49]

The details of the agreement did not bother the growers, as long as the government succeeded in raising leaf prices. "How the government does it," the *News and Observer* commented, "by what agreement with the buyers, the growers do not care." Ehringhaus stressed this at the hearings in Washington. The growers had fully complied with the government's requests; they were receiving the wages of a peon and a slave and the government must end that situation, but "so far as methods are concerned . . . [we are] in a sense not interested. We say to the government the problem is yours."[50]

The tobacco manufacturers were, however, far from indifferent to methods. Their spokesman at the hearings, S. Clay Williams, accepted the need to pay higher leaf prices, but claimed that the AAA agreement would not raise prices, since there was no "proviso whatever in that agreement to the effect that anybody shall buy a single pound of tobacco." But what really worried Williams were the clauses about consumer protection and access to books. The power of the Secretary of Agriculture to restrict cigarette price increases and to have free access to company books would take the running of the tobacco industry "out of the hands that have handled it . . . and [give] it over to the position where the management cannot operate, but the government controls the operation.'' He believed that behind these provisions lay the reformers who wanted to make the tobacco companies cut down their advertising spending by controlling cigarette prices. He threatened that if the manufacturers had to submit to this sort of control they would immediately stop buying tobacco and start instead to reduce as quickly as possible ''the whole lot of excessively big inventories that they have got now.''[51]

The manufacturers were nevertheless prepared to make alternative proposals. They would buy a specific amount of the current crop at a specified minimum price: as much tobacco in the remainder of the season as they had used the previous year, for which they would pay a minimum average price of seventeen cents a pound. On the question of access to books, they would report to the secretary the amount of tobacco they had used the previous year, the amount they were buying, and the prices they were paying. To check this, the secretary could have access only to those records which related to such information. The manufacturers would be further protected by a clause guaranteeing their right to ''manage, conduct and operate their respective businesses with freedom of business policy as heretofore.'' The secretary would have no control over cigarette prices.[52]

The manufacturers were offering the growers more money than the growers would receive from the AAA agreement and were prepared to pay more than the AAA ever thought they would. The reason for this shift from the earlier intransigence was the threat of regulation implicit in the agreement proposed by the AAA. The manufacturers were hoping to avoid this control by making a generous cash offer to the farmers. They could afford to be generous in any case. There was the chance that the 1934 crop might be reduced (although they were skeptical about the government's ability to achieve crop control), and their profits were large enough to absorb increased leaf costs without any difficulty. As Clay Williams admitted later, it did not matter to the manufacturer how much more he had to pay for his leaf requirements under the marketing agreement, as long as his competitors had to pay the same. Indeed, there might be a desirable side effect of increased leaf costs. The Big Three could absorb them easily, but the manufacturers of the cheaper cigarettes might find their narrow profit margins eroded and thus be squeezed out of business.[53]

The AAA accepted many of the manufacturers' proposals, and a quick solution of the growers' problems seemed likely. The 17¢ proposal was not only more than the AAA had hoped to give the grower, it also obviated the necessity for the cumbersome enforcement machinery that the AAA had proposed. On the question of cigarette prices the manufacturers conceded some government restriction of price increases, but basically achieved the price freedom they wanted. The AAA proposal had been that the cigarette prices should not be raised above the 15 September level without the secretary's consent. The manufacturers argued that this was an abnormally low price at which they would not be able to afford to purchase the amount of leaf that they promised. In an effort to fight off the challenge of the cheaper cigarettes the manufacturers had reduced their prices on 3 January 1933 to $6.00 per thousand from $6.85 per thousand. There had been a further reduction on 11 February to $5.50. This last price would be the basic price under the AAA agreement. The manufacturers wanted instead to raise their prices to the higher 3 January level and to add charges to cover increased costs arising from the operation of the AAA and the National Recovery Act. The AAA conceded this, since Hutson did not believe that competitive conditions would allow the manufacturers to raise their prices to the maximum permitted level in any case.[54]

The manufacturers would not, however, make any concessions over "freedom of business." They insisted on a clause similar to the one they had drafted. In effect they wanted the Secretary of Agriculture to waive his right to license the manufacturers for the duration of the agreement. It seemed as if the AAA would back down in the face of this intransigence, since the alternative to an agreement would be slow, cumbersome, and expensive. The government would have to license the buyers to pay a minimum price for their leaf and almost certainly have to go on to the market itself. Hutson feared that might "eventually lead us to take over the whole tobacco industry and handle it as a government monopoly." Rather than face that prospect, it looked on 27 September as if the AAA and the manufacturers would sign the marketing agreement.[55]

Instead, negotiations broke down as the government continued to balk at the freedom-of-business provision and hardened in its determination to maintain the right to intervene in the industry. Hutson was increasingly concerned that the growers, whose support was essential for future production control, would be suspicious of an agreement that incorporated so many of the manufacturers' proposals. Secretary

Wallace felt the government would be open to the criticism of "validating perhaps $40m of profit for the big tobacco companies and that only $25m, or perhaps even less, will be secured additionally for the farmers." The consumers' counsel division of the AAA objected that the cigarette price provision sanctioned a return to the companies' 1928–29 profit levels, which would be particularly rash without access to the manufacturers' books to find out the true cost of producing cigarettes.[56]

The government's concern to protect its right to intervene in the tobacco industry might appear excessive in relation to this particular agreement. The agreement, after all, was only for a limited period of time; it did not confer antitrust exemption on the manufacturers, and it waived licensing powers, which the AAA did not wish to exercise in any case. But the tobacco agreement was just one of a number of marketing agreements and codes that the AAA was negotiating with processors. Already there had been considerable dispute within the AAA over an agreement with the meat packers. The young lawyers in Jerome Frank's legal division and Frederic Howe's consumers' counsel division were anxious that the agreements should not allow the processors to increase their profits at the expense of consumers. The right of access to the processors' books and control over the prices they charged were crucial to ensuring this. Tugwell and Wallace supported them in their struggles against businessmen, who regarded their demands as presumptuous and irrelevant to the task of restoring farm prices. George Peek, however, sympathized with the businessmen. His sole concern was to raise farm prices, whereas he believed the lawyers were a "collectivist group" trying to instigate some form of socialistic control of the industry. Thus, the tobacco agreement was a battleground between Peek and the reformers. On the one hand, the AAA legal division feared a surrender of any powers that might be construed as a precedent in negotiations with other industries. On the other, Peek and the tobacco manufacturers saw the demands for "incessant inspection" of books as a threat to "take over control of the industry" and as the thin end of the wedge that would open the door to government intervention in other industries. Much more was at stake than simply the mechanics of securing better leaf prices for tobacco growers.[57]

Once the negotiations had broken down, the AAA drew up a license prescribing a minimum price that the domestic buyers would have to pay for their tobacco and prepared to enter the tobacco markets to purchase leaf if necessary. Faced with this threat and its long-term implications for government control of the industry, the manufacturers reconsidered and indicated on 2 October that they were prepared to make concessions on the question of access to books. Whereas previously they would only allow the Secretary of Agriculture access to records relating to the purchase of leaf, they now agreed to the government's request to have access to all records relating to the whole agreement,.which, of course, included material relating to their costs and their pricing of cigarettes. An agreement between the companies and the AAA was reached on 6 October and presented the next day to a committee of growers drawn mainly from the committee of the North Carolina Tobacco Growers' Association.[58]

The growers had had serious misgivings about the agreement and had listened sympathetically to a proposal put forward by Frank Hancock. Hancock had tried to persuade the AAA that the government should purchase any leaf of a particular grade that failed to reach the parity price and then resell it to the tobacco companies. Such a scheme, forerunner of the postwar stabilization plans, would have left the companies under no obligations to purchase any leaf, and the growers' committee was persuaded to reject it and accept the marketing agreement.[59]

While the growers returned to North Carolina confident that the agreement would be signed within twenty-four hours, the old stumbling blocks returned, and the protagonists took their dispute to the White House on 8 October. Once more, the crux of the matter was cigarette prices, which under the agreement were to be restricted to the 3 January 1933 level, adjusted to account for increased costs incurred by the operation of the Agricultural Adjustment Act. Clay Williams interpreted this section to mean that not only was this a maximum limit for the tobacco companies, but that the Secretary of Agriculture accepted that maximum and agreed for the duration of the agreement not to interfere with price rises up to that maximum. He insisted that this agreement to allow any price rise that did not go above the maximum was essential if the manufacturers were to sign the marketing agreement. The AAA legal division disagreed with this interpretation and wanted a specific clause stating that the section did not limit the secretary's powers. They were not primarily concerned with protecting consumers in this particular agreement, but they did want to protect the secretary's powers as a matter of principle, and they did not want him signing away powers that he might want to exercise in code negotiations with the tobacco manufacturers, which he could conduct under the National Recovery Act. Clay Williams refused to allow the insertion of any statement asserting the secretary's residual powers.[60]

The White House meeting brought no solution, and neither side gave way when Wallace, Tugwell, Frank, Peek, Hutson, and Williams met again the following day. On Wallace's instructions, Hutson therefore resumed work on drafting the license. On 10 October, however, Roosevelt suggested to Wallace that he "go slow" on issuing the license, presumably in order to placate Peek and Williams. Since something had to be done for the growers quickly, Wallace therefore scrapped the license and went ahead with the marketing agreement, although he did secure one concession from the manufacturers. While there was no assertion of the secretary's residual powers in the section on cigarette prices, he was able to add a general rider after his signature stating that it was "obvious that no officer of the government can by agreement limit or curtail any authority vested in him by law, nothing contained herein shall be construed by the parties to this agreement as attempting to limit or curtail such authority."[61]

Thus, the marketing agreement was eventually signed on 12 October. The domestic buyers agreed to purchase at the markets between 25 September 1933 and 31 March 1934 an amount of flue-cured tobacco at least equal to what they had used in the twelve months ending 30 June 1933, for which they would pay an average price of at least seventeen cents a pound. The agreement was to end on 31 March 1934. The export buyers had maintained throughout the negotiations —and the AAA accepted their argument—that they could not sign a marketing agreement, because foreign purchasers, especially government monopolies, would not approve. However, they promised to make their purchases fully conform with the agreement.[62]

Success

The delay in Washington in reaching an agreement seemed interminable in North Carolina. By the time the agreement was signed the markets had already been open for over two weeks. Such was the discontent when the market opened on 25 September with prices at their preholiday level that Governor Ehringhaus feared violence might erupt. At Wendell an angry crowd of two thousand farmers actually forced warehousemen to stop sales for the afternoon. Their action seems to have been fueled more by heavy drinking and the counterattraction of a local baseball game than by serious hopes of a second marketing holiday, and no other market followed Wendell's example. Prices remained low, however, and rapid sales made the situation even worse. Growers began to suspect that the manufacturers were stalling the negotiations in Washington in order to buy as much of the crop as possible before signing the agreement.[63]

Ehringhaus was "pounding Washington" to try to convey the growers' concern and the need for urgency. He reported market conditions to Chester Davis on 26 and 27 September, stressed that the government might have to intervene in the markets again, and eventually wired Roosevelt on 2 and 6 October to emphasize the "utmost gravity of the situation." Each day he hoped for an announcement from Washington, and each day his hopes were dashed. It was not surprising that when the agreement was eventually announced he was less than enthusiastic.[64]

If Ehringhaus was unenthusiastic, Frank Hancock, who had seen his own stabilization scheme rejected, was contemptuous of the marketing agreement. In a lengthy and bitter condemnation he denounced it as "a sop to the grower and a flop by the AAA . . . a pitiful effort and a pathetic fall down" that gave the grower no hope of obtaining parity. Hancock was swiftly answered by Con Lanier in what was a unique public outburst by an AAA official against a tobacco congressman. He accused Hancock of trying to wreck the crop reduction campaign and asserted that the growers stood to gain millions of dollars. The only thing that could stop them was "the success of a plan to mislead the farmers by loose talk."[65]

Lanier was proved right, and Hancock wrong, in his assessment of the effects of the marketing agreement. An early visit to the Greenville market led Lanier to predict that tenants would be able to buy some of the luxuries of life after three years of subsistence living and that landlords would be able substantially to reduce their debts and make long-delayed improvements to their farms. By 16 November, he was reporting to Warren that this optimism had been justified. Eastern North Carolina was, he concluded, "transformed." Senator Bailey similarly told Roosevelt of the dramatic change that had overtaken the section, "Eastern North Carolina, a very large section devoted to agriculture has been prostrated for five years. This year the people are really prosperous. . . . With one accord they give the credit to the President." In the words of the Greensboro *Daily News*, "The flat country is no longer flat," or as the *News and Observer* put it, "Happy Days" were back again in the tobacco belt. As New Belt farmers crowded into stores to spend their new-found wealth, supply merchants reported that business was double that of the previous year. Necessities like shoes and sheets could be purchased for the first time for many months. One Pitt County black tenant farmer announced, "The first thing I'm gonna buy is some good ol' long draws. I nearly froze to death last winter." In the Christmas shopping spree, used car lots were cleared for the first time in a decade. Railroad traffic increased, bank deposits in some areas doubled, and taxes were being paid three times as fast as in earlier years. The Regional Agricultural Credit Corporation reported a 99 percent collection of loans due on the year's crop—the best record of any region in the country. The *News and Observer* went so far as to claim that the eastern part of the state was nearer a cash basis than at any time since the Civil War.[66]

The leaf prices confirmed these impressions. On 24 October, more money was paid out on the Kinston market than on any day since the bumper year of 1919. In November, daily averages on the markets were frequently over 20¢ a pound. On 5 December, the AAA issued figures to show that the flue-cured grower was receiving for his 1933 crop two and a half times the money he had received for the 1932 crop and twice as much as he had received in 1931. In the end, the average price for flue-cured tobacco was 15.3¢ a pound as compared with 11.6¢ in 1932 and 8.4¢ in 1931. The crop as a whole brought in $112.1 million, compared with $43.4 million in 1932 and $56.4 million in 1931. North Carolina growers received $85.6 million compared with $34.9 million in 1932. On the New Belt alone, the flue-cured crop yielded $47.9 million compared with $18.9 million the previous year. All this and more—because the growers had yet to receive any rental or benefit payments or price-equalization payments for those who had sold their crop before the marketing agreement took effect. In no other major commodity were the benefits of the New Deal in terms of prices and cash receipts for the crop seen so tangibly or so quickly.[67]

The Scramble for Credit

An even better indication of the success of the tobacco program was the way in which politicians, manufacturers, and warehousemen seeking the support of the tobacco growers scrambled to try to gain the credit for instigating the program.

After a conversation with Graham A. Barden about a visit Barden made to Washington to talk to AAA officials, Governor Ehringhaus asked the future third district congressman to write a detailed account of that visit. Ehringhaus particularly wanted for the record Barden's statement that AAA officials had admitted that "they were doing nothing about this year's crop and had not thought anything could be done until I [Ehringhaus] came and persuaded them." Barden duly obliged. Senator Bailey was also anxious to secure testimony to his worth from the AAA. He asked for, and received, a letter of appreciation from Con Lanier that told Bailey that he "should be proud of your contribution toward this program." Bailey sent this letter immediately to the Washington correspondent of the Greensboro *Daily News*, who published it in an article that played up Bailey's role in the program. The letter was also used in Bailey's 1936 campaign advertising. Congressman John Kerr wanted a letter too. He had to remind Hutson of his promise to provide him with a letter that he could show his friends. Finally, he actually wrote the letter which he wanted Hutson to send. Kerr was unstinting in his own praise: he had left "nothing undone" in his efforts to secure better tobacco prices, and his constituents were congratulated on their good fortune on having him as their congressman. Hutson was more restrained, but his praise was still fulsome.[68]

Bailey and Kerr were busy obtaining their letters, because it was becoming clear that the chief political beneficiary in North Carolina of the success of the tobacco program was Governor Ehringhaus. Correspondents informed the governor that he had pulled off a political masterstroke in leading the tobacco growers' fight. In doing so, he had removed those suspicions of the 1932 primary in the tobacco belt that he had been too closely associated with Max Gardner and the Tobacco Trust. On 10 November, Ehringhaus was feted as guest of honor at the Golden Weed Jubilee at Farmville. The press wrote him up as the prime mover of the drive to get better leaf prices. By the end of the year there was considerable speculation that he would capitalize on this popularity and run for the Senate against Bailey in 1936.[69]

While Ehringhaus was being acclaimed, Bailey and Kerr found themselves under attack for their roles in the marketing crisis. Bailey, of course, had voted against the Farm Act and had particularly scorned the domestic allotment plan, which was the foundation of the tobacco program. He had also played no part in the delegations and negotiations that had led to the marketing agreement. After attending the 31 August meeting in Raleigh he had left for a fishing holiday in Morehead City and had remained there through the crisis. He had not been invited to join the growers' delegation to Washington, and he attributed this to a "nice political maneuver" by his opponents, who then made political capital out of his failure to attend. Bailey, in the future, made sure he did not make the same mistake again. He attended every tobacco meeting whether he was invited or not and paid assiduous attention to the wishes of his tobacco-growing constituents, at least until he was safely reelected in 1936. Bailey also stressed that it was monetary policy, rather than production control or marketing agreements, which was responsible for the rise in tobacco prices. He himself had advocated currency inflation at the start of the tobacco crisis. He maintained that it was the devaluation of the American dollar that led to the success of the tobacco program, for "while it appeared that the price for our cotton and tobacco went up in terms of American dollars, it was equally clear that neither of these crops went up appreciably in terms of British pounds or Japanese yen."[70]

Kerr, like Bailey, found himself criticized for not going to Washington with the growers, but he also found that he was accused of being active on behalf of the manufacturers not the farmers. The charge arose out of a visit Kerr made with leaf dealer James I. Miller to Governor Ehringhaus after the markets reopened. Kerr was alleged to have asked Ehringhaus to support the manufacturers' proposals. Kerr replied that he had not joined the growers because it had originally been decided to exclude politicians from the delegation; he had merely visited Ehringhaus to see what the governor intended to do about poor leaf prices; finally, he had been responsible on his own for bringing the tobacco companies and the Department of Agriculture back to the negotiating table when talks had broken down. This heroic effort was accomplished when "several gentlemen who are trying to get credit for it knew nothing whatsoever about it."[71]

The politicians were not the only ones trying to claim credit for the tobacco program. When, after 1933, the manufacturers and the warehousemen attempted to secure the support of the tobacco growers and the AAA for measures in which they were interested, they tried to do so by claiming for themselves the responsibility for the increased tobacco prices. In 1934 when the manufacturers were trying to obtain a reduction in the federal cigarette tax, Clay Williams claimed that it was the voluntary cooperation of the manufacturers who had come "forward wholeheartedly and executed a contract" that was responsible for the increased prices. When the warehousemen opposed compulsory government grading in 1934 Lindsay Warren, on their behalf, told the AAA that "without the wholehearted and unanimous cooperation of the warehousemen the tobacco program . . . could never have been put over."[72]

In fact, the major credit for the tobacco program and its success belongs to the one institution that made no great effort to claim responsibility—the federal government.

Obviously, Ehringhaus and the growers were important agents. When the governor declared a marketing holiday and led the growers' delegation to Washington, the AAA had given up any real hope of obtaining higher prices for the 1933 crop. Their strategy of trying to negotiate with the manufacturers to increase prices had failed. The resulting decision to impose a processing tax—the announcement of which was precipitated by the Raleigh mass meeting—was not itself going to raise prices for the 1933 crop. Nor did it seem likely that the manufacturers would pay higher prices because the government was preparing a crop control program for 1934, since the companies doubted the feasibility of any acreage-reduction scheme. It was the mass meeting, the marketing holiday, and the subsequent discussion in Washington that radically changed this.

Ehringhaus himself was responding to pressure from below. He had shown no special interest in the tobacco growers' plight until the Raleigh mass meeting and had played no part in organizing the earlier protest meetings. The credit for those rested with the growers themselves. In turn, it is unlikely that the growers would have been so well-organized and determined if it had not been for the largely unheralded efforts of L. V. Morrill, Jr., supported by Jonathan Daniels and the *News and Observer*.

Yet these mass meetings had occurred only after Administration spokesmen had specifically asked the growers to indicate what sort of tobacco program they wanted. Without such requests and the implicit promise of government action it is unlikely that the mass meetings would have taken place. Certainly, without the assurance that there was a responsive and sympathetic administration in Washington that had secured for itself legislative authority to act, it is inconceivable that the growers would have risked keeping their tobacco off the markets.

Also, once the growers had signed the preliminary contracts, Ehringhaus and the growers constantly reiterated their intention of letting the AAA find its own methods of securing better prices. Indeed, the final results could be seen merely as the fulfillment of the AAA's earliest avowed aims: raising the prices for the 1933 crop by negotiation with the buyers and instituting a crop reduction plan for 1934. The growers' action merely gave this program substance and credibility. As Hutson said of the growers, "They were not pressuring for any particular kind of action, but were rather requesting that some action be taken." A pattern therefore emerged. There was grass roots pressure from below by the growers, but in many ways it was stimulated and encouraged by the AAA, which could then respond in the way it wanted to the pressure that it had itself created.[73]

A similar pattern can be seen in the development of a growers' organization. One of the problems the AAA sometimes faced in consulting farmers about new commodity programs was the absence of a commodity organization or recognized spokesmen for the farmers. This was the case in tobacco. Dean Schaub arranged county meetings that would elect delegates to form a tobacco growers' organization, precisely because the AAA wanted some evidence of grower interest in a tobacco program. In instigating the establishment of the North Carolina Tobacco Growers' Association he was creating an organization by which growers could put pressure on the AAA. The AAA, in turn, encouraged this. For example, the North Carolina representatives on the flue-cured growers' advisory committee that met in Washington on 14 August had simply been nominated by Schaub. When the growers were asked to approve the marketing agreement on 7 October, however, the executive committee of the new growers' association was represented, led by Claude Hall. Soon, that committee became recognized by the AAA as the official state tobacco advisory board. Finally, when the AAA formalized its ad hoc advisory committee structure and set up a Four-State Tobacco Growers' Advisory Committee, Hall became its chairman. In other words, the AAA deliberately fostered, and later institutionalized, the growth of a growers' pressure group.

A similar process occurred in the corn belt when A. G. Black for the AAA stimulated the formation of state and national corn-hog committees.[74]

The manufacturers' claim that their voluntary cooperation was responsible for the growers' increased prices in 1933 is, at best, misleading. In fact, the manufacturers only cooperated under threat of drastic regulatory action by the government. At the meetings of 27 July and 30 August the manufacturers refused to make proposals that would increase prices to the growers, thus thwarting the government's whole strategy of securing increased prices by agreement. It was only when the growers had held their tobacco off the market and signed up to reduce their 1934 acreage and when the AAA had taken the unprecedented step of submitting a proposed marketing agreement of its own that the manufacturers submitted proposals to improve the growers' position. It was their intransigence over "freedom of business" that caused the negotiations to break down. They were forced back to the conference table by the threat of a government license, and they then had to back down: partially over consumer price protection, completely over access to books. This scarcely added up to the wholehearted cooperation on which they later prided themselves.

The cooperation of the warehousemen, who were almost as much a target of the growers' rhetoric as the manufacturers, was essential to the success of the marketing holiday. If they had defied the governor and kept the markets open, the holiday would have collapsed. It was undoubtedly in their interests to cooperate. The prosperity of their communities depended on prosperous tobacco farming. Better prices for the grower meant better commissions for the warehousemen. They also had extensive business and credit ties with the larger planters.

As a Virginia grower suggested, however, the warehousemen may have cooperated because they feared government action to change the system of selling tobacco if they did not. There was support both inside and outside the government for compulsory government grading of tobacco. The Growers' Advisory Committee on 14 August favored a uniform system of grading. Secretary Wallace reported to the buyers on 30 August that he had found a "very intense dissatisfaction with the auction system" on his recent visit to the tobacco belt. At the Raleigh mass meeting a resolution passed calling for a uniform belt-wide system of grading. Any of the proposed stabilization schemes would have involved standardized grades. The consumers' counsel division of the AAA wanted government grading as part of its alternative to the marketing agreement. Threats like these clearly worried the president of the United States Tobacco Association, and it is against this background that the cooperation of the warehousemen in the 1933 crisis must be seen. When they had cooperated, all the AAA did was to finance additional government grading on four North Carolina markets to check on compliance with the marketing agreement.[75]

Senator Bailey's emphasis on the importance of monetary policy and devaluation, rather than the activities of the AAA, was also misleading. Devaluation helped, but it was not crucial. Devaluation did not force the foreign buyers to pay parity prices; it made it easier for them to do so. They were forced to pay parity prices because the domestic manufacturers were paying those prices for a significant section of the crop. The fact that devaluation had not helped prices rise before the marketing holiday and that prices remained high even after 1933, when exchange rates were no longer so favorable, also suggests that Bailey was wrong.[76]

In the final analysis the most important aspect of the 1933 crisis was the extent of government intervention in the production and marketing of tobacco. Mass meetings had been held before. The growers' discontent had been as great, if not greater, on earlier occasions. What was different in 1933 was federal government action, taking advantage of the opportunity created by Governor Ehringhaus. The government transformed the marketing position of the tobacco grower. In persuading the growers to sign up to reduce their acreage, the federal government did what state governments and the growers had long wanted to do, but had been unable to. The growers were organized for the first time as a direct response to the likelihood of government action. By the marketing agreement the government exerted controls over a group of manufacturers who had long been considered immune from government action.

The full import of this government intervention was not perhaps fully realized at the time. One warehouseman did see the possibilities: "Never again will they [the tobacco growers] be required to accept less than living prices for weed unless they decline to cooperate with the government." What the federal government had done was to accept an open-ended commitment to ensure that the flue-cured growers were paid a decent price for their tobacco. It was a responsibility that the government has maintained to the present day.[77]

Chapter 3

Compulsory Crop Control

Despite the euphoria in the tobacco belt as leaf prices rose, the crucial test of the tobacco program was still to come. Could production control be made to work? A leading buyer from one of the manufacturers bet John Hutson six cartons of cigarettes that the tobacco growers would in fact increase their crop in 1934. The contract that the growers had signed in September 1933 was only tentative. The details—the exact amount of acreage to be taken out of production and the size of the payments to be made to the growers—had still to be decided. Would the growers, who had so willingly agreed to reduce their acreage when the markets were closed and prices had been low, sign the final contract now that the marketing agreement had raised prices so effectively? Even if they signed, would they actually keep to the contract and cut back their 1934 tobacco production?

The Program for 1934

The final contract was drawn up in the tobacco section of the AAA after consultation with the committee of the North Carolina Tobacco Growers' Association and the leading extension officials in the four main flue-cured states. Its intention was to reduce flue-cured production in 1934 to under 500 million pounds. To achieve this the growers who signed agreed to reduce their acreage and production by 30 percent of their average acreage and production in the previous three years. The acreage taken out had to be left idle or planted in home-used feed crops, and the growers could not increase their acreage of other crops that were being limited by the AAA. In the event, because bad weather seemed likely to reduce production even further, an administrative ruling in the spring allowed growers to increase production to 80 percent of their base, although the benefit payments they were to receive were correspondingly reduced.[1]

In return for reducing his crop the grower would receive two payments: the first, a rental payment of $17.50 for every acre taken out of production; the second, a benefit payment of 12 percent of the selling price of his tobacco (the maximum price for this calculation was 21¢ a pound). He would also receive a price-equalization payment if he had sold his 1933 tobacco before the markets closed and prices rose.[2]

The "historic base" method of calculating allotments and the treatment of small farmers and tenants and sharecroppers under the contract was later criticized. The "historic base," by which the grower's allotment of acreage and production depended on what he had grown between 1931 and 1933, was arbitrary, and it tended to freeze agriculture into the pattern of those years. At the time, however, it was an inevitable, if temporary, expedient. As Rexford G. Tugwell explained to Senator Bailey, the government could scarcely be expected to pay growers not to produce tobacco if they had not produced tobacco in the past. In an effort not to penalize those farmers who had reduced their acreage before the Agricultural Adjustment Act, the growers were given alternative methods of calculating their base acreage and production. A further problem with the base was that the allotment went with the land rather than the producer. A small farmer or tenant who moved from farm to farm had no allotment rights himself. It had been decided that to allot to both the land and the farmer would lead to confusion and to an increase in the base, which would defeat the purpose of the program.[3]

There was some effort to protect small growers and tenant farmers. Hutson maintained his insistence that a flat-rate reduction should be applicable to all growers, but small growers with a base acreage under four acres did receive additional benefit payments. The treatment of tenants and sharecroppers was a problem that was also exercising the cotton section of the AAA. As in the cotton contract sharetenants and sharecroppers in tobacco did not share in the rental payments, but they were to receive the benefit and price-equalizing payments in proportion to their share in the crop. Hutson reduced the amount of the rental payment in order to increase the benefit payment, so that the tenants would receive a greater share of the payments. Despite AAA legal division objections, these payments were not to be made directly to the tenant but to the landlord, who would have to be designated as a trustee by the tenant. The landlord was not to reduce his number of tenants because of acreage reduction, but he could displace a tenant if he replaced him with a tenant of similar status, or if he removed him for any reason other than the reduction in acreage.[4]

The technical details of these contracts and the various alternatives they offered were not easy to understand. In order to persuade the growers to sign, Hutson recognized the need for "a rather thoroughgoing educational campaign" through the press and local meetings. As Con Lanier noted, "I am convinced that not more than one person in ten in the tobacco area understands the program. . . . Each leader in the community has his own explanation of the program and in most cases his explanation is faulty." Details of the program were released to the press, and extension editors were briefed so that they could write explanatory articles for the farm pages of the local newspapers. On 25 November, Henry Wallace wrote to all the growers urging them to sign up, pointing out that the price rises after the markets reopened had been entirely due to the signing of the preliminary agreement.[5]

The county agents were finally briefed on 4 December in Raleigh, and then they returned to their counties to sign up the growers. The growers had to come in to local community centers where local committeemen were available to help them fill in their contracts with the necessary data about past acreage and production and sign them. In contrast to September, progress in this sign-up was slow. By 24 December the *News and Observer* warned that "there is a distinct possibility that a substantial number of the farmers who enthusiastically signed preliminary agreements in September will refuse to keep their word and sign the permanent contracts."[6]

"Compulsion is distasteful to most of us"

It was against this background that the first demands for compulsory control of tobacco production began to be heard. The essence of the plan presented to the growers, and its great virtue in the eyes of AAA theorists, was that it was entirely voluntary. If a grower chose not to sign a contract he was free to plant as much tobacco as he wanted. He would, of course, receive no rental or benefit payments, but he would benefit from the probable price increase that the general acreage reduction might bring about.

From the start, growers who were prepared to cooperate with the government were unhappy about this. In the preliminary sign-up, questions had been asked about what would happen to nonsigners. Threats of various forms of unofficial action against them had been made. At the meeting in Raleigh on 4 December, when the county agents had discussed the final contract with the AAA, they had sought unsuccessfully an assurance, which they in turn could give to the growers, that in 1934 nonsigners would not be permitted to sell more than 70 percent of their 1933 crop.[7]

This concern was not restricted to tobacco. On 24 December Clarence Poe, editor of the *Progressive Farmer*, was responsible for presenting to the AAA the resolutions of a conference of national farm leaders in Washington. One of those stated that "we should prevent the non-cooperating or non-signing crop growers from planting to the limit and thereby a) defeating the general program of crop adjustments and b) securing larger benefits from the AAA than cooperating farmers themselves." Poe, in a comment to Chester Davis, specifically related this resolution to tobacco. He wrote that he saw no alternative except to license the noncooperating farmer, while he suggested that an agreement might be reached with the manufacturers whereby they would buy a specified minimum of their orders from cooperating growers. Poe's plan was enthusiastically endorsed by the instigator of the August mass meetings, L. V. Morrill, Jr.[8]

On 11 January 1934 the North Carolina State Tobacco Advisory Board, which was, in fact, the executive committee of the North Carolina Tobacco Growers' Association, urged the AAA to take complete control immediately of the production and marketing of both signers and nonsigners. Dean Schaub reported that there was "almost unanimous sentiment" among the tobacco growers for legislation to control nonsigners. By this time, congressional hearings were being held on Senator John Bankhead's plan for the compulsory control of cotton production by taxing the production of cotton by nonsigners. On 8 February, therefore, Claude Hall, chairman of the North Carolina Tobacco Growers' Association, was urging growers to put pressure on their congressmen for a similar tax on the tobacco of nonsigners in order to discourage "chiseling." The response to Hall's request had a semiofficial tone. All the AAA township committees in Lenoir wired Senator Bailey in favor of compulsory control, while the county agent in Pitt made public the telegram that the chairman of his county committee had sent Lindsay Warren. The congressmen responded to the pressure. On 10 February, John Kerr conferred with Hutson in Washington, and from then on there were daily conferences between the tobacco congressmen—Kerr, Hancock, Warren, and Umstead—and the AAA. These congressmen were reported to be "besieged" by the growers' demands.[9]

It is not immediately clear why these demands by the growers and their representatives were so forceful. It is probable that in the early stages they were stimulated by the slowness of the sign-up. The threat of compulsory control by taxing nonsigners could be used to persuade reluctant growers to come into line and sign. However, as early as 9 January it was clear that the vast majority of growers had signed. The state AAA tobacco chief, E. Y. Floyd, estimated that by then 90 percent of the North Carolina growers had come forward. By the end of February, 95 percent of the eligible farms were covered. It seemed unlikely that 5 percent of the growers could make a significant difference to the size and price of the flue-cured crop, yet the growers continued to demand compulsory control.[10]

The more the growers signed up, in fact, the greater was the hostility to the nonsigner and the greater the reluctance to let him gain any advantage from opting out. Although the numbers of nonsigners were small, the growers still maintained that hundreds of them would increase their plantings above their 1933 acreage. Because tobacco was an intensively cultivated crop, a small increase in acreage by these nonsigners could still yield a decisive increase in poundage. The growers also feared an influx of new farmers; for example, those whose land had been taken out of cotton and were tempted by the relatively high tobacco prices. Dean Schaub received reports almost every day that many people were planning to go into tobacco production for the first time. He cited the instance of a physician who owned a two-thousand-acre farm that had never grown tobacco before and who was now constructing fifty curing barns on it. In one county where there were only fifty tobacco growers the county agent had reported two hundred or more farmers getting ready to put up curing barns. Others particularly feared an increase in the Florida and Georgia belts, which were relatively new to tobacco production. Unless something was done, argued Schaub, there was "no way . . . by which the production may be held down to a minimum during the coming season."[11]

The control program was also new and unproven. The flue-cured growers had bitter memories of acreage-reduction programs that had come to nothing. They did not yet know whether even those growers who had signed contracts would actually comply with them. Compulsory control might make the reality of production control that much more certain.

Whatever the growers felt, the AAA had considerable doubts about the desirability and efficacy of compulsory crop control. A major aspect of the appeal of the domestic allotment plan had been that it combined production control and voluntarism. Government opinion in favor of continuing with voluntary methods was succinctly expressed by the director of extension:

> The theory of crop control which affects all producers alike is excellent, but the making of allotments to every producer on a satisfactory basis to all concerned, and the enforcement job would be tremendous. . . . We do not feel that voluntary control has yet had sufficient trial to justify its abandonment and going over to more drastic measures. Furthermore, there is a very general feeling here that while many people favor compulsory control in principle, there probably would be a rather prompt and general reaction against it once it was put into practice.[12]

Secretary Wallace had been confronted with the idea of compulsion in November 1933, when five midwestern governors had demanded that the government license farmers under a code that would have allocated each individual farmer a production quota. Such dictatorial authority for the Secretary of Agriculture was repugnant to Wallace, but he also did not believe that anyone could mount the necessary police action to enforce such a measure. He shuddered at the administrative complexity of the task, the necessity of a police force of half a million men, and the racketeering and bribery "which always exist when compulsion is being exerted in defiance of economic fact and emotional tendency."[13]

Senator John Bankhead's proposal to control the production of cotton by nonsigners forced Wallace and the AAA to rethink their position. Bankhead had first raised the idea in September 1933, when

Roosevelt rejected it. When Bankhead raised the matter again, Wallace sent down his economic adviser, Mordecai Ezekiel, to try to convince him "that it was an undemocratic approach to force a man to reduce whether he wanted to or not and was contrary to the philosophy of the Wallace regime." Wallace himself opposed Bankhead's bill before the Senate Agriculture Committee, but Bankhead and the cotton growers persisted, so that shortly afterward Wallace promised to send out a questionnaire to check on the apparent growers' demand for compulsion. When the returns indicated overwhelming support for compulsory control, Wallace offered the department's aid in drafting and enacting the measure, and the President eventually endorsed the bill, in principle at least.[14]

Nevertheless, Wallace scarcely concealed his doubts and reluctance. He insisted on a referendum provision in the bill and maintained that compulsion would be unacceptable if a sizable minority of farmers opposed it. As late as 23 April 1934 he described the Bankhead bill as a frankly experimental step into the unknown and appealed to farmers of other commodities not to follow the cotton growers' example until the results of the experiment were known. Roosevelt shared his caution. "It is still my earnest conviction," he wrote, "that we should not try to impose compulsion on the farmers and that compulsion should not be adopted until farmers in general know all that is involved and willingly accept it."[15]

For all this reluctance to support compulsory control for cotton, when the tobacco growers approached the AAA in January 1934, the AAA cooperated closely from the start in drawing up a program of compulsory control for tobacco.

It seems that the tobacco section was less imbued with the spirit of voluntarism than Wallace. As early as 11 November 1933 Con Lanier had said that the AAA was considering "the possibility of handling these chiselers when they come to sell their tobacco next fall," and he foresaw possible legislation. On 10 January 1934, before the growers' demands were by any means insistent, Frank Jeter, extension editor, reported from Washington that the tobacco section expected to have congressional authority to deal with nonsigners. When asked about the prospect of nonsigners marketing their tobacco, one government official had replied, "I wouldn't risk my money that way." It seems likely, therefore, that members of the tobacco section were already working along similar lines to the growers, despite their repeated insistence that they acted only in response to the growers' demands.[16]

It is unlikely, on the other hand, that the AAA accepted the growers' arguments about the danger to the program from overproduction by nonsigners and new growers. In early February 1934 Hutson wrote to Clarence Poe that he did not believe these groups could increase production enough to threaten the success of the program, and, in any case, a small allowance for this had been made in the reduction plans. The later administrative ruling, allowing contracting growers to plant up to 80 percent of their base, did not indicate any great concern about increased production by nonsigners. The tobacco section was rather more guarded in its report on the eventual compulsory control bill. It said that it was very difficult to determine how much nonsigners and new growers might plant, but it admitted that, because of the intensive cultivation, tobacco could be more easily increased than any other crop.[17]

What the tobacco section was really concerned about was the attitude of the cooperating growers. The growers' belief in overproduction by nonsigners, however unfounded, was in itself grounds for action. Their "widespread fear . . . appears to justify" compulsion. "A few isolated examples [of non-compliance] in each community may become a very real menace in the minds of those participating in the program." The growers' reaction already had shown that. The refusal of a small minority to take part in the program appeared to have so irritated those who were participating that some growers feared "that any substantial increase of production by non-signing growers . . . may result in lawlessness."[18]

The attitude of these participating growers was important, because their continued cooperation in the future was essential if the tobacco program was to be successful. In September 1933 Hutson had given a pledge that the program would ensure a larger income to those who participated than to those who did not. Compulsory control was the means of fulfilling that promise. Its principal objective, said the tobacco section, was "to make certain that neither of these two groups [nonsigners and new growers] is allowed to so take advantage of the adjustment programs that they will be able to obtain a larger income than those participating in the adjustment programs." Hutson had hoped that he would be able to make sufficiently large rental and benefit payments to ensure that growers who participated in the program would get as large a return as those who did not participate. This would ensure that they would continue to participate in the future. It became clear to him in early 1934 that there was not enough money available under the Farm Act to make high enough payments under the tobacco program to guarantee that the growers would cooperate in the years ahead. This was a different fear from that expressed by the growers. They feared that increased production by nonsigners and new growers would wreck the program and lower prices in 1934. The AAA did not think this would happen, but they did perceive that if nonsigners were seen to receive a higher income in 1934 than participating growers, it might be impossible to secure voluntary participation in acreage-reduction programs after 1934.[19]

The argument most used by the AAA in defense of this position was that a bill proposing a tax of 30 percent on the sale of tobacco of nonsigners was not, in fact, a compulsory measure. "It has been pointed out that if outside growers received as much after paying the tax as they would have received had no program been offered, that the principle of compulsion would not be involved." In other words, it was argued that the proposed tax was not sufficiently high to prevent anyone from growing tobacco. It was calculated that the acreage reduction of 30 percent would lead to a price increase of 30 percent. If the noncooperating grower was taxed at 30 percent of the selling price of his tobacco, he would receive a price equal to what he would have received if no crop reduction program had been in operation. The argument that the tax was not prohibitive and that therefore the control was not compulsory was the linchpin of the AAA's public defense and reconciled the stand of the tobacco section to the voluntarism of the Wallace regime.[20]

For these reasons the tobacco section was prepared to work with the growers. At the 4 December meeting with the county agents, James E. Thigpen for the AAA had told them that they could rely only on community sentiment to persuade nonsigners to participate. But when the growers' representatives made their demands for compulsion in early January 1934, the AAA was prepared immediately to work on a draft control bill. A draft was ready for discussion with tobacco congressmen by 10 February. A final draft was ready for a meeting on 20 February of the AAA, the congressmen, and the executive committee of the North Carolina Tobacco Growers' Association. By cooperating with the growers from the start, the AAA tobacco section was able to guide the bill in the direction it wanted. The growers wanted a tax on the sale of tobacco by nonsigners of 50 percent, which was the rate laid down in the Bankhead bill. The AAA persuaded the growers to accept a tax rate of 30 percent or less, which squared more easily with the argument that the control was not, in fact, compulsory. The other concession to voluntarism was that the continuation of the tax would depend on the support in a referendum of those who controlled two-thirds of the tobacco acreage. John Kerr announced on 22 February that he would introduce this bill in the House.[21]

John H. Kerr and the Growers

Kerr's role in the development of compulsory control legislation was to be a source of controversy. He repeatedly boasted that his second district was the largest tobacco-growing district in the country, but 1934 was election year, and in the winter of 1934 Kerr was in political trouble because of his alleged lack of zeal on behalf of the tobacco growers. The issue at stake was the role Kerr had played in the marketing crisis of the previous fall. The man most responsible for organizing the farmers then, L. V. Morrill, Jr., was now circulating stories to the effect that Kerr had taken the manufacturers', not the growers', part throughout the crisis. One of the sponsors of the Raleigh mass meeting that had led to the marketing holiday announced his candidacy against Kerr. Something needed to be done to restore the congressman's credibility as a friend of the farmer.[22]

Never one to hide his own light under a bushel, Kerr soon issued a letter to key constituents in which he rewrote the history of the fight for better prices. He emerged as the central hero who had, almost single-handed, saved the farmers: "My activity in recent months brought many millions of dollars to the tobacco growers in Eastern North Carolina." He sent copies of the letter he had solicited from Hutson, praising his contribution to the tobacco program, to a number of his supporters. As he said, "This will prove the falsity of the statement of some of my enemies who are circulating among the people that I have been of no service in securing better prices for our tobacco farmers." His friends, in turn, made sure that the local press knew about the letter.[23]

Nevertheless, Kerr was still worried. Later in the campaign, and in a future campaign, an opponent, Oscar Dickens, asserted that Kerr sponsored the compulsory control bill purely as a political measure to gain reelection, and that he had nothing to do with the drafting of the bill. While there is evidence that as far back as September 1933 Kerr was concerned about the problem of noncooperating growers, it is also true that the growers and their leaders had called first on the AAA, not on the congressman, for initial action and that the AAA had the drafting of the measure well under way before Kerr appeared for consultation. Indeed, Kerr seems only to have been aware of the tobacco section's efforts through the local press. Once the bill had been drafted it made sense to choose Kerr as its sponsor. Of all the tobacco congressmen he was the one least hindered by other legislative chores, and it was prudent that the bill, whose whole rationale was the growers' demand for it, be introduced by a man from the principal tobacco constituency. In no sense was Kerr responsible for the tobacco control legislation in the way that John Bankhead had fostered compulsory cotton control. Regardless of the role he played in its origins, Kerr's sponsorship of the bill thrust him to the forefront of the fight for better tobacco prices at a convenient time for his electoral prospects.[24]

Kerr's first step after introducing the bill was to assemble a legislative steering committee of congressmen from all the tobacco-growing areas, in order to emphasize that there was no intracommodity conflict. Demand for compulsory control had come mainly from the flue-cured region, but there were also demands from other areas. The sponsors avoided potential sources of opposition by excluding Maryland, Virginia sun-cured, and cigar leaf tobacco from the immediate operation of the bill in 1934. This tactic was later rewarded in the debates in the House and Senate when speakers from tobacco-growing constituencies in Georgia, Kentucky, Massachusetts, South Carolina, and Virginia supported the North Carolinians.[25]

Kerr's strategy was to slip the bill through after the Bankhead bill in an effort to capitalize on a favorable vote on that measure. He even rejected the offer of subcommittee hearings by the House Agriculture Committee so that the bill might not be delayed. However, hopes of quick passage soon evaporated, and the bill had to move through regular channels.[26]

The first major obstacle was Marvin Jones, chairman of the House Agriculture Committee. Jones was not sympathetic to New Deal agricultural policy in general, although he masked this by his loyalty to the

Administration, but he was particularly opposed to the principle of compulsion in the Bankhead bill. He agreed to it eventually, but he expressed the hope that it would be tried for a year for cotton before any similar measure was enacted for any other commodity. He finally agreed not to oppose the Kerr bill, but he insisted that it operate only for two years. This reluctant acquiescence reflected his style of running the Agriculture Committee. "To a great extent, we listened to members of Congress who represented tobacco-producing districts and relied on their viewpoint as to the necessity for special tobacco provisions."[27]

Nevertheless, his lack of enthusiasm held up the bill. He insisted on having subcommittee hearings, but delayed in naming the subcommittee. Rather than report the bill out, he referred it back again to the subcommittee. Even when it was reported out, he wanted action by the Rules Committee on another bill first. Such delay was critical to a bill that was engaged in a race against time and adjournment. At one stage, the Greensboro *Daily News* reported that there was not "a ghost of a chance" of action on the Kerr bill. As it was, the bill was finally reported out of the Agriculture Committee at the last committee meeting of the session.[28]

Progress on the Rules Committee was much simpler. The death of Edward W. Pou had deprived North Carolina of the chairmanship of the Rules Committee, but the committee was prepared to grant a favorable rule to the Kerr bill as soon as the Agriculture Committee released it. Another North Carolina tobacco congressman, J. Bayard Clark, had moved onto the committee at Pou's death, and Pou's successor as chairman, William Bankhead, sympathized with the compulsory control principle espoused by his brother.

Since the Kerr bill was introduced late in the session, it was essential that there should be no disagreements among its proponents if it was to be passed before the adjournment. There were two threats to that unity: supporters disagreed over the treatment of small growers and the amount of the tax on nonsigners.

Some growers were to be exempt from the bill. The bill provided for some tax-exempt warrants to be allocated to growers who had not in fact signed contracts. These could amount to 5 percent of the total quantity allotted to the growers under contract in any county and would go to growers who could not obtain an equitable base under an acreage-reduction contract. These would, in the main, be small grow-

ers. This provision had been vigorously supported by William Umstead, whose sixth district lay in the Piedmont where the small growers
were the most numerous, but it was opposed by Claude Hall for the
Growers' Advisory Committee, who did not want any exemptions at
all. The tobacco section reported that the growers were divided over
this question of additional allotments. At the House subcommittee
hearings Umstead argued for an increase in these exemptions to 7
percent of the county allotment, but the subcommittee left it at 5
percent. Later, the Senate increased this to 6 percent provided that at
least two-thirds of the grants were made to growers who produced
under fifteen hundred pounds.[29]

Far more controversial was an effort by Umstead to secure exemption for all growers who produced under three acres of tobacco.
This move was immediately denounced by Con Lanier, who said that it
"would completely destroy the bill." The subcommittee largely went
along with Umstead, inserting an amendment providing tax exemption
for those growing under two thousand pounds of tobacco. Kerr was
opposed to this, as was Hall, who thought it would "defeat the purpose of the bill since it opens up so many loopholes by which the
growers could escape." But the Agriculture Committee insisted on
retaining the amendment, threatening to oppose the bill if attempts
were made to remove it.[30]

It was an important amendment. Nearly half the tobacco growers
had allotments under two thousand pounds. Hutson thought that opposition to the amendment came not only from the large growers, who
feared an unlimited number of new growers, but also from some small
growers, who themselves had contracted to produce under two thousand pounds. They could not expand those allotments, but resented the
prospect of nonsigners planting up to two thousand pounds tax free.[31]

On the other hand, Senator Bailey was immediately interested in
the two-thousand-pound amendment. He had tried to exempt all growers who produced under six bales of cotton from the Bankhead Act and
had long advocated exemption of five-acre tobacco growers from crop
control legislation. He received complaints from small growers that
the Kerr bill ignored them. One had asked Kerr to exempt all those
who grew tobacco on less than one-quarter or one-fifth of their acreage, but he felt that Kerr was opposed to the nonsigner to the end.
Another complained that Kerr never talked to the little farmers; one
more reported that the two men most active for the Kerr bill in Wayne
and Lenoir counties were the two largest growers in the tobacco belt.[32]

The tobacco section finally opposed the amendment. Hutson had written to the county agents asking for their assessment of grower feeling on the two-thousand-pound amendment. Although none of their replies survive, it is clear that they reported general hostility by the growers to a clause that effectively destroyed the point of compulsory control. At the insistence of the AAA the amendment was removed in the Senate. The fifteen-hundred-pounds provision in the additional allotment clause was a small concession to its supporters. In the give-and-take of securing passage on the last day of the session, Kerr managed to keep the amendment out of the final version of the act.[33]

The other threat to the unity of the bill's supporters came from the growers who wanted a more punitive tax than the 25–33⅓ percent provided in the final draft. On 3 March the Tobacco Growers' Association called for a 35–50 percent tax. A 13 April meeting of growers' representatives in Raleigh called for a 40 percent tax, and Governor Ehringhaus took up their claim in Washington. The county agent in Craven County reported that large numbers of growers could not understand why the tax should not be prohibitive, but the AAA would not concede on this point. It was a central argument in favor of the bill that the tax was not prohibitive and that therefore the control was not compulsory. The growers were confronted with a choice of the existing tax rate or no bill at all. They had to be content with the lower tax.[34]

The growers' activities at this time suggest the AAA's directing hand behind their pressure. The meeting at Raleigh on 3 March called for a higher tax and also established the North Carolina Tobacco Growers' Association on a permanent basis—and the men who did this were the AAA county committeemen. The county agents were also there, even though they did not vote. County agents played their part in instigating pressure. As the Craven County agent wrote Schaub later in the month, "I have just received from Mr. Floyd copies of the petitions to be sent to Judge Kerr and we will get a good number of signatures mailed out of here Monday night." It is also clear from Pitt and Lenoir that these petitions in favor of the Kerr bill were distributed among the growers by the county agents and the county and township committeemen. In other words, Floyd, as state head of the AAA tobacco program, was deliberately organizing growers' pressure on congressmen. Once again, this raised the question of whether the AAA was responding to grass roots pressure or was creating it, in order to win support for legislation that it was anxious to enact in any case.[35]

Senator Bailey's Volte-face

The bill passed in the House on June 6 by 205 votes to 144, the Democratic ranks largely holding firm in the face of routine Republican claims that it meant "the enslavement of the American farmer" and "the complete regimentation of the agriculture of this country." In the Senate Kerr had persuaded "Cotton Ed" Smith, chairman of the Senate Agriculture Committee and testy opponent of AAA theorists, to sponsor the bill. Smith approved the bill because of his tobacco-growing constituents in South Carolina and because he was a good friend of Kerr. He also had better relations with Hutson and the tobacco section than with most of the New Deal's other agricultural officials. The prospects of success in the Senate, however, depended much on the attitude of Senator Bailey.[36]

Bailey's dislike of compulsory control was ill-concealed in his private correspondence. It ran, he said, "counter to every principle of American liberty." "If the government can tell a man what he should plant and how much or whether he can plant anything or not, I do not know what has become of the doctrine of liberty to preserve which this government was formed." He agreed with a correspondent who talked of the "half-baked communistic control of agriculture," and he predicted "thousands of injustices" from control. However, to avowed supporters of compulsory control like Charles Sheffield, secretary of the North Carolina Tobacco Growers' Association, and Clarence Poe, Bailey added cautious riders. To Sheffield he wrote that "nothing short of dire necessity will move me in this matter," but admitted that perhaps dire necessity might arise. To Poe, after much soul-searching, he conceded that they might "temporarily" be justified in interfering with the liberties of the people, since it had happened that "the farmers themselves have decided upon this course, and that the large majority of them have voluntarily, by contract, limited their liberties in this respect for the current year, and that they have done this in the public interest, and are, therefore, entitled to the public cooperation."[37]

In public, Bailey was even more guarded. At the initial meeting of congressmen, growers, and the AAA on the Kerr bill, his questions were critical, but he indicated that he would probably support the measure. Kerr certainly expected Bailey to take the lead in pushing the measure through the Senate. The weekend before the Senate voted on the Bankhead bill for cotton control Bailey was still reported as undecided, although his interruptions in the debate had generally been interpreted as hostile.[38]

Then came Bailey's outburst. He not only voted against the Bankhead bill, which embodied the same principles as the Kerr bill, but he also delivered a violent speech denouncing the principles behind the bill. He based his arguments before the Senate not on economic grounds, but on constitutional grounds: "The real question is [not] the question of cotton or the prices of cotton . . . [it is a] question of human liberty." The Bankhead act was unconstitutional. It presented Congress with a choice between constitutional government and tyranny. If the federal government could determine how much cotton a farmer may gin, "we do not have a republic we have a tyranny. If the Federal government can do that there is not a vestige of states' rights left in America . . . it is going to be a free republic or regimented socialistic communism." Secretary Wallace would be the "Commissar of Agriculture." Bailey could not possibly vote for such a bill because of the oath which he had sworn to uphold the constitution. Those who were asking him to support this legislation were "asking me to take from the American people powers which I solemnly swore I would never take from them when I swore to support the constitution."[39]

His specific objections were that the bill was unfair to nonsigners, who had not been faced with the alternative of taxation when the sign-up campaign was started; that it was being passed after planting had finished and was unfair to those who had already paid for seed and fertilizer; that one could not create wealth by reducing production; that the South would lose its foreign markets; that it was unfair to tenants and sharecroppers; and that it discriminated against small farmers, leaving them with not enough to support themselves. All his objections applied equally to the Kerr bill for tobacco with one exception; the Kerr bill had a provision for a thirty-day grace period in which previous nonsigners could sign up. Bailey made it clear after his Senate speech that he was equally opposed to the Kerr bill.[40]

Bailey had to defend his views on the Bankhead bill in North Carolina. To charges of disloyalty to the party he pointed out correctly that the bill was not a presidential measure, that Roosevelt had only endorsed it in "principle," and that Wallace was skeptical about its merits. He cited the failure of crop control in other countries and the need to expand domestic and foreign markets. He reiterated his absolute constitutional objections to it. He also claimed that opinion in the state was divided; of the hundreds of letters he was receiving, more praised his stand than opposed it. He claimed the support particularly of those who had already diversified their crops and small tenant farmers.[41]

The prospect of Bailey actively opposing the Kerr bill was a daunting one for its supporters. To get it through the Senate at such a late stage in the session would take unanimous consent. The determined opposition of one senator could be fatal, especially the opposition of a senator from a tobacco state.

After his outburst on the Bankhead bill, Bailey refrained from specific comment on the Kerr bill. He contented himself with statements in his letters that the bill was unlikely to go through with tobacco already planted and that it seemed unlikely that the bill would emerge from the House Agriculture Committee, let alone reach the floor of the Senate.[42]

Yet, in the end, Bailey voted for the Kerr Act. He claimed that he had "no desire whatsoever to obstruct this measure," but he did more than merely not oppose the bill. He actively worked for it. Indeed, his positive intervention could be said to be decisive, since it was he who persuaded Senator Fess to withdraw his objection to unanimous consent and thus enable the bill to be considered. This was a volte-face. Bailey had voted for a bill whose principles were exactly the same as those of the Bankhead bill, which he had felt bound by his solemn oath to oppose because it was unconstitutional.[43]

It was true that some provisions made the Kerr bill a slightly more moderate measure—the lower tax rate, the grace period for signing up, and the provision for additional allotments. But at no time did Bailey accept the AAA's argument that the lower tax rate eliminated the compulsory features of the bill. His explanations for his shift were unconvincing. He had once said that only dire necessity would cause him to vote for compulsory control. Yet after voting for the Kerr bill, he claimed that the bill was superfluous, as a short crop was likely in any case. He then said he could scarcely oppose a bill that all the growers were supposed to support and that was endorsed by the entire House delegation from North Carolina and by the Department of Agriculture. Yet the Bankhead bill had also supposedly been supported by the growers, all the North Carolina delegation, and the department, and Bailey had had no qualms in opposing that. On the contrary, he had boasted that "if every man in America should ask me to vote to destroy the liberties of the American people, I would not do it."[44]

The key to Bailey's change of heart was his tricky political situation. He had opposed the Farm Act, which was the basis of the tobacco program, and he had been absent from the fall drive for a control program. Two people prominent in the fight for better tobacco prices, Governor Ehringhaus and Lindsay Warren, were increasingly mentioned as potential opponents for Bailey's Senate seat in 1936. Now the issue was simply resolved. Bailey could not afford politically to oppose another measure favored by tobacco growers. The dire necessity against which Bailey had guarded had come about; it was not the dire necessity of avoiding low tobacco prices, it was the dire necessity of avoiding electoral defeat. His oath suddenly became unimportant in the face of genuine political pressure. Few men have professed themselves so courageously independent of popular whim, yet been so carefully attuned to constituency pressure. He was now able to say on the one hand to an opponent of compulsory control that he "was not for the . . . bill" and on the other to a supporter of the bill that he had "manifested no opposition whatsoever to the Kerr-Smith bill."[45]

Once Bailey had moved in support, all that remained was the technical problem of steering the bill through in the hectic last days of the session. This problem was aggravated by the fact that on the planned final day of the session Senator Smith's daughter was getting married—an occasion at which the Senator's presence was deemed essential. Fortunately, the pressure of legislation delayed the adjournment over the weekend, and Senator Smith was able to perform his paternal duties and still introduce the tobacco control bill. The bill passed without a roll-call vote, and Kerr ensured that the House agreed to the Senate-approved amendments.[46]

The Kerr-Smith Act finally provided for a tax to be levied on the sale of tobacco of between 25 and 33⅓ percent of the sales price. The Secretary of Agriculture was to determine the rate, and he immediately announced that the tax would be levied at the 25 percent rate. The justification for the lower rate was that it was late in the season and a higher rate would not measurably affect production. On the other hand, it was high enough to ensure that cooperating growers received more than nonsigners. It would also not penalize too much those who had been unable to sign equitable contracts, but for whom there were not enough special exemption warrants.[47]

The tax was to be applied in 1934 to all types of tobacco except Maryland, Virginia sun-cured, and cigar leaf. For a tax to be levied on the 1935 crop, the support of those "who own, rent, share crop or control three fourths of the land customarily engaged in the production of any particular type of tobacco'' had to be secured. Tax-exemption warrants would be issued to contracting growers to cover their allocated production. Additional warrants could be given to non-signers who could not secure an equitable allotment under the Agricultural Adjustment Act. These could cover up to 6 percent of the county's allotment, provided that two-thirds of the amount allotted in any county was allocated to growers whose allotments were fifteen hundred pounds or less. The act was only to be in operation for 1934 and 1935.[48]

The Practice of Crop Control

Meanwhile, the task of actually putting production control into practice had been going on since the sign-up started the previous December. Translating the overall goal of acreage reduction into detailed application to thousands of individual growers was a sizable and complex task at the local level. The heaviest part of this burden fell on the county agents, who were the key figures in the local administration of the flue-cured program. At the state level, as in the cotton program, the state extension director or his nominee headed the AAA. In North Carolina this was the extension service tobacco specialist, E. Y. Floyd. At the county level the county agents were the official local AAA representatives. They, in turn, selected local growers to serve on county and community committees to help administer the program. Local administrative expenses were paid by the AAA.[49]

Thus, the county agent in the tobacco program played a far more important role than in other AAA programs. For other commodities, the cooperating growers usually formed production control associations and elected their own community committees. Delegates from these then formed county committees, which served as the official local AAA representatives. The county agents often serviced these county committees, but sometimes the growers kept them out of the administration altogether. Local administrative expenses were paid by the farmers themselves.[50]

In North Carolina the county committees were in a sense elected by the growers. The county agents usually named as members of their county committees those delegates who had been elected at the county mass meetings of growers called by extension director Schaub back in September 1933. It was these growers who had gone on to form the North Carolina Growers' Association. Thus, at the local level these growers were given a formal official role, just as at the state level the executive committee of the Growers' Association had been made by the AAA into the State Tobacco Advisory Board, and eventually into part of the Four-State Growers' Advisory Committee.

When the growers had signed up in December 1933 the administrative headaches of the county agents were just starting. The first task was to check the accuracy of the information that the growers entered on their contracts about their past acreage and production. This had to be checked by a member of the local committee familiar with the farm, then by the county agent, and finally by the state office. There was an immediate problem in that most growers overestimated what they had grown in the previous years. Few had kept records themselves. It was also the avowed aim of several county agents to give ''the farmer the advantage in any way that they could,'' while local committees were often anxious to help growers who had had abnormally low yields on their acreage during the base period. In some cases there were simply deliberate overestimates.[51]

Where state and local records did not tally with the growers' calculations the county agents returned the contracts either for the grower to produce records of his production or to agree to a downward adjustment of his figures. Even then, the estimates of yields per acre accepted locally were markedly higher than the yields finally decided by Washington. This meant that in March each county had to scale down its allotments to meet the Washington figure. The county agent was left to work out the specific individual adjustments as best he could, either by individual adjustment and negotiation or a flat-rate cut for every grower. Despite the time and expense involved, most agents decided to try to work out individual adjustments with each grower. The growers were invited to come in and discuss their contracts with the committeemen. Few were able to bring the production records that might have solved the problem. One county agent attempted to resolve the discrepancies by putting notices of the allotments in the local stores and inviting growers secretly to inform him if their neighbors were overestimating. Even with all these individual adjustments, some considerable flat-rate cuts had to be made at the end to bring estimates into line with Washington figures. Nevertheless, the agents were probably right to go to such lengths. The Vance County agent, who decided on a simple flat-rate cut in the beginning for everybody, merely provoked "uproar" among all the cooperating growers. Whatever the method they used, the county agents found the adjustment of the contracts "the hardest and most disagreeable" task of the year.[52]

These tasks put the Extension Service under a considerable strain. All the counties involved had agreed to fund county agents, but few provided clerical help for them. An estimated $300 had to be spent in each county to provide clerical help, while in the headquarters at North Carolina State College emergency statisticians had to be employed to check and calculate allotments. About $12,500 was provided for the expenses of committeemen to help the county agents, but even with their assistance Dean Schaub reported that his agents were seriously overworked, especially in the fifty or so counties where they had to conduct both cotton and tobacco sign-up campaigns. Invariably they had to abandon completely their normal extension work. Schaub feared for the physical health of his men and suggested that the only way they could cope was for Congress to legislate a forty-eight-hour day.[53]

Nevertheless, there were compensations for the agents when the rental checks arrived after the contracts had been accepted. These provided growers with an unusual source of cash income in April and May. Schaub had hoped that the checks would be sent to the growers directly, rather than to the county agents, but the agents did not begrudge the task of disbursing them. One present-day extension official recalls the farmers queuing up outside the Northampton County agent's office to receive their checks from the agent, who was clearly enjoying every minute of his newfound role as dispenser of government largesse. The Mecklenburg County agent insisted on delivering the checks in person. On each visit he took the opportunity to put over the extension message and encourage the recipients to plant and can some fruit and vegetables. County agents were seeing more farmers than ever before through their AAA work, and their status and power were immeasurably increased.[54]

In June, when the Kerr-Smith bill was passing through Congress, these agents were just beginning the task of ensuring that the farmers had complied with their contracts. It was a troublesome and time-consuming task to measure some 500,000 fields in the cotton and tobacco counties of North Carolina. In a tobacco county like Nash or Pitt as many as ninety compliance supervisors were employed. These had to receive hurried training from local committeemen, who had, in turn, just been instructed by state officials and the county agents. The inexperienced supervisors, often students, had to measure rolling and irregular fields. There was surprisingly little complaint from the farmers, who rarely asked for a field to be remeasured by a surveyor. It was also surprising how few farmers had failed to comply with their contracts. In Martin County, for example, only 3 out of 1,409 growers failed to meet their contract requirements. Most noncompliance was unintentional, and the farmers were only too anxious to destroy their excess tobacco in order to comply, or to take advantage of the increase in allotment to 80 percent at the cost of some downward adjustment of their benefit payments. Even when confirmation of the checking came so late that the farmer had to burn excess tobacco that had already been harvested, there was no complaint. This high degree of compliance in the flue-cured tobacco program merely reflected the AAA's experience in other programs like cotton and wheat.[55]

The actual passage of the Kerr-Smith Act simply brought new tasks for the hard-pressed county agents. As Dean Schaub lamented, "To handle the distribution of tags for old cotton and the applications for allotments under the Bankhead bill, and applications and allotments under the Kerr Tobacco Bill, distribution of checks, the issuing of marketing cards for tobacco, and the many other activities we are called upon to handle during the next sixty days is more than one organization can possibly accomplish with the limited trained personnel and funds available to us."[56]

Under the compulsory control act, the county committees had to handle applications for tax exemption from those growers who had not been able to sign contracts because of an inequitable base. The committees very rarely, in fact, used the full 6 percent of the county allotment that was available to them. On the whole, they seem to have granted allotments to over two-thirds of the applicants, but in at least one county, Edgecombe, the committee, with the backing of the county agent, only granted one of the sixteen applications. They took the attitude "that if the bars were let down this year and the price of tobacco should continue higher in 1934 that an immense acreage of tobacco would be planted in 1935 by non-signers."[57]

One potential problem arose from the provision that not more than 6 percent of the county's *contracted* acreage allotment could be used. In other words, the fewer the growers who signed up, the smaller was the amount available. Thus, the more growers who could not sign contracts because of an inequitable base, the less the acreage available to compensate them. This was a real problem in the Burley program, but the completeness of the sign-up in the flue-cured areas eradicated this as a source of discontent.[58]

When the tobacco was finally sold, each grower had to receive a master marketing card from the county agent with the total of his production allotment on it. Landlords had to get their tenants to sign this to designate them as trustees in order to receive the benefit payments. When the marketing card was returned to the county agent he then issued allotment cards. At the warehouse each sale was recorded on this by an agent of the Secretary of Agriculture, and tax-exempt warrants were issued to cover the sale. These were finally handed in to be checked by the county agent. Details of the sales could then be entered on the marketing card and sent off to the state office as the basis for the distribution of benefit payments. If the agent was lucky he might finish these tasks by the end of the year.[59]

The national director of extension had feared that in enforcing compulsory control the Extension Service "would have a job just about as popular as prohibition enforcement, and quite possibly no more successful." In fact, the administration of the Kerr-Smith Act for tobacco had gone smoothly and involved the county agents in little unpopularity. This was partly because there was so little excess tobacco produced by nonsigners. Approved production under contract was 534.5 million pounds. Actual production was 556.8 million pounds. As a result, very little tax had to be collected. Compulsory control of tobacco therefore provided fewer headaches at the local level than the administration of the Bankhead Act for cotton. Cotton control was hampered by the late arrival of tax-exemption certificates, the low estimates of yields per acre, which angered growers, and the delay in using the state's 10 percent reserve allotment, which was meant to compensate them.[60]

"Relatively the most prosperous people in America"

One reason why tobacco growers were satisfied with the administration of the Kerr-Smith Act, irrespective of the red tape involved, was the price they received on the markets at the end of the day.

The AAA had not been absolutely confident that production control would bring good prices and had attempted to negotiate a new marketing agreement with the tobacco buyers just in case. In two conferences in July, however, the tobacco section and the growers' representatives failed to persuade the tobacco manufacturers to sign another agreement. The companies argued that there was no need for one since the Farm Act was going to work, and a marketing agreement might even hamper free buying by the manufacturers. The AAA acquiesced in the buyers' refusal, but reserved the right to seek a marketing agreement or impose a license if prices were not satisfactory.[61]

In the event, there was no need for further action. The average price for flue-cured tobacco was 27.3¢ a pound, and the total receipts for the crop were $151.7 million, over three and a half times the 1932 receipts. North Carolina received $118 million compared with $34.9 million in 1932. The Durham *Sun* argued that "even the grower who was careless enough to neglect to sign a crop production contract can pay his special tax and net more than twice what he was paid last year." The Kinston *Daily Free Press* summed up the situation for eastern North Carolina by saying that "today we are relatively the most prosperous people in America." The prosperity was revealed in a number of ways. A Goldsboro storekeeper reported a boom in the sale of nails as farmers began to undertake long-delayed repairs and improvements to their farms. Bank deposits in Pitt County reached all-time records. In Greenville, the Flanagan Buggy Company won a prize for selling more new Fords than any other agency in the country. The proprietor, E. G. Flanagan, a close friend of Lindsay Warren, attributed his success simply: "High prices paid for tobacco did it."[62]

The experience of a black small farmer, Ed Long of Rougemont, perhaps best showed what a difference the AAA had made. In 1932 five acres of tobacco had brought him $11.30. In 1933 five acres of equal-quality tobacco had yielded $480.00, but in 1934, even with his acreage cut, he received $1,472.00. He was going to be able to pay off the large hospital and doctor's bills incurred during his wife's seven-month illness, pay off some long-term debts, and "then have a little change after I buy Santa Claus." His analysis of his success would have pleased the AAA and the Extension Service. "I feel all this is due to this 'sign business' and I will follow your advice, Farm Agent, for I did not know about that 'sign business' until you explained it to me."[63]

The situation in cotton was not so satisfactory. Numerous complaints of hardship in the South led to a drive to suspend the operation of the Bankhead Act. Naturally, Bailey was at the forefront of this agitation, since he saw the complaints as a justification of his vote against compulsory cotton control, and he maintained that people now recognized him as a prophet. He claimed that this dissatisfaction also extended to the Kerr-Smith Act. He admitted that the tax-exempt warrants had been handled more gracefully in tobacco than in cotton, but he still insisted that there was considerable complaint against tobacco control. The other tobacco representatives could find no evidence of this. On the contrary, wrote Lindsay Warren, "every tobacco farmer is tickled to death."[64]

Even Bailey had finally to admit this. He wrote to Henry Wallace that the tobacco farmers of North Carolina "feel that they have been almost miraculously delivered. They are grateful to the Government for the part it has played and many of them are grateful to God." In private, it was clear that Bailey attributed the greater role to God. The Kerr bill had had "nothing whatever" to do with the increase in the price of tobacco, for "if we could raise prices by legislation, then it is a strange thing that for two thousand years the civilized world failed to do such a good thing."[65]

Publicly, however, Bailey had to recognize the popularity of the Kerr-Smith Act. In the referendum in December 1934 growers voted overwhelmingly to continue the tax on the tobacco of nonsigners. Those who controlled 96.5 percent of the eligible tobacco acreage voted. Of that percentage, those in favor of the tax represented 99.1 percent of the acreage. One of the most striking features of the vote was the absence of any extensive propaganda campaign, in contrast to later years. Growers were just mailed a sample ballot, notice of the polling places, and a statement by Secretary Wallace. There is evidence of only an occasional explanatory meeting. As one editor wrote, there were "no long-winded orations at the various meetings, no speech-making at the county seats. Farmers were asked to vote and they voted."[66]

Bailey had more hopes that the cotton growers would vote against compulsory control. He was skeptical of Charles Sheffield's claims that 90 percent of North Carolina cotton farmers favored the continuation of the cotton act. But Sheffield was right, and 90 percent of the state's cotton growers who voted did vote in favor. They did so, however, only after the AAA had agreed to press for exemption from the Bankhead Act of those who produced under two bales, and after the Extension Service and the cotton section launched a campaign to counter what "appeared to be growing opposition to the act in various parts of the state." State and national officials addressed growers' meetings, and the Extension Service provided press material designed to show the planters how they were benefiting from the Act.[67]

These two manifestations of his constituents' support for compulsory control made Bailey very cautious. After the referendum results he withdrew an article he had submitted to the *South Atlantic Quarterly* in reply to Clarence Poe's "The Bankhead Act and Democracy." He was anxious not to arouse his rural constituents, whatever his real views about compulsory control might be. "I am bearing in mind that our farmers are very sensitive about changes in the Bankhead bill and the Kerr bill and I do not wish to take any steps that would be interpreted as in any way impairing these acts."[68]

These signs of growers' support for compulsory control could only please John Kerr. Although friends of L. V. Morrill, Jr., and other tobacco growers continued to attack Kerr, Kerr beat Oscar Dickens in June with a comfortable, if decreased, majority. He was voluble as usual about his work for the tobacco program. As he later said, "When I retire I can go home, prop up my feet on my front porch and look back with the utmost pride on this great program." There was no doubt that he would remind the tobacco growers of his contributions again— when the 1936 primary election loomed large.[69]

In 1934 the tobacco growers had therefore successfully reduced their acreage and fulfilled their promise of September 1933. They were rewarded with the highest leaf prices for fifteen years. In the process the AAA acquired another weapon to control production, the power to tax the sale of tobacco by nonsigners under the Kerr-Smith Act.

The AAA claimed that compulsory control legislation had only been passed "at the request of the tobacco growers." As Wallace said, "The idea of compulsion is distasteful to most of us. However, we have been repeatedly requested during the past few months by the tobacco growers . . . to work out some plan that would protect them from growers who were not cooperating in the production adjustment program.'' Certainly the Growers' Advisory Committee, the county committees, and the county agents had demanded such legislation, but, as in 1933, this growers' pressure had been institutionalized and encouraged by the tobacco section of the AAA. The tobacco section had its own reasons for supporting compulsory control legislation. Whereas the growers had feared that production by outside growers would wreck the program and reduce leaf prices, the AAA feared that it would be unable to guarantee cooperating growers a larger income than the nonsigners would receive, which would damage the prospect of cooperation from the growers in future reduction programs.[70]

The tobacco section's attitude can be contrasted not only with the initial hostility of the Department of Agriculture to compulsory control for cotton, but also with Hutson's own response to demands for compulsory control for potatoes. Potato growers, dissatisfied with a marketing agreement, wanted production control along the lines of the Bankhead and Kerr-Smith acts, particularly in North Carolina and Virginia. The AAA refused to support their demands, but Congress conceded compulsory control to the growers in the Warren Potato Act (Title II of the Agricultural Adjustment Act Amendments in 1935). When the act was passed, Hutson simply refused to implement it, much to the annoyance of its sponsor, Lindsay Warren.[71]

Whatever the AAA's attitude in the case of tobacco, the reality of the growers' pressure was eloquently demonstrated by, on the one hand, the alacrity with which John Kerr took up the cause of compulsory control legislation at a time when he was in electoral trouble and, on the other, by Senator Bailey's decision to support the Kerr-Smith Act in contradiction to his deeply held views in opposition to the Bankhead Act.

The struggle for compulsory control had revealed unity in the ranks of the growers and their representatives. This was not always to be the case.

Chapter 4

Divisions in the Ranks

Christiana Campbell has suggested that one of the main reasons for the favored treatment of tobacco growers during the 1930s was the degree of unity among the growers and their representatives and the virtual absence of any intracommodity conflict. Events during 1934 and 1935 put that harmony under strain on a number of occasions. Disagreements arose among the growers themselves, between the growers and their representatives, and among the growers, their representatives, and the tobacco section of the AAA. In particular, the proposals to reduce the federal cigarette tax, the proposal for compulsory government grading of tobacco, and the plans for the 1935 reduction program provoked dissent. Nevertheless, these disputes took place within a context of overall loyalty to the AAA, as indicated by the growers' spirited defense of the AAA and their overwhelming vote in favor of continued crop control in 1935.[1]

Cigarette Tax Reduction

Robert L. Doughton, North Carolina's ninth district congressman, often did not understand what the New Deal was doing, but, as chairman of the House Ways and Means Committee, he was a loyal supporter of the President and his party. While he jealously guarded his committee's prerogatives, he rarely took independent initiatives himself. In early 1934, however, he appointed a subcommittee to hold hearings on proposals to reduce the federal tax on tobacco products. His motives were mixed. As a farmer and country banker he was always interested in helping the tobacco growers. As a politician who had come to national prominence by leading the fight against the federal sales tax in 1932, he was always opposed to any form of sales tax. He was also sympathetic to the tobacco manufacturers. Ever since he had become chairman of an influential committee he had been assiduously courted by North Carolina manufacturers in general and by S. Clay Williams of Reynolds Tobacco Company in particular.[2]

The federal tobacco tax had been substantially increased during World War I. In 1919 the tax on cigarettes stood at $3.00 per thousand or 6¢ per pack of twenty. Although other wartime taxes had been removed, the tobacco tax had never been returned to its prewar rate of $1.25 per thousand, since it was far too attractive a source of revenue for the Treasury. Indeed, various attempts to increase the tax had been made, but these had been successfully resisted by North Carolina congressmen. There had been no determined drive by the cigarette manufacturers to reduce it, although manufacturers of other tobacco products, like plug and chewing tobacco, whose products were doing less well, had tried to reduce the excise rate on tobacco generally.

Nineteen thirty-four was a promising year for the cigarette manufacturers to press their case. As one leaf dealer noted, such was the impact of the marketing agreement and increased leaf prices that "never before . . . have I seen manufacturers build up for themselves as much good will with the farmer and the public generally . . . as . . . in the bright flue-cured district since September 1933 until now." The manufacturers wanted to exploit the mellow feelings of the tobacco growers in order to build up the necessary political pressure to reduce the tobacco tax.[3]

The manufacturers disagreed over what sort of reduction they wanted. The Big Three who produced cigarettes selling at 15¢ per pack wanted a straightforward horizontal reduction that would keep the flat tax-rate on cigarettes irrespective of their retail price. The independents who produced cigarettes at a price of 10¢ per pack also wanted a substantial tax reduction. Their narrow profit margins were now threatened by higher costs under the NRA, higher leaf costs as a result of the AAA, and the processing tax. They favored, however, a graduated reduction that would result in a differential tax, whereby their cheaper cigarettes would be taxed at a lower rate than the Big Three's standard brands.

When it came to enlisting the support of the tobacco growers, the Big Three were in a much stronger position than the independents. The

Big Three based their case for the horizontal reduction entirely on the benefits that would accrue to the growers from the increased consumption of cigarettes and thus the increased purchases of leaf by the manufacturers. In contrast to this apparent display of altruism, the independents had to argue for the graduated reduction on the grounds of their own self-interest. Supporters of the flat-rate cut made the graduated proposal seem merely a device for "causing tobacco manufacturers to make more money."[4]

The whole tone of the tax reduction drive was set by Fred Vinson, one of Doughton's most trusted committee colleagues, when he opened the subcommittee hearings. "This is," he said, "the first time an approach to the reduction of the tax on tobacco and tobacco products has been made from the viewpoint of the grower." The Big Three succeeded in their efforts to make the growers' viewpoint sympathetic to the horizontal reduction. On 3 March 1934 Clay Williams had persuaded the Growers' Advisory Committee in Raleigh to call for a tax reduction of between a third and a half. At the subcommittee hearings the growers' representatives turned up in force to testify— Claude Hall, Earl Vanatta of the state Grange, J. Y. Joyner, and L. V. Morrill, Jr., who had been so prominent in the fall campaign for better prices. They were joined by the tobacco congressmen, and all enthusiastically put forward the views that were expressed by the Big Three manufacturers. They favored the horizontal reduction, because it would lead to increased cigarette consumption and increased purchases of those higher-quality leaf grades that gave the growers their best prices. A graduated cut, on the other hand, would merely lead to increased consumption of the 25 percent of their tobacco for which they received low prices in any case.[5]

Some witnesses wondered what guarantee there was that the benefits of the tax reduction would be passed on by the companies in lower retail prices and eventually be seen by the growers, but most seemed to accept the promise of the Big Three's spokesmen that cigarette prices would be lowered and leaf purchases increased. The only fundamentally challenging testimony came from an academic, G. W. Forster, the agricultural economist from North Carolina State College. Forster saw no probable increase in consumption coming from lower cigarette prices, since the demand for cigarettes was essentially inelastic. What the growers needed was increased competition in the buying of their leaf, and the best way to ensure this was by means of a graduated tax reduction that would maintain the existence of the cheaper independent cigarettes. He was unworried by the Big Three claim that they would then have to stop buying the higher leaf grades. He did not think they would need to move away from the demonstrably profitable and viable market for higher-priced cigarettes. But if they did move into the lower grades, competition from the independents would force those leaf prices up in any case.[6]

The subcommittee, however, dismissed these arguments in its report as the arguments of "so-called economists" in defiance of "age-old economic laws." The subcommittee came out instead in favor of the horizontal reduction, stressing the benefit to, and support of, the tobacco growers and "without any thought or purpose that the tobacco manufacturers will retain any part of the taxes reduced." Vinson prepared a bill providing for a 40 percent flat reduction that was favorably reported out by the full Ways and Means Committee.[7]

The subcommittee hearings had been an impressive public relations demonstration of the case for a horizontal reduction on behalf of the growers. What was going to matter, however, was the attitude of the Administration, and the Administration basically favored a graduated reduction.

Government officials supported the graduated cut, because they wanted to maintain competition in the tobacco industry. This had led the consumers' counsel division of the AAA to endorse a graduated cut in September 1933 and had prompted Secretary of the Treasury Henry Morgenthau to propose such a reduction to the Senate Finance Committee in March 1934. Hutson for the tobacco section originally accepted the argument that the horizontal reduction would lead to increased leaf purchases, but he felt that competition in leaf buying was more important, and he did not feel that the independents could sustain their cheaper cigarettes, in the face of heavy advertising of the standard brands, if a horizontal tax was introduced. Roosevelt also favored the graduated tax. Characteristically, he doubted that a horizontal reduction would increase consumption, since he did not think that he would smoke two packs a day instead of one.[8]

Doughton and Vinson visited both Hutson and Roosevelt and felt they successfully converted them at least to not opposing the horizontal reduction. They were joined in their efforts by Clay Williams. Publicly, he had had little to do with the tax-reduction drive, leaving the limelight to the growers' representatives, but now he moved in to convince Rexford Tugwell and Roosevelt of the wisdom of the horizontal cut. He was at pains to stress that the manufacturers were following the socially responsible policy of cooperation that they had pursued in September 1933. They were, he maintained, "on high ground in this." They did not "have the big stake in this matter," whereas the tobacco growers did, and the farmers were unanimously in favor of the horizontal reduction despite "a very heavy campaign of propaganda . . . in the tobacco-growing districts" by the advocates of the graduated tax.[9]

The AAA and the President were prepared to be conciliatory to Doughton, Vinson, and Clay Williams, because they knew that the man whose opinion really mattered was the Secretary of the Treasury. Williams completely failed to impress Morgenthau even after Elliott Roosevelt had visited the secretary on Williams's behalf. Morgenthau was merely exasperated by such lobbying attempts by members of the President's family. He was chary of any tobacco tax reduction. He had had to make his peace with Doughton after his advocacy of the graduated tax, but he could see no virtue in the horizontal reduction. All he could see was that the Treasury would lose revenue it could ill afford. As he explained to Vinson, the Treasury would lose $75 million in order to give the farmers $10 million. As for the manufacturers, the figures for their profits, he said, showed that they at least could look after themselves.[10]

Some of the growers' representatives also shared the AAA's and Morgenthau's skepticism of the manufacturers' disinterestedness and doubted the arguments that a tax reduction would automatically lead to increases in leaf prices. They wanted more than personal assurances from Clay Williams that the companies would lower their cigarette prices. Governor Ehringhaus and a delegation of growers wanted a legislative guarantee that a tax reduction would be accompanied by benefits to the growers. When Vinson maintained that such a legislative guarantee was impossible, resolutions and telegrams from the growers demanded that the AAA protect the growers' interests in the event of any tax cut.[11]

Their doubts were academic, since the revenue situation in 1934 was too grim for Morgenthau to sanction any tax reduction. The following year the bill that Vinson introduced for a horizontal reduction contained the guarantee the growers wanted. The reduction was conditional on the lowering of cigarette prices to the levels promised by industry spokesmen in the tax hearings. Faced with making good on their promises to the growers, the manufacturers suddenly lost interest in tax reduction, and Vinson's bill went no further. A bill for a graduated reduction also made no progress, despite a propaganda drive in eastern North Carolina by the manufacturers of the cheaper cigarettes, since the federal government remained desperately short of revenue.[12]

The unwillingness of so many of the growers and their representatives to consider that the manufacturers had a vested interest in tax reduction, their unwillingness to support measures which might in some small way have helped break up the oligopolistic structure of the industry, their willingness to accept the manufacturers' assurances about leaf prices—all are testimony to the skillfulness of the manufacturers' propaganda and to the limitations of agrarian radicalism. When they are compared to the violent antitobacco company spirit of August 1933 and earlier crises, they are testimony to the tremendous change that higher tobacco prices had brought. To an old enemy of the Tobacco Trust like Josephus Daniels, watching from Mexico City, it was an aberration. He thought that the Administration had saved the growers after the North Carolina congressmen had been stampeded, but he was sure that the growers now realized that "all this talk about increasing the price of tobacco to the farmers only through reduction of the taxes on cigarettes was bunk." But the basic conservatism of the growers would become more apparent as the years went by.[13]

The Warehousemen and Government Grading

In October 1933 Charles Gage of the Bureau of Agricultural Economics contributed an article to the *Progressive Farmer* on "Changes Needed in the Tobacco Auction System." Gage's main complaint was against the speed of selling. As much tobacco as possible had to pass through the market in the short selling season to offset the high cost of investment in the warehouses. As a result, he noticed, most tobacco boards of trade established a *minimum* selling speed of 300 to 350 lots an hour, which it was the responsibility of the supervisor of sales to maintain. Such speed was bound to be unfair to the grower. Gage demonstrated that government grading, when accompanied by regular market reports showing what particular grades were fetching, brought the grower higher leaf prices. He criticized other aspects of the system: the practice of warehousemen operating their own leaf accounts, thereby becoming dealers rather than commission agents; the warehousemen's links with speculators; and the lack of representation of farmers on the tobacco boards of trade. The government must reform the warehouses, he concluded.[14]

A small step had already been taken under Gage's direction with the introduction of government grading for those growers who wanted it on a limited number of markets. By giving the grower an objective standard by which to judge the fairness of the bids he received for his tobacco, it was hoped that one of the weaknesses of the grower's marketing position would be eliminated. Few growers, however, had taken advantage of the service. They had to pay for the service themselves; the buyers paid no attention to the government grades; and not enough growers used the service to provide an intelligent comparison of bids and prices. There had been suggestions at the time of the 1933 marketing crisis that grading be established on a wider scale, but the warehousemen cooperated with the government and the growers during the marketing holiday so that no reforms were introduced.[15]

In early 1934 therefore members of the tobacco section cooperated with Representative John Flanagan to draft a bill to regulate loose-leaf auction sales. Flanagan represented the "fighting ninth" district of Virginia, opposing the Byrd machine, and sat on the House Agriculture Committee. His bill provided for the Secretary of Agriculture to license warehousemen, weighmen, and buyers and to inspect warehouse scales; to order mandatory grading of tobacco and to determine selling charges, regulations, and the opening dates of markets. Flanagan hoped to improve prices to the growers by opening the markets earlier, thus avoiding congestion, and by slowing down the speed of selling. Standardization of grades would eliminate wide fluctuations in price and enable growers to make intelligent and informed rejection of bids.[16]

The measure aroused the bitter opposition of the warehousemen and the North Carolina congressmen. Lindsay Warren was the first to become aware of the bill, tipped off by his friend, Con Lanier. In turn, Warren warned the warehousemen in his district and encouraged them to organize opposition to the bill. He himself described it as an "attempt . . . to destroy the auction system." As such, he regarded it as "damnable" and "thoroughly vicious and uncalled for." As with the manufacturers, so with the warehousemen: Warren reminded the AAA of the wholehearted and unanimous cooperation the warehousemen had provided in the fall of 1933 as a justification for scrapping the proposed reforms. Hancock, Umstead, and Kerr, who saw the ghost of cooperative marketing lurking behind the bill, joined Warren's denunciation of the Flanagan proposal.[17]

North Carolina warehousemen spoke for themselves at hearings on the bill before an agriculture subcommittee. They testified that the reforms were unnecessary. There was already an adequate North Carolina state law covering warehouse charges, while most of the other abuses were being dealt with in the NRA code that they were in the process of negotiating with the government. In the face of their opposition and the vocal dissent of the North Carolina congressmen, there was no chance of passing such a controversial measure late in the 1934 session, unlike the Kerr-Smith Act.[18]

The Flanagan bill was not, however, without effect. It almost certainly hastened agreement on an auction and loose-leaf tobacco code. Negotiations had been going on since December 1933, and agreement was finally reached in July 1934. The code limited the speed of selling to a maximum of 375 lots an hour, gave growers up to fifteen minutes to reject a bid, and licensed weighmen. Various abuses—the granting of rebates, speculation by warehousemen, and the paid soliciting of tobacco—were outlawed. There was little in this to offend the warehousemen. The abuses were competitive tricks that most warehousemen were only too pleased to see abolished. The code had no provision, on the other hand, for government grading, and it was virtually self-enforcing. The voting members of the code authority were to be elected by the warehousemen's associations, and the first administrator was to be Con Lanier, who had done so much to secure agreement on the code and who was well known as a friend of the warehousemen. It seems that just as the warehousemen had cooperated with the government and the growers in 1933 in the face of the threat of government grading, so in 1934 the fear of licensing under the Flanagan bill encouraged them to reach agreement on a code. In the place of unpredictable regulation by the Secretary of Agriculture, they were now able to regulate themselves.[19]

At the same time, Representative Joseph Byrns of Tennessee had introduced a more limited measure providing solely for compulsory government grading. The Tobacco Growers' Advisory Committee endorsed it, Lindsay Warren spoke in its favor, and there was every indication that the warehousemen would be prepared to support it. It made no progress in 1934, but when Flanagan introduced a similar bill in 1935, after Byrns had become Speaker, there seemed likely to be very little opposition. The bill provided for compulsory government grading on markets designated by the Secretary of Agriculture with the cost to be borne by the buyers.[20]

Whatever sympathies the warehousemen might have had with the Byrns bill in 1934 when they were confronted with the prospect of government licensing, in 1935 they had no intention of supporting compulsory grading sponsored by their nemesis, John Flanagan. The tobacco boards of trade in eastern North Carolina quickly sponsored resolutions condemning the measure outright. Grading had been tried and had failed. It would be an unnecessary financial burden on an already overtaxed industry, and the government would be unable to find enough qualified graders. Behind these objections lay the feeling that the grading scheme was a precursor to the cooperative marketing they had fought so bitterly in the 1920s. Such fears were naturally strongest in Wilson and were echoed by John Kerr, who denounced the Flanagan bill as "nothing but an endeavor on the part of some of the old cooperative marketing crowd to get the Federal Government to accomplish what they failed to accomplish in their association which cost the farmer many thousands of dollars."[21]

The warehousemen's most effective argument was that, although the bill was designed to benefit the growers, many tobacco growers did not, in fact, want it. A mass meeting of two hundred growers from all over the New Belt at Farmville voted to oppose the Flanagan bill as "savoring of cooperative marketing." Petitions and letters were sent by the thousand to congressmen. Graham Barden, third district congressman, received two to three thousand letters from growers opposing the bill before he received one in favor. L. V. Morrill, Jr., warned Warren emphatically that the growers in his district were against the bill, while John Kerr maintained that twenty-two thousand growers in the second district were adamantly opposed. At the subcommittee hearings only two North Carolina growers spoke for the bill, while one hundred turned up to protest the measure. The North Carolina House of Representatives voted to memorialize all the state's congressmen against the bill. It seemed from the Craven County agent that what the farmers feared was that the cost of grading would be passed on by the buyers to the growers and that the buyers would continue to purchase leaf as in the past, irrespective of what grades were decided upon by the government.[22]

Some growers, however, supported the grading bill. Harold Cooley, fourth district congressman and a new member of the House Agriculture Committee, polled the members of the Regional Growers' Advisory Committee when they were in Washington and found them unanimously in favor of it. Individual members of the state committee reiterated this support in letters to their congressmen and the governor. Cooley wrote to two hundred leading growers in his district, who replied in favor of the bill. Clarence Poe and the *Progressive Farmer* had long championed government grading and continued to do so. There was no reason, Poe asserted, why the tobacco farmer "should not be given as full knowledge of what his product should bring as the buyer possesses." The state Grange, which had always shared Poe's views, went on record for the bill, as did some of the county Granges. Two AAA county committees in Pitt and Wayne also endorsed the Flanagan bill.[23]

These growers who supported compulsory grading were frankly suspicious of the apparent opposition of so many of their fellow farmers. They were convinced that this was not spontaneous, but that the growers were victims of the warehousemen's propaganda. John Flanagan himself believed that, although the opposition was represented as coming from North Carolina growers, the real opposition came from "the Tobacco Association of the United States, composed of manufacturers, warehousemen and 'pinhookers,' a type of tobacco broker, and 'warehouse pets,' large growers who by reason of their influence over other growers are accorded special treatment by warehouses and buyers." These interests had deliberately misled the growers by telling them that grading would cost 5¢ per pound and that the Secretary of Agriculture could close up warehouses and prevent barn sales.[24]

There was plenty of evidence that the warehousemen were circulating and preparing the petitions that were meant to come from the growers. But, while Jonathan Daniels could write to the state's congressmen that he did "not believe such petitions represented the feelings of the growers or at least the feelings of the growers if they understood the full meaning of the bill," it was difficult for congressmen to make that distinction. As Graham Barden replied, "If it [the Flanagan bill] is a good thing, apparently the farmers have not been so informed and are not of that opinion at this time." In fact, grower

opposition to government grading, or more probably grower indiffer-
ence, was not the result of a conspiracy by the warehousemen, but a
natural result of the influence the warehousemen had always wielded
among the growers, especially in the New Belt.[25]

Faced with such apparent opposition, Cooley moved to modify
the bill in order to meet any possible objections from the growers. He
insisted on three amendments before the bill was reported out of the
Agriculture Committee: that a referendum of growers on each market
should be held before compulsory government grading was established
(Lindsay Warren added a requirement of a two-thirds majority), that
the government, not the buyers, should bear the cost of the grading,
and, finally, that there should be an explicit statement that no warehouse could be closed.[26]

It was difficult to see what objections could now be made to the
measure by tobacco congressmen, but these amendments did not satisfy
the bill's opponents. Kerr remained adamant in his opposition, and he
was joined by J. Bayard Clark. William Umstead also came forward
with an amendment making grading optional even after a referendum.
There followed the rare sight of an open split among the tobacco
congressmen on the floor of the House.[27]

Flanagan, supported by speakers from Kentucky, Georgia, and
South Carolina, repeated his charges that the opposition was made up
of warehousemen, manufacturers, and large growers who were misleading the ordinary grower by complete misrepresentation and false-
hoods. The North Carolina congressmen were split. Clark denounced
the bill as "the most unconstitutional measure that has yet been proposed in this House." Kerr condemned it for its "purpose . . the
breaking up of the warehouse system of marketing tobacco." Lindsay
Warren and Barden were unenthusiastic, but prepared to vote for the
bill in the expectation that the growers would defeat grading on any
referendum on North Carolina markets. Only Frank Hancock spoke
out strongly in favor of compulsory grading, complaining bitterly that
the warehousemen were now opposing a measure they had earlier
promised to support when they wanted to defeat government licensing.
His attack on the warehousemen in general, and Con Lanier in particular, drew spirited responses from Barden and Warren.[28]

Umstead's amendment, which Flanagan argued would "absolutely destroy the bill," was defeated. Of the North Carolina delegation
only Hancock, Cooley, and Lambeth voted against it, however. De-

spite the misgivings of the rest of their colleagues, the bill then passed without a record vote. In the Senate progress was even quicker, without any debate at all. Bailey, whose private views about compulsion were quite clear—"I think the grower should have the right to grade his tobacco for himself and I do not think the government or the Congress has the power to compel him to have his tobacco graded by somebody else"—nevertheless announced his "unqualified approval of the bill." In 1935 Bailey had become very solicitous of his constituents' feelings. "My view is that the farmers should have this grading if they want it and should not have it if they do not want it." The provision for referenda therefore suited him admirably.[29]

The warehousemen were not prepared to give up without a struggle. The battle was merely transferred from Washington to the markets. When the Department of Agriculture offered government grading on four North Carolina markets in 1936—Oxford, Farmville, Smithfield, and Goldsboro—Lanier protested violently that the methods of conducting the referenda were a "travesty on fairness and justice." He deeply resented the "unfair coercive methods now being used by agent Wilkinson [the man responsible for the government's system of grades]." The department replied that government officials were merely available to explain the operation of the inspection act and to counter the misleading statements of the warehousemen.[30]

At Goldsboro, the one market where government grading had not been offered before, the evidence did not support Lanier. There was a campaign for grading, but it was mounted by the local newspaper and the chamber of commerce, who saw it as an attraction to entice more growers to use the market. It was only *after* the farmers had voted for grading that Wilkinson came down from Washington to speak to meetings of businessmen and farmers to explain how the system would operate.[31]

Oxford, Farmville, and Goldsboro voted for grading by large majorities; Smithfield did not. Not content with this, Lanier joined the warehousemen in a court challenge to the constitutionality of compulsory grading. In late 1936 the district court issued a restraining order on the federal grading services in four warehouses in Oxford. This decision infuriated Frank Hancock, confirming his earlier contention that "powerful interests" would stop at nothing to halt grading. He predicted that growers would insist on having grading on every market within two or three years. His assessment of grower sentiment was in this case more accurate than that of Con Lanier. The court ruling was soon overturned. By 1941, fourteen market areas had voted for government grading when it was offered in the flue-cured belt. During 1941 a further twelve areas voted for it. In 1942, the remaining seventy-five markets were offered grading and accepted it, although thirty-eight could not receive it at once because of the shortage of qualified graders. By 1946, it was available on all markets as an essential part of the postwar stabilization program.[32]

The 1935 Program

During the formulation and implementation of the 1935 crop reduction program the tobacco growers and their representatives attempted on four occasions to change the plans of the AAA. In the fall of 1934, when the 1935 plans were first being discussed, the growers' representatives tried to have an immediate sign-up of farmers for the 1936–39 program. In the 1935 program itself they tried to secure greater exemption for small growers. They also wanted a much smaller crop in 1935 than the AAA proposed. Finally, in the fall of 1935 when leaf prices were relatively low, they attempted to secure some kind of emergency AAA action to raise them. On all four occasions they failed to move the AAA.

The contract the growers had signed in the early months of 1934 was due to expire with the marketing of the 1935 crop. In October and November 1934, when the details of the coming 1935 program were being discussed, advocates of crop control in North Carolina thought that it would be an advantage to look ahead to the period *after* 1935 and to present the growers immediately with a long-term contract for those years, which could be signed at the same time as the Kerr-Smith referendum in December 1934. By capitalizing on the current enthusiasm for the tobacco program they would be able to commit the growers to a long-term program of control and persuade the buyers of the growers' determination to restrict crops for the foreseeable future.

The Tobacco Growers' Association, a mass meeting of growers in Farmville, and, in response to the growers' demands, Governor Ehringhaus, all pressed the AAA for an immediate sign-up of a long-term control program. But Hutson was unmoved by this pressure. The AAA could ill afford the time and effort preparing contracts for 1936 when it had not organized many commodities yet for 1935. Any long-term contract would have to be tentative, since the AAA did not know what processing tax revenue was likely in the future or whether the Kerr-Smith Act would be in force for 1936.[33]

So the growers had to wait. They were eventually polled on the continuation of a crop control program in the summer of 1935. Their favorable vote led to the announcement of a 1936–39 program and contract, which the growers signed in the following fall.

A more immediate concern of the growers was the actual program for 1935. There was a growing conviction that the time had come to consolidate the tobacco program by ironing out the defects that had been highlighted in the day-to-day running of crop control programs. Most problems centered on the use of the "historic base" in calculating allotments of acreage and production. This tended to freeze the program by benefiting most those farmers who were well situated in the years 1931–33. The large commercial farmer who planted most of his cropland in tobacco was the principal beneficiary. In North Carolina the county agents, the congressmen, and even the Growers' Advisory Committee recognized that certain groups of farmers were unduly penalized: the grower who had reduced his acreage before the base period, the grower who followed the advice of the Extension Service, diversified his crops, and planted a small percentage of his acreage in tobacco, the grower whose farm had been foreclosed during the depression, the tenant farmer who had been displaced, the tenant farmer who had moved to a farm that no longer grew tobacco, the tenant who now owned and operated his farm, the farmer who had abnormally low yields during his base period, and, finally, the young farmer attempting to start working his own farm. All these farmers received unfavorable allotments if they received any at all. All were small farmers whose plight had exercised Umstead and Bailey the previous summer. One solution was to give every farmer the chance to plant three acres of tobacco without tax or reduction.[34]

The program for 1935 announced by the AAA had no special provisions for these growers. The AAA's reluctance to make special concessions was partly due to its fear of the reaction of the larger farmers. With a three-acre exemption for growers, the large producers might resent bearing the whole brunt of acreage reduction, withdraw from the program, perhaps even increase their acreage, and thus wreck the scheme. Alternatively, they might split their farms into smaller units and thus evade reduction. If all growers planted three acres there would be almost automatic overproduction. In part, however, the AAA was also anxious to protect the tenant farmers. Since the large farms were farmed on a sharecropper or tenant basis, a reduction that hit the largest producer hard would also hit the small tenant farmer hard. There were other practical considerations. An exemption for small growers would certainly shift the balance of tobacco production from the New Belt to the Old and Middle Belt where the small growers predominated. Did the tobacco growers really want that adjustment? Also, if the small growers did not reduce their crops, they could scarcely qualify for government rental and benefit payments.[35]

The AAA did, however, take up one of the suggestions made by the North Carolina county agents, and supported by the Growers' Advisory Committee, that all those who had base acreages under three acres should be allowed to plant up to their base acreages. An administrative ruling allowed anyone with a base acreage of 3.2 acres or under to plant up to their base acreage or 3 acres, whichever was the smaller. The growers who took advantage of this were to forego payments that would have been made to them under the 1935 contract. This concession was, of course, very different from allowing anyone to plant up to 3 acres. As Lindsay Warren said, "This will help some, but it did not go as far as I would like to see it."[36]

To ease slightly the position of those penalized by the "historic base," the AAA gave permission to county committees to make upward adjustments in base acreages if they felt that the grower had an abnormally low base acreage for reasons beyond his control. Once again, the grower would forego payments under the 1935 contract, and the total increase in base acreage and allotments could not exceed 3 percent of the state's total allotment. Allotments would also be given to those growers who had not signed contracts, but received special exemptions from the Kerr-Smith Act because of their inequitable bases. This was specifically to benefit those types of growers whose plight concerned the county agents and the congressmen, but there was an automatic restriction in that special tax-payment warrants could be issued only up to 6 percent of the county's allotment. None of these concessions significantly eroded the principle of the "historic base," and none of them provided the kind of blanket exemption for small growers that Warren, Umstead, and Senator Bailey seemed to want.[37]

The aspect of the 1935 program that disturbed the growers and their representatives much more than the fate of the small grower was the increase the AAA had decided to allow in the size of the 1935 crop.

Hutson had indicated that a considerable increase in the crop for 1935 was planned when he visited the flue-cured belt in October 1934. It was not a popular idea. A meeting of growers on 8 November asked for only a small increase in the crop, a modification of an earlier flat demand for no increase at all. Claude Hall warned Hutson of dissatisfaction with the planned increase; growers were already complaining that the announcement was having a deleterious effect on current market prices. L. V. Morrill, Jr., wrote Warren that every time Hutson talked of an extra hundred million pounds in the crop he was "waving a red flag in the face of every loyal signer."[38]

Nevertheless, when the Regional Growers' Advisory Committee met in Washington they were persuaded to recommend what Hutson wanted: an allotment for 1935 that was 85 percent of the base acreage. This compared with the 70 percent of the base that had been the target in 1934.[39]

The AAA wanted the increase to bring production into line with increased domestic and foreign consumption, which was indicated by the shortage of normal carry-over stocks. It was feared that artificially high prices would lead to the loss of foreign markets and also to a long-term increase in production by encouraging new growers and increased output by noncontracting growers. In addition, there would not be enough revenue from processing taxes in 1935 to fund a larger reduction.[40]

The growers and their representatives saw the matter in a much less complex light. As Graham Barden said, they simply wanted "to keep the flue-cured market a sellers' market instead of a buyers' market." After hearing of the dangers of overproduction for so long, they were at a loss to understand the wisdom of an increase in production. Even if they were prepared to accept that lower prices than those in 1934 were desirable, they were nevertheless worried that the AAA might have overreacted and prices might revert to pre-1933 levels.[41]

North Carolina congressmen expressed these fears, but failed to move either Hutson or the regional and state growers' advisory committees. There was therefore a mass meeting of businessmen and growers from twenty-three tobacco counties in Farmville on 10 February

1935. The growers elected a committee of their own to go to Washington and put their case against the increase, which they felt had not been put by the advisory committees. They invited Ehringhaus to head the delegation and Jonathan Daniels and L. V. Morrill, Jr., to accompany them. Various members of the General Assembly added themselves to the party, and Senator Bailey said he would attend whether he was invited or not.[42]

The delegation's fear of a "paralyzing surplus" failed to disturb Hutson, but he did take the precaution of reconvening the Growers' Advisory Committee. The committee, resentful of the interference by the governor's delegation, restated its acceptance of the crop increase but did agree to hold a mass meeting in Raleigh that would be addressed by Hutson and Secretary Wallace.[43]

When Hutson and Wallace spoke to the five thousand growers in Raleigh, they simply reiterated their determination to increase the crop by 20 percent. This left the North Carolina speakers with little to say, since the most ardent advocates of the smaller crop were among the most loyal supporters of the AAA. They therefore vied with each other in expressing their gratitude for what the AAA had done in the past, their concern that a mistake might have been made in calculating the size of the crop, but their determination to give continued support to the Administration and the crop control program.[44]

Wallace must have been rather bewildered by much of what he heard at the Raleigh meeting: references to cooperative marketing, the cigarette tax, and taxation revenue in North Carolina and New York, all of which had their special connotations in internal North Carolina politics. What his presence at the meeting indicated was that the dispute over the crop increase was not simply a dispute over the best means of securing better prices for tobacco growers, but had wider implications for AAA policy as a whole.

Planners in the AAA were already worried by the tendency of producer groups to regard the commodity programs as "simply a mechanism for grinding out checks to farmers" without any regard to the AAA's long-term aim of adjustment. The tobacco growers, or the producers of any commodity, ought not to be allowed simply to push up their prices by rigid production controls. First, it was not in the long-term interests of the tobacco growers themselves. Production control had been designed as an emergency measure to bring supply into line with demand, not as a permanent method of creating artificial prices through scarcity. Agricultural economists, and certainly Wallace himself, doubted that any farmers could sustain the control necessary for a monopoly control over supply for very long. Even if the markets were not lost by the high prices, production control would collapse as growers tired of the rigors of restriction and new growers and noncooperating growers increased production to capitalize on the high prices.

Second, the AAA had a responsibility to other groups, not merely the tobacco growers. Its aim was to restore a balance between agriculture and the rest of the economy, reflected in the parity goal. Tobacco prices ought to fulfil that aim. The AAA ought not to tolerate an attempt by a pressure group to force prices up to whatever level the pressure group thought desirable. The AAA had wider loyalties, not only to other farmers, but to consumers and even the manufacturers.[45]

Wallace had attempted to put some of this across to the Raleigh meeting. He was more direct in a speech to the Foreign Policy Association shortly afterwards. There he complained that "spokesmen of one commodity have begun to organize a drive to restrict production still further in the hope of raising prices still further. . . . Men who engage in political manipulation of this sort are of course interested in personal power rather than bringing a long-term balance among economic groups." The United Press identified the commodity as tobacco and one of the men as Ehringhaus.[46]

This speech upset Ehringhaus, who protested that he had no political ambitions and was loyal to the AAA. Whereas Wallace saw fundamental differences of policy between them, Ehringhaus merely saw a disagreement over the best means of improving leaf prices. Wallace could praise Ehringhaus's "single-minded devotion" to the cause of the tobacco growers. What Ehringhaus could not understand was that it was precisely that "single-minded devotion" which meant there would be basic differences in their conceptions of the function of the AAA.[47]

The prices on the New Belt markets in 1935 seemed to confirm the growers' worst fears that the AAA had made a mistake when it set the size of the crop. They wanted the tobacco section to take effective remedial action.

When dissatisfied growers met at Wendell on 12 September, Ehringhaus reported that they were "distressed, protesting and very restless" at 15¢ and 16¢ prices. But after his experience of the previous

February, the governor was wary of leading another growers' protest. Instead, the growers appointed a committee that was to wait and see whether prices improved. When prices did not advance, they called a mass protest meeting in Raleigh on 21 September. What they expected to get from the AAA was not clear, but three general demands seemed to emerge: that the growers sign their 1936–39 contracts immediately, helped by a marketing holiday if necessary; that a stabilization corporation lend money to the growers to keep their leaf off the market; and that the AAA admit its mistake and announce at once that the 1936 crop would be cut by 30 percent. The growers' mood was not improved by repeated assertions from Wallace that prices were in fact above the parity level, which he defined as 19.87¢ per pound.[48]

The mass meeting was a futile exercise. Hutson refused to take any immediate action, and the congressmen warned the growers to be cautious in criticizing the Administration. Eventually a committee was elected to go to Washington with an innocuous set of resolutions about keeping the surplus off the market, an immediate sign-up, better methods of calculating parity, and better consultative procedures between the growers and the tobacco section. In Washington the committee achieved nothing. The AAA doubted that the crop would be as large as the growers feared; E. Y. Floyd pointed out that almost all growers would have signed up within the week; and the manufacturers forecast as usual that prices would improve.[49]

The failure and collapse of the growers' agitation illustrated a division between the growers and their representatives over the best way of dealing with the AAA. Ehringhaus, still smarting from what he considered to be a public rebuke from the government for his earlier activities, felt that the AAA should frankly admit its error about the 1935 crop and accept blame for the low prices. Many growers agreed with him. Others like Clarence Poe, who supervised the organization of the mass meeting and led the delegation to Washington, the *News and Observer*, and the state's congressmen were loath to criticize the AAA, since it was the only hope of the tobacco growers for better prices.[50]

The failure to change the AAA's mind on almost everything involving the 1935 program cast doubts on its responsiveness to grower pressure, whether the growers were divided or not. It was true that the growers in 1935 had no very specific remedy for their plight, but they had also had none in 1933. In 1933, however, the growers' pressure could be used by the AAA to help put into operation something the AAA wanted to do in any case. In 1935 the AAA did not want to intervene. Therefore, it could ignore the grower pressure. It had no intention of acting, and it did not act.

The events of 1935 also cast doubts on whether the growers' advisory committees, either the regional four-state committee or the state committee, really represented the views of the growers. In February they had been accused of misrepresenting the wishes of the farmers over the proposed acreage increase. In September there were references to their members as "the fair-haired boys" of the AAA. Other committees were chosen that month to arrange mass meetings and to go to Washington. The subcommittee that organized the Raleigh meeting told the AAA bluntly that the existing committee procedure was "wholly ineffective as the means for a systematic and organic relationship between the grower and you." Clarence Poe, who drafted this complaint, wanted annual meetings of growers in each county to elect a state committee that, in turn, would choose an executive committee that would confer with the AAA. But perhaps the tobacco section did not want "a systematic and organic relationship" between itself and the grower. Perhaps it preferred to consult a committee that it could always persuade to do what it intended to do in the first place, a process that gave the impression of consultation and consent.[51]

Finally, what made the growers' pressure abortive in 1935 was that there was no crisis. The anxious rhetoric was artificial, because leaf prices were reasonable. Throughout September John Kerr had pointed out that although prices per pound were lower than in 1934, the size of the 1935 crop meant that growers would receive in aggregate more than they received for the 1934 crop. He was right. Prices averaged only 20¢ a pound compared to 27.3¢ the year before, but with an 811.2 million–pound crop the growers grossed $162.2 million, an increase of $10.5 million over 1934.[52]

The Defense of the AAA

Whatever disagreements the growers and their representatives might have had with the AAA, they came wholeheartedly to its defense in 1935 when it was threatened, first by a drive to repeal the processing tax on cotton, and then by an attempt to defeat the AAA amendments.

The determined effort in the spring of 1935 by textile interests to eliminate the processing tax on cotton alarmed representatives of the tobacco growers, who saw it as the first stage of a move to remove the processing tax altogether and eventually to destroy the tobacco as well as the cotton program. They were embarrassed by the action of the North Carolina General Assembly in memorializing Congress for the repeal of the tax, and, led by Clarence Poe, the state Grange, and the *News and Observer*, they mounted sufficient pressure to persuade the Assembly to reverse its action. In Congress, Lindsay Warren took to the floor specifically to defend the AAA. The processing tax was a matter, he argued, of simple justice to the farmer. Its elimination on cotton would lead to its elimination on tobacco and be the first step in the destruction of the farm program as a whole. Warren's speech won him the gratitude not only of the AAA, but also of the North Carolina Tobacco Growers' Association.[53]

The processors' drive also prompted North Carolina farmers to join the Plowman's Pilgrimage, a curious episode when five thousand farmers turned up in Washington on 14 May to lobby Congress in defense of the AAA. Opponents argued that this supposedly spontaneous demonstration was in fact sponsored by the AAA itself and the county agents, who paid the farmers' expenses. Certainly the county agents coordinated the fifteen hundred North Carolina farmers who went to the capital, but it is more likely that the farmers paid the agents' expenses. The largest delegation came from Pitt, where the county agent was always closely involved in the growers' pressure group activity. The tobacco section also helped by arranging a Growers' Advisory Committee meeting for the day on which most of the farmers were due to arrive.[54]

The threat that most roused the tobacco growers was the attempt to defeat the amendments designed to prolong the life of the AAA in the summer of 1935. The amendments were necessary to try to protect the licensing and taxing powers of the Secretary of Agriculture, which were under challenge by the processors in the courts. While the AAA defended them as simply clarifying amendments, Clay Williams for the manufacturers attacked their "revolutionary character." His objective was simple. He wanted the processing tax on tobacco removed. He argued that the tax was being imposed illegally, since leaf prices were over parity, and he said that the manufacturers would reduce their leaf purchases if the tax became permanent. What was worse was the "cover-up on all past illegal acts" in the attempt to prevent suits for the recovery of processing taxes already paid.[55]

This time the growers' representatives did not accept Williams's arguments that he was really concerned for the tobacco grower. Harold Cooley, fourth district congressman, maintained that the processing tax was essential for keeping prices at the parity level, while the public would not tolerate an attempt by the manufacturers to recoup taxes that they had already collected from the consumers, although he had "no doubt that some manufacturers would like to enlarge their already abundant incomes by a Treasury raid of this kind."[56]

Once again, the proposed legislation put Senator Bailey in an awkward position. It is clear from his private correspondence that he basically agreed with Clay Williams's arguments. But as in 1934 with the Kerr-Smith Act, thoughts of the 1936 primary loomed large in Bailey's mind, and the attitude of the tobacco growers was crucial to him. He had no great respect for their thoughts. Benefit payments and the huge AAA machine, which extended to every county, had given the Department of Agriculture an influence which it would not otherwise have had. It had convinced the farmers that the amendments meant something to them, so that Bailey realized that "if we voted against the AAA amendments, certain self-appointed friends of the farmers will tell them that we are not in sympathy with the farmers." He was right. When the AAA amendments reached the floor of the Senate, Claude Hall of the Growers' Association urged all county committees to wire their senators in support of the amendments. Bailey was then flooded with telegrams from the chairmen of county committees. As one grower said, "From all reports there is a concerted effort on the part of the manufacturers and others to wreck our farm program." Thus, Bailey was confronted with constituency pressure from the growers on one hand and Clay Williams on the other.[57]

To counter this, Bailey devised a shrewd strategy of supporting efforts to emasculate the amendments, but finally voting for the bill. His rhetorical opposition to several proposals was strident. The idea of prohibiting suits to recover processing taxes, he said, "strikes down the soul of the American Republic, compromises us in our own eyes and presents us defenseless before the bar of the moral law." The power to fix prices by license was "an inducement to bring about what has heretofore been known as 'cooperative marketing,'" and North Carolina's own experience of the Tri-State Cooperative "practically ruined the farmers for a period of three or four years.'' Despite this opposition and his role in the Republican-Democratic coalition that tried to wreck the amendments, Bailey indicated that in the final analysis he would vote for the bill, because the growers wanted it; but he made it clear that he did not think that the growers knew what they were talking about. ''I think that the farmers of my state desire that I shall support this legislation. I think that they, without having examined the details of this system of raising and lowering taxes, would rather that I support it.''[58]

This strategy enabled Bailey to write to an AAA enthusiast, ''I am happy to say that I supported this bill,'' while writing to textile manufacturer, Charles Cannon, who wanted to scrap the AAA, that his tactics had been the most effective way of limiting the AAA: ''We did our best to restrain the AAA within definite bounds. Any effort to defeat the bill would have prevented us from doing this: that is to say we had to be for the bill in order to get rid of some very obnoxious features.'' Clay Williams did not appreciate the strategy and was disappointed that Bailey had given up the fight. Bailey had patiently to remind him that the President had threatened not to lend money on cotton if the amendments had not passed. In the circumstances, he argued, they had pushed their opposition as far as they could. In 1935 Bailey was conscious that the tobacco growers outnumbered the holders of tobacco stocks among his constituents. After 1936 he had no need to be so cautious.[59]

The tobacco growers' support of the AAA was not merely demonstrated by Senator Bailey's perception of their wishes. In June 1935 they had voted to continue the production control program. Of those eligible, 83.3 percent voted, and 98.2 percent of them voted in favor of the AAA. Contracts for 1936 to 1939 were presented to the growers in August. They provided for crop reductions of not more than 35 percent in any one year from the old acreage and production bases. By December 1935, 85 percent of the flue-cured growers had signed up.[60]

Chapter 5

The Aftermath of Hoosac Mills

"The Supreme Court," said Harold Cooley, "voted against the Triple A by a vote of 6 to 3; the farmers voted for the Triple A by a vote of nineteen to one, yet the Triple A is no more." Whatever support the tobacco growers had given the AAA was indeed rendered meaningless on 6 January 1936, when the Supreme Court handed down its decision finding the 1933 Farm Act unconstitutional in the Hoosac Mills case. Both the production control and processing tax provisions were knocked down by the Court in *U.S.* v. *Butler*. In the light of that decision, Congress rapidly repealed the Kerr-Smith and Bankhead acts.[1]

The decision caused consternation among the North Carolinians in Congress. Warren, who announced the decision on the floor of the House, immediately denounced it as a "sickening and deadly blow." Cooley called it a "calamity," and Doughton predicted it would have a "paralyzing effect." Even when the immediate passion subsided, the Court's decision was not held in high repute. Hancock believed that the Court had taken "an untenable and absurd position in holding that agriculture was a local rather than a national problem." Kerr maintained that the Court could have ruled favorably but "for the fact that they are politically biased and determined to assault our administration." Cooley promised a constituent that he would "remember you to the Court. You actually have no idea how many people would like to get a crack at at least six of the old boys."[2]

The reaction was similar back in North Carolina. The *News and Observer* headed its editorial "Back to Despair." Dean Schaub described the situation as "precarious," "alarming and serious." A

Nashville farmers' meeting called the decision a "death blow to our hopes." A traveling salesman in Wayne County summed up the general reaction when he lamented: "I couldn't do any business at all. All I could do was to listen to talk about the death of the AAA. How it was bound to ruin us right quickly. I didn't do a bit of business the next day after the decision. I finally snapped my bags shut about 2 p.m. and came on home." Both Schaub and Lindsay Warren asserted that the growers would not tolerate a return to pre-1933 conditions, and the message that came from the various township meetings of farmers, held in the wake of the Supreme Court decision, was that the tobacco growers wanted some sort of substitute for the AAA. This their representative promised them. Warren had already vowed to keep Congress in session until the following Christmas if necessary to secure redress. Even Senator Bailey agreed that "parity is nothing more nor less than justice" and promised that Congress and the President would pass all laws necessary to secure it.[3]

After initial confusion, the efforts to try to retrieve the situation after the crushing blow of Hoosac Mills concentrated on five main lines of approach: support of the soil conservation program as a stop-gap measure; an attempt to secure crop control by means of a compact among the tobacco-growing states; a drive to organize tobacco farmers in the Farm Bureau; support for the President's plan to reform the Supreme Court; and support for a permanent replacement for the AAA, which would include compulsory crop control for tobacco.

The Soil Conservation and Domestic Allotment Act

The North Carolina tobacco congressmen soon realized that it would be very difficult to secure special legislation for a single commodity. They therefore solidly supported the government's substitute proposal for the AAA, the Soil Conservation and Domestic Allotment bill. Utilizing and adding to existing soil conservation legislation, farmers would be paid for planting certain soil-building crops, but more important they would be paid for taking certain soil-depleting crops out of production. Tobacco was one of the soil-depleting crops. It was thus hoped that production would be controlled indirectly under the guise of soil conservation.

North Carolina congressmen regarded the measure as an indifferent replacement for the old AAA. Cooley described it as a ''very poor substitute [but the] best we could do under the present circumstances,'' while Clark admitted that it was not ''so practical or so effective or so satisfactory'' as the AAA. It was not self-financing, and the congressmen doubted that enough money would ever be appropriated to provide the sort of payments that would be necessary to persuade growers to reduce their acreage sufficiently. Similar fears were expressed by farmers at county program-planning committees. Senator Bailey, on the other hand, responded enthusiastically to the new scheme. In part, this was the result of the exigencies of election year and his perception of his constituents' wishes, but it was also clear that while the state's congressmen acquiesced in the soil conservation measure for want of something better, Bailey regarded it as a sound program in its own right, shorn of the obnoxious compulsory features of the old AAA.[4]

Much of what the new legislation did out of constitutional necessity had long been advocated as desirable policy by planners in the AAA. They had been anxious to shift from the short-term emphasis on production control (which simply raised prices) to the longer-term aim of genuine adjustment, which would create an American agriculture in which farmers produced what they were best equipped to produce at the lowest cost. To that end, the planners had already launched an educational program of regional adjustment studies, county program-planning committees, and discussion groups. The 1936 act gave this program a positive legislative stimulus. Whereas the former commodity programs had been rather indifferent to what farmers did with their rented acres, the new program provided for incentives for genuine conservation practices. To get away also from the simple commodity orientation, farmers were now offered a single contract for their whole farm rather than a separate contract for each commodity. The new work sheets offered a more flexible and integrated program of farming than had the rigid ''historic base'' of the old contracts.[5]

Nevertheless, North Carolina tobacco farmers, like their congressmen, regarded the new program as a production control program rather than a charter for better farming. E. Y. Floyd estimated that between 75 and 80 percent of flue-cured growers participated in 1936 and reduced their acreage by 23 percent. Some 136,100 acres in the state were diverted from tobacco under the program. This, combined with bad weather, kept the overall flue-cured crop down to 682.9

million pounds. But very few of the farmers took part in the positive side of the program—the establishing of soil conservation practices. In part, this was because the payments for soil-building practices were far less than the payments for soil diverting. According to county agents, the program was also implemented so late that many farmers did not understand it and were unaware that merely taking acreage out of production was not the whole program. Many were simply not interested in soil conservation.[6]

As part of the shift away from the narrow emphasis on individual commodities, the administrative structure of the AAA was changed under the new program. The old commodity sections disappeared and were replaced by regional divisions, although these had strong ties with particular commodities. North Carolina came under the East Central Region, and the chief importance of tobacco was acknowledged with the appointment of Hutson as regional director. State AAA committees and state executive officers were appointed after consultation with the Extension Service. In North Carolina, J. F. Criswell, who had been in charge of the cotton program, became executive officer while E. Y. Floyd chaired the General Program Committee and overlooked advanced planning. In practice, Floyd retained his responsibility for matters concerning tobacco and took charge of the new tobacco program when it was launched in 1938. Under the 1936 act the program was due to be handed over to the states in 1938, financed by grants-in-aid to state agencies conforming with federal standards. This plan was later scrapped, and the federal government retained control.[7]

Locally, the administration shifted to formally elected committees. This had been foreshadowed in the tobacco program for 1936–39, but had not yet been implemented. Cooperating growers were to be members of the County Agricultural Conservation Association. At community meetings they were to elect community committeemen. In turn, the chairman of the community committee would be on the board of directors of the county association, which would elect a county committee. In North Carolina these committees invariably then chose the county agent as their secretary. He was thus the servant of the county committee rather than the designated AAA representative as he had been under the tobacco program. The break was not a sharp one in North Carolina. The program was established so late in the planting season that vital administrative tasks had to be carried out by the existing machinery. Elections frequently returned the same county committee, particularly in counties with one major commodity where members of the county committee for that program simply continued under the new program.[8]

The Extension Service had mixed feelings about the shift. Dean Schaub was reluctant to let the reins of administration pass from his county agents to the county associations, but at the same time he complained of a lack of interest in administration by the farmers: "The agents report that most of the farmers are 'fed up' with meetings and they are having trouble in getting out a reasonable number to select committeemen." Yet he complained when the farmers were enthusiastic. He reacted with horror to reports that people were actually campaigning for election to committees, canvassing the entire community, and providing cars to haul voters to the meeting. He was told that some "very undesirable persons" had been campaigning. In fact, the Extension Service would remain firmly in control of the local administrative procedures, and this would bring the organization headaches as the program itself ran into difficulties.[9]

The Tobacco Compact

In an effort to secure production control that was more substantial than the voluntary and indirect restriction provided by the soil conservation scheme, the North Carolina congressmen worked for congressional authorization of a compact among the tobacco-growing states, by which the states would agree to their own compulsory crop control.

The idea of such a compact seems first to have been broached in the summer of 1935 by a North Carolinian, John Hester, who was working in the Reconstruction Finance Corporation and who wrote to the state's press suggesting ways in which the New Deal could obtain objectives in the constitutional framework left by the Schecter case (which had invalidated the NRA). He suggested, for example, that the tobacco-growing states could enter a compact to implement the Kerr-Smith Act, with the Secretary of Agriculture designated as the enforcement agent to secure uniform enforcement of the state laws. John Kerr noted the letter and sent a copy to Hutson. No more was heard until the Hoosac Mills decision was announced, when Kerr said that he hoped a compact among the tobacco states might be reached. By the end of

January 1936 he had introduced a bill granting congressional authorization for such a compact.[10]

There were two immediate obstacles. Neither the Georgia nor the North Carolina legislatures were in session, and it was doubtful if either could be called back to enact control legislation in order to enter a compact. Governor Eugene Talmadge's hostility to the New Deal in general and crop control in particular made it certain that he would not call a special session in Georgia. The situation was less clear in North Carolina. It might have been expected that someone who had played as decisive a part in the tobacco growers' fight for better prices as Governor Ehringhaus would take the lead in the battle for the compact. But since the summer of 1935 he had been resisting pressure to call a special session to take the state into the Social Security system. His ostensible reason was that a special session was unnecessary because the state already had adequate enabling legislation, but his real reason was that, like Max Gardner in 1931, he feared a special session would undermine the state's fiscal soundness. By retrenchment and the imposition of a sales tax in 1933, Ehringhaus had managed to balance the state's budget. He had protected that achievement in 1935 when he fought off a sustained drive to repeal the sales tax by anti-administration forces led by Ralph W. McDonald. Ehringhaus feared that a special session would reopen the sales tax issue (and also the controversial liquor-control question) and might jeopardize the budget, which he had balanced at great political cost to himself. It remained to be seen whether the governor would risk this on behalf of the tobacco growers.[11]

Early meetings in Washington among representatives of the flue-cured states made limited progress. There was no prospect of official Georgia action, although growers from that state thought they might be able to form a cooperative association that might come to a private agreement with the other states. One solution to this problem was for the federal government to control the interstate commerce of tobacco to and from noncompacting states, but most of the congressmen present doubted this could be legally done. Most important, Ehringhaus clearly had serious reservations. Nevertheless, when he returned to North Carolina he posed two questions to the growers and indicated that he would be guided by their replies: Were they prepared to form a compact without Georgia? Were they prepared to form a compact if both Georgia and South Carolina stayed out?[12]

The replies can have left the governor in no doubt that the growers would form a compact without Georgia and that they wanted the governor to call a special session immediately. He received this message from many of the men who had backed him in the tobacco growers' fights in the past. There were also similar demands from newly formed units of the Farm Bureau. The North Carolina Farm Bureau had come out in favor of a compact and a special session and was linking its organizational drive to the drive for a compact. The state Growers' Advisory Committee echoed their demands.[13]

Further testimony to the growers' desire for a special session was the way in which both anti-organization candidates in the gubernatorial primary attempted to capitalize on such sentiments. In that primary two candidates, Ralph McDonald and A. H. "Sandy" Graham, were attempting to exploit anti-administration feeling against Clyde R. Hoey, Gardner's brother-in-law and clearly the organization candidate. McDonald had called for a New Deal in North Carolina and had long wanted a special session to take the state into the Social Security program. Both he and Graham now came out strongly in the tobacco belt for a special session to enact compact legislation. Both complained that North Carolina should have taken the lead in the move for a compact, and both argued that Georgia's production would not be sufficient to destroy the compact's effectiveness.[14]

At the same time some progress was also made in Virginia toward solving the problem of Georgia. While the Virginia law still required reciprocal legislation by North and South Carolina before a compact could go into effect, legislation by Georgia was no longer required. For the crop year of 1936 it was left to the discretion of the governor of Virginia merely to satisfy himself that effective means of controlling production in Georgia existed. The way was now open for some form of cooperative association there.

In response, Ehringhaus announced in a statewide broadcast on 7 March that he would call a special session as soon as it became clear that a compact could be made effective. But he argued that there was no point in such a session until Congress had authorized compacts, since neither the Virginia nor South Carolina laws could go into effect without that authorization, and until South Carolina had acted, since their legislature was already in session. Furthermore, both Congress and South Carolina would have to act by 1 April; otherwise planting in Georgia would have started and no compact could be effective in time.[15]

It was convenient for Ehringhaus to shift the blame for delay to Washington, but he needed an alternative to a compact to demonstrate his real concern for the growers. On 16 March therefore he called for a voluntary sign-up of North Carolina growers to reduce their acreage to 70 percent of their base. A meeting of farm leaders next day appointed a steering committee to start a sign-up campaign, but this flopped dismally. It was called off before it started, because neither Virginia nor South Carolina showed any interest, nor did many North Carolina growers. Instead, the steering committee pressed Ehringhaus to call a special session.[16]

Just as his alternative to a compact had failed, so the governor's alibis for inaction also tended to disappear. Bad weather delayed the planting of crops and made the 1 April deadline irrelevant. At last there was also progress in Congress. The North Carolina delegation secured the support of Marvin Jones, the House Agriculture Committee chairman, the Department of Agriculture, and Speaker Joseph T. Byrns. Jones had his doubts about the bill, but, as he explained, he had also had doubts about the successful Kerr-Smith Act, so that he did not regard himself as infallible. In order to get the bill passed, however, the delegation had to sacrifice the provision regulating the interstate commerce of tobacco to and from noncompacting states. The congressmen had been reconciled to this, and, in any case, the department felt that its loss would not impair the effectiveness of the compacts. As Cooley pointed out, at the time of year when North Carolina growers marketed their tobacco, they would not want to, and could not, sell it elsewhere.[17]

The bill was assured passage in the Senate by the backing of Senator Ellison D. Smith, Bailey, and the Senate leaderhsip. It was delayed merely by a series of calendar obstacles, including the start of a baseball season, an impeachment, and the filibuster of another measure by Senator Robert Reynolds. This filibuster caused the junior senator from North Carolina some embarrassment. He had little personal knowledge of, or interest in, tobacco legislation. He routinely voted for what the growers and the House delegation wanted. To his horror he discovered that some of his constituents thought that his filibuster against the Kerr-Coolidge bill, which concerned his favorite subject of immigration and aliens, was in fact against the Kerr compact bill. He immediately leapt to his feet in the Senate, waved the Kerr bill in the air, and tried to get it passed at once, oblivious of the patient work done by the leadership to get the bill passed as soon as possible. In due course, the Senate passed the bill as promised on 21 April.[18]

Progress was halting in South Carolina. While Ehringhaus interpreted this as a justification of his own inaction, South Carolina advocates of the compact blamed their difficulties on Ehringhaus's refusal to call a special session in their neighboring state. How could South Carolina, they argued, be expected to pass a compact bill if the country's major flue-cured growing state was not prepared to act?[19]

Ehringhaus's excuses for not acting had gone with the assurance of congressional action and the delay in planting. Even supporters of the organization candidate Clyde Hoey, like Lindsay Warren and William Umstead, both friends of the governor, were urging him to call a special session. It was now clear that he had no intention of calling a special session under any circumstances.

Supporters of the compact, however, believed that they could force the governor to act. The drive to do so came mainly from Pitt County, in the very heart of the tobacco belt, which was also the starting point of the newly formed state farm bureau. On 15 April the Pitt Farm Bureau held a mass meeting of fifteen hundred growers in Greenville. The local president told them that Ehringhaus "had opposed the will of the majority of the state's farmers in failing to call a special session to enact tobacco control legislation . . . now let's see who's the biggest." The place to test this challenge was to be a mass meeting of growers in Raleigh on 21 April when they would confront the governor.[20]

Feelings ran high in the tobacco belt. One grower warned Ehringhaus that the meeting might get out of hand. The Pitt farmers aimed to attract ten thousand growers to the meeting with the slogans "On to Raleigh" and "It's time to go." A committee arranged to provide one thousand cars to transport the farmers. In Greenville the mayor proclaimed a general business holiday for the day of the meeting; a judge postponed his court; the Alcoholic Beverage Control stores shut for the day. On 21 April the town was reported to be like a deserted village. Business holidays were proclaimed all over eastern North Carolina. Half the businesses in Wilson were shut after the county commissioners urged the growers to go to Raleigh. In Lenoir the Farm Bureau, the Grange, and the AAA county committee jointly asked the growers to attend.[21]

At the meeting in Riddick Stadium at North Carolina State College the growers made plain their views. Ovations greeted the speakers, who all urged the governor to call a special session. These included members of the Growers' Advisory Committee and sponsors of the 1933 Raleigh meeting. Some reminded Ehringhaus of his leadership then, some asked if he knew better than the entire congressional delegation, and some asked what plan he had as an alternative to a compact.[22]

The more they asked for a special session, the more determined Ehringhaus became not to concede anything. He spared no one in a bold and unrepentant reply. It was clear that in his view whatever happened in Georgia, South Carolina, and Congress would be irrelevant. He dissected the compact idea as embodied in the Virginia law and the model Department of Agriculture statute. The compact would not, he argued, bring the compulsory control its supporters wanted. The penalty on noncooperators was trifling; it affected only their excess tobacco, not all their tobacco, unlike the Kerr-Smith Act. Noncooperators could plant as much as they liked and evade the act by shipping it across state lines and selling it in a noncompact state like Tennessee or Georgia. North Carolina growers would be putting their heads in a noose and in the long run might lose their dominance of flue-cured production, in the same way they had lost their share of cotton production by their voluntary reductions in the 1920s.

The frustrations of four years of office and constant criticism surfaced as he launched a bitter personal attack on the growers' leaders with whom he had worked so enthusiastically in the past. He lashed out at Dean Schaub, Claude Hall, Hutson, and Wallace. It was the large crop for 1935, which they had sanctioned and which he had opposed, that had put the growers in the trouble they faced that day. These leaders, searching for an excuse, had shamefully turned on the governor who had fought for the growers all along. He seemed willingly to accept the martyrdom they had prepared for him and compared himself to Christ.[23]

This speech killed all hopes of implementing a compact for the 1936 crop. All that remained was for the congressional delegation and the governor to trade insults in an attempt to avoid the blame for the failure. The most bitter and sustained of these exchanges occurred between Kerr and Ehringhaus. Kerr argued that the governor had had every opportunity to get the compact legislation he wanted, but instead had "all along endeavored to make this compact impossible." Ehringhaus retorted by dragging up again Kerr's alleged role on behalf of the manufacturers in 1933 and his support of the large crop in 1935. Kerr defended this assault and denounced the governor with even greater vehemence. Kerr was once again having to defend his record as a friend of the tobacco farmer in a congressional primary, and he never forgave Ehringhaus for balking the compact and reviving past controversies. In future years, he blamed most of the growers' problems on the governor's failure to act in 1936.[24]

In the event, the predictions of disaster which everybody freely threw around came to nothing. The 1936 crop brought higher average prices than the 1935 one. Total income was down by $10 million from the 1935 total, but it nevertheless matched the bumper year of 1934. These figures were later taken by Ehringhaus as a justification of his refusal to act in the spring. But he had then been as gloomy as anyone else about the growers' prospects, which he had described as "tragic and desperate." Although his analysis of the weakness of the compact approach was in many ways, if not completely, correct, his failure to act still requires explanation. The dangers were no greater than the potential disasters that might have resulted from his decisive action in closing the markets in 1933.

For a critic like Jonathan Daniels the explanation was simple. The governor had been caught between the "conflicting interests of the industry-banker crowd which put him in office and the farmers." In 1933 Ehringhaus had been able to help the farmers without antagonizing the wealthy interests. In 1936, however, helping the farmers required the calling of a special session to which the special interests were bitterly opposed, because they feared it might bring about fundamental changes in the economic power structure of the state by repealing the sales tax. Ehringhaus could not help the farmers without alienating these groups to whom his first loyalty lay.[25]

A simple picture of Ehringhaus as a tool of the special interests is not entirely satisfactory. It is certainly not clear that Ehringhaus himself felt that he was under pressure from the "industry-banker" crowd to oppose the special session. The financial interests of Winston-Salem led by Robert Hanes of Wachovia Bank were believed to be supporting Sandy Graham in the gubernatorial primary, and Graham had endorsed a special session. Men close to O. Max Gardner and his candidate Clyde Hoey, like Lindsay Warren and other members of the state congressional delegation, also favored calling the legislature back.

What was more important was Ehringhaus's personal fiscal conservatism, which had for so long been at odds with his own moderate New Dealism. He had vigorously supported many New Deal programs and cooperated with New Deal agencies. At the same time, however, he had balanced the state budget and aroused considerable opposition from state liberals appalled at the social cost involved. This fiscal conservatism had also led to many disputes with impatient Washington officials over North Carolina's reluctance to contribute financially to federal programs. His reluctance to call a special session reflected his increasingly obsessive concern with maintaining the fiscal credit of the state, which he had built up at great political sacrifice. It is difficult not to sympathize with Ehringhaus in his predicament. In many ways a loyal supporter of the New Deal, he had received credit for this neither from the liberal faction in the state nor from the federal administration, while far less steadfast supporters of reform, especially in the congressional delegation, had been amply rewarded. No wonder he felt frustrated at the farmers' meeting in Raleigh. The compact crisis was the final blow. Increasingly politically isolated and unappreciated, he found himself alienating the very tobacco farmers whose cause he had once championed with such courage and determination.[26]

Ehringhaus derived some comfort from the remarkable speed with which the agitation for a special session died down after his firm stand. Perhaps, as one of his correspondents assured him, it had all been the work of a "few agricultural leaders, including some county agents [who] can always work up a minority and make public sentiment seem what they wish it to be." Any such doubts about the reality of the tobacco growers' pressure for a compact in 1936 were heightened by the sorry history of the attempt to secure compact legislation in 1937. Ehringhaus must have permitted himself a wry smile as advocates of the compact came up against insurmountable obstacles after he left office. The failure in 1936 had demonstrated the difficulty of coordinating action among the states in an emergency situation. The failure in 1937, when there had been adequate time for preparation and when all the legislatures were in session, illustrated the difficulty of securing production control by state rather than federal action even under the most favorable circumstances.[27]

The tobacco growers had plenty of time to prepare for compact legislation in 1937. In September 1936 the Farm Bureau sponsored a meeting in Washington with representatives of all the tobacco states. Agreement was reached on the administrative structure in each state and on the type of control to be used. At this point, Hutson was reported to be "completely optimistic" that a compact would be put into operation.[28]

What was acceptable in an emergency, however, was not necessarily satisfactory in a permanent program. In particular, there were now doubts·in North Carolina about the proposals for acreage reduction in the new model state bills. In the original proposals there had been merely a penalty for marketing excess poundage using the old AAA bases; in the new state bills there were provisions for acreage allotments and penalties for overplanting. This brought up the whole question of the "historic base" as a method of calculating allotments and the treatment of the small grower.

Jonathan Daniels was worried that the "historic base" created "vested rights for certain farmers." He noted that land with acreage allotments had already increased in value compared to·land without that advantage. Clarence Poe and the state Grange wanted to protect the small farmer against the large farmer, who had planted most of his cultivated acreage in tobacco. The small farmer should not be expected to bear the same burden of reduction. They wanted allotments to favor those who planted a small percentage of their acreage in tobacco and to take into account the number of members of a family who were dependent on that allotment for their income. The data used to calculate these allotments should be publicly displayed in the townships to make sure there was no favoritism to the larger planters. These problems of the small farmer, the historic base, and local administration had always been present, but up to 1936 they received a low priority because of the emergency nature of the growers' position. In a nonemergency situation supporters of control could afford to pay more attention to them. They would plague the production control program in the next few years.[29]

The Grange had proposed a minimum four-acre allotment and a gradual reduction of allotments so that by 1940 no farm would have an allotment that exceeded 25 percent of its cultivated acreage. At hearings on the compact bill attended by three thousand growers in Raleigh in January 1937, Claude Hall and E. Y. Floyd maintained that the calculation of allotments was a routine administrative matter. They defended the allotment procedure laid down in the bill. It essentially provided for the existing AAA bases to be adjusted by a tobacco commission, in order to cope with blatant inequities and to make room for new growers. But such was the clamor from those who believed that they had been discriminated against under the old AAA that a subcommittee had to be established to draft compromise amendments. These amendments were acceptable to the Grange and provided that no grower with a base acreage under 3.2 acres should be cut, that no tobacco allotment should exceed 35 percent of a farm's cultivated acreage, and that the data for calculating allotments should be publicized in the way that Clarence Poe had suggested. The 35 percent maximum provision was turned down by the North Carolina House Agriculture Committee on the advice of James E. Thigpen, who had been sent down from Washington by the AAA to supervise proceedings. He had no objection to limiting a grower's tobacco to 35 percent of his cultivated acreage, but pointed out that this would in fact discriminate against the small grower whom it was meant to help. He showed that in a county like Sampson, whose representative was pushing for the change, the small growers tended to have over 35 percent of their acreage in tobacco. Even so, the representative from Sampson persisted in presenting this amendment on the floor. Other amendments called for a minimum allotment of four acres and the inclusion of dependents in the allotment calculation. These were all narrowly defeated. The compact bill then passed the House and the Senate easily. A supplementary bill established a review and equalization board to hear complaints about allotments.[30]

All the debate in North Carolina, revealing divisions that were to grow in importance, was to no avail. There was strong opposition to a compact in Georgia, and the new governor, E. D. Rivers, was not going to jeopardize his other reforming legislation by a fight over the compact. No sooner, therefore, had the compact bill passed in North Carolina than it was clear that there was no hope of reciprocal legislation in Georgia, or for that matter in South Carolina. The compact was dead.[31]

Interstate compacts have never been very satisfactory. At best, they require lengthy and patient preparation to secure the participation of the states concerned. They tend to be clumsy instruments. Interstate differences often have to be resolved by giving member states veto powers. Disputes then take on an interstate quality. Overall, they accentuate parochial rather than national interests. The history of the attempt to secure production control by means of a compact among the tobacco-growing states indicates the virtual impossibility of achieving crop control by action at the state level. In 1936, Ehringhaus had demonstrated the inherent weaknesses of the compact idea. Even under the stimulus of an emergency, compact advocates were unable to secure sufficiently quick action by the states. In 1937, in more favorable circumstances, it was still impossible to achieve uniform action by the various legislatures. It was clear that, if the tobacco grower was to win the crop control he wanted, he would have to look to federal legislation for it.[32]

The Formation of the
North Carolina Farm Bureau

One direct consequence of the Hoosac Mills decision was the organization of the North Carolina Farm Bureau. The main reasons for its formation and its chief aims were to secure legislation that would replace the Agricultural Adjustment Act and restore compulsory crop control for tobacco.

It was clear that this goal could not have been achieved by the existing farmers' organizations in North Carolina. The state Grange had neither the capacity nor the interest. It had been revived in North Carolina in 1929 at the instigation of a committee of farm leaders, including Clarence Poe and Dean Schaub. It had the full backing of the Extension Service and by 1933 had 12,500 members. It had, however, no particular appeal to large tobacco growers. At a state level the Grange had less interest in crop prices than in general rural welfare concerns: rural electrification, the provision of mutual insurance and exchanges, and the incidence of state land taxes. Its membership was scattered all over the state, and it boasted that its main concern was for the family-sized farm. At the national level the Grange, by 1936, was opposed to the New Deal. It was scarcely likely to fight for a crop like tobacco, which its national master thought should never have been a basic commodity in the first place.[33]

The North Carolina Tobacco Growers' Association, which had been spawned by the great marketing crisis of 1933, clearly wanted to restore crop control, but lacked the organizational strength to exert any pressure to achieve that aim. Whatever authority and power it had had came from above: from, on the one hand, the AAA, which had given its committee a formalized position in the decision-making process of the tobacco program as the Growers' Advisory Committee, and, on the other, from the county agents, who had selected its delegates as county committeemen to administer the control program. The association's authority did not come from below as elected representatives of a viable grass roots organization of growers. Before Hoosac Mills, this did not matter. What mattered was the ability to influence decisions that were made within the government. The association's committee had a sufficiently influential position in administration counsels to do that. After Hoosac Mills, what mattered was the ability to convince legislators, not government officials, of the necessity of crop control. To do this a demonstrably powerful pressure group was needed.

Such a pressure group seemed to be available in the American Farm Bureau Federation. By associating itself from the start with New Deal farm policy, the Farm Bureau had hoped to capitalize on the New Deal's popularity and also make itself indispensable to the New Deal as its foremost supporter. In particular, the bureau had recognized in the AAA a great opportunity to increase its membership, especially in the South, by exploiting the AAA's own work of organizing farmers. While the Farm Bureau in general attempted to capitalize on the organization of the AAA to extend its membership, in North Carolina it attempted to launch itself on the tide of the growers' desire to revive the AAA. The formation of the North Carolina Farm Bureau was fundamentally linked to the need to secure production control once more for tobacco.[34]

The movement started almost within the AAA. In January 1936 the Pitt County agent, E. F. Arnold, discussed with his county committeemen the need for a farmers' organization that would secure substitute legislation for the AAA. They first thought of a temporary lobbying organization in Washington and wrote other county agents with the idea that each tobacco county be responsible in turn for sending a delegation each day to the capital for the next two or three months, until replacement legislation was passed. But they also wanted a more permanent and visible pressure group. They therefore invited county committeemen from twenty-five eastern Carolina tobacco counties to a mass meeting at Greenville on 9 February to hear Edward O'Neal, president of the American Farm Bureau Federation. The resolutions passed by the county committeemen at this meeting indicated that their main aim was to bring about renewed production control. They voted to cooperate fully with any federal program for 1936, to reduce tobacco acreage in 1936 to 70 percent of their base, to contact credit agencies to ensure that credit was given only on such a basis, and finally to form whatever organization might be necessary "in order to perfect substitute legislation or plans which will fully control the surplus in all basic crops produced in 1936." A meeting was arranged the following week, also addressed by O'Neal, which set up a state farm bureau federation under the chairmanship of J. E. Winslow, a leading Pitt tobacco farmer.[35]

The link with tobacco and with production control was clear. As far as the new secretary, E. F. Arnold, was concerned, control for tobacco was the major objective of the new organization. He considered his job to be done when a new farm act introduced that control in 1938. Winslow, who became president of the permanent organization, had been an AAA tobacco committeeman in Pitt and was a member of both the state and regional growers' advisory committees. Claude Hall, chairman of the North Carolina Tobacco Growers' Association, was a director, as were six of the sponsors of the original 1933 mass meeting. The organizing campaign of the new body focused on tobacco. It concentrated on twenty-eight counties around Pitt in the tobacco belt and was tied in immediately with the drive for a tobacco compact. As a local paper explained, growers were joining the new organization because they believed it would assist them in restricting acreage.[36]

The Farm Bureau boasted of its close connection with the North Carolina Extension Service. The letterhead of the state Farm Bureau proclaimed that it was "Cooperating with the Extension Service for the Advancement of Agriculture," and the national organizers clearly believed that the state's county agents were "their" representatives, whose functions were to attract new members to the bureau. Despite the bureau's feeling that the agents were not doing this successfully enough and despite occasional disclaimers by county agents that the Farm Bureau was purely a farmers' movement, the county agents did take a full part in helping the Farm Bureau organize. They arranged meetings and speakers, occasionally collected dues, sometimes turned official AAA meetings into bureau gatherings, and generally encouraged farmers to join. The close institutional links, however, which existed in other states between the Farm Bureau and the Extension

Service were absent in North Carolina. North Carolina county agents were never the mere tools of local farm bureaus, which they were in some northern states. Similarly, local North Carolina farm bureaus were never merely the paper creation of the county agent, which they were in some southern states. Whatever the North Carolina Farm Bureau may have claimed, the Extension Service encouraged farmers to join the Farm Bureau in the same way that it had always encouraged farmers to organize, whether in the Grange or in the North Carolina Tobacco Growers' Association.[37]

To the extent, however, that a close link between the two organizations was either perceived by opponents or exploited by the Farm Bureau, the position of the Extension Service and, indirectly, the AAA was weakened. For the Farm Bureau failed. After three months it had attracted only four thousand members, and although a year later it claimed a membership of fifteen thousand, this was a doubtful figure and certainly rapidly declined afterward. For all its lobbying activities and well-publicized meetings and resolutions, it failed to develop any grass roots strength among the tobacco growers. Its local organization remained almost as much a paper creation as the North Carolina Tobacco Growers' Association. The secretary, Arnold, was something of a disaster. He certainly enjoyed lobbying trips to Washington—in one year he was reported to have made thirty-three trips to the capital on behalf of tobacco and peanut legislation—but he had a knack of offending people, was a hopeless organizer, and knew nothing about, and had no interest in, local organization. By 1939 the southern regional organizer of the American Farm Bureau Federation called the North Carolina Farm Bureau a patient that was "sick unto death." O'Neal admitted that no other state organization had given him so much worry.[38]

The bureau's formation and the link it claimed with the Extension Service injected a note of divisiveness into the drive by the tobacco growers for crop control. As the *News and Observer* noted in November 1936, the Farm Bureau could be identified as representing the time merchants, warehousemen, and large farmers. As such it would conflict with the Grange, which was the self-styled defender of the family-sized farm. This conflict had exacerbated the tensions over the treatment of small growers that had arisen in the fight for the tobacco compact. On the one hand, prominent members of the Farm Bureau simply could not understand what Jonathan Daniels was worried about

in the "historic base"; on the other, the Grange resented being excluded from the meetings that drafted the proposed compact bills and
believed that the small grower had been ignored as a result. The more
often disputes like this occurred, the harder it was for the Extension
Service and the AAA to retain an impartial image in the administration
of production control programs. The results of this were seen in the
defeat of crop control in 1938.[39]

Some of the divisiveness could be seen in the personal antagonisms that members of the Farm Bureau aroused from the start. The
men who organized the Farm Bureau had greatly offended their local
congressman, Lindsay Warren. Warren wrote on a letter of support
from Winslow: "This two-faced rotter. I wouldn't believe him on
oath. He has always hated me." He also regarded the local president of
the Pitt Farm Bureau, Haywood Dail, as an ingrate who had asked
Warren for many favors, but had never paid the attorney whom Warren
had secured for him to reduce Dail's tax assessment. Similarly, Con
Lanier regarded the secretary, Arnold, as a "little squirt" and expressed a desire to ram his teeth down his throat. To people like Lanier
and Warren, the organizers of the Farm Bureau were merely interested
in collecting membership dues and were using the issue of crop control
as a bait with which to attract the tobacco growers. It was not surprising that an opponent of crop control like Senator Bailey should also see
the organization as a group whose "main business is to raise a racket
and collect dues." Bailey had a particular reason to be annoyed with
the Farm Bureau. At the organizing meeting in February 1936 O'Neal
had claimed that he had "raised Cain" with Bailey with the result that
the senator now supported agricultural legislation. Bailey maintained
that "O'Neill [sic] is unknown to me . . . I have no recollection of
ever having seen him." Bailey may have been angry that O'Neal had
drawn attention to the discrepancy between Bailey's professed independence and his susceptibility to political pressure near election time,
but the early history of the North Carolina Farm Bureau does little to
contradict the suspicions of men like Warren, Lanier, and Bailey. In
the long run, despite its clear aim, its formation made the task of
bringing back and retaining tobacco production control in North Carolina more difficult.[40]

Supreme Court Reform

Within the constitutional framework laid down by the Hoosac Mills decision, the tobacco growers had been unable to secure the production control that they wanted. Indirect control under the soil conservation scheme and direct control under the compact had proved either inadequate or impossible. One possible solution was to change the constitutional framework. For this reason the tobacco growers and their representatives supported the President's plan to reform the Supreme Court in 1937. Advocates of reform argued that the only way the growers could gain the control legislation they wanted was to change the Court.

The President's plan was revealed at the very time that the attempt to implement crop control by the compact was breaking down in February 1937. The *News and Observer* explained to the growers in one of the first of its editorials supporting the reform plan that it was precisely to meet that sort of situation that Roosevelt had made his proposal to reform the judiciary. If the growers waited for a constitutional amendment they might have to wait ten or twenty years to get what they wanted. Meanwhile, they might starve to death. Presumably the Court would regard the starving of farmers as a "purely local activity." Claude Hall of the Growers' Advisory Committee also drew the connection between crop control and Court reform when he wrote his fellow committeemen that it was important for all farmers who wanted crop control to get in touch with their congressmen at once to support the President. The Farm Bureau came out for reform. It claimed that it had not found a single farmer in the state "who opposes the President's efforts to adjust the Court [so] that Congress may pass laws to protect labor and farmers in their struggle for economic existence." It was significant that the state Grange, whose national organization bitterly opposed Court reform, made no public comment on the Court issue, while several of its local units came out in favor of the President.[41]

The behavior of the North Carolina congressmen suggests that they also thought that their constituents favored the reform. When the plan was introduced only Hancock of the tobacco representatives gave it his unqualified support. He became a member of the steering committee of supporters appointed by Maury Maverick's group of liberal congressmen. Hancock had personal reasons for supporting judiciary reform. He had been intensely angered by District Judge Isaac Meekins' restraining order preventing compulsory government grading of tobacco at the Oxford warehouses, especially since Meekins so delayed signing the order that an appeal before the end of the marketing season was impossible. As a result, Hancock had already introduced with Senator Kenneth McKellar a bill to restrict the power of lower court judges to declare legislation unconstitutional. Roosevelt's plan therefore struck a responsive chord with Hancock. The two other North Carolina congressmen to declare their views quickly, Zeb Weaver for the measure, A. L. Bulwinkle against, had little to do with tobacco.[42]

Two of the tobacco congressmen, however, found that their constituents' feelings allowed them to support the President. Both Kerr and Cooley had expressed themselves with some vehemence on the Hoosac Mills decision, but they were initially noncommittal on the Court reform proposals. On 23 February, however, one of Kerr's most loyal political henchmen reported to him that 95 percent of the people in the district favored reform. Kerr replied confidentially that he was inclined to back the President, and he soon moved from that reticent position to become one of the more outspoken partisans of the plan. Cooley likewise returned to his district to find that the overwhelming majority of people favored reform, especially farmers and laborers.[43]

The other North Carolina tobacco congressmen remained silent in public. Of these, Warren certainly was opposed to the reform. He admitted to Speaker Bankhead that he had no reason to like the Court after the way it had dealt with agricultural legislation, but he would rather be defeated than vote for the President's plan. It is probable that Clark and Umstead also opposed the scheme, but it is not known what Barden's views were. Their unwillingness to express their views openly reflects their high degree of party loyalty, but it also probably reflects their perception that a large number of their constituents supported reform. Certainly, the letters to both Warren and Barden opposing reform came in the main from outside their tobacco-growing districts, usually from the industrial Piedmont. On the other hand, their tobacco-growing constituents cannot have felt as strongly on the subject of Court reform as they had on other subjects that had more directly affected them, since they failed to put these congressmen under heavy pressure to come out for Roosevelt. Warren at least masked his opposition well enough for the North Carolina Farm Bureau to praise him, along with Kerr, Hancock, and Cooley, for backing the President.[44]

Unlike the tobacco congressmen, Senator Bailey openly denounced the Court-packing plan without reservation. He became a key member of the steering committee that coordinated the opposition's strategy in Congress. The state Farm Bureau was appalled, but whereas Bailey had assiduously courted his tobacco-growing constituents before 1936, in 1937 he did not worry about constituency pressures of this sort.[45]

By keeping his pre-1936 criticism of the New Deal largely to his voluminous correspondence, Bailey had been able to run successfully for reelection in 1936 as a loyal New Dealer, capitalizing on his votes for some of the major pieces of New Deal legislation and benefiting from New Deal patronage. Liberals in the state had been unable to find a strong, identifiable pro–New Deal candidate. The candidacies of Ehringhaus, Warren, Hancock, and even Josephus Daniels had been floated at various times, but had all been headed off. In the end Bailey had been opposed by Richard T. Fountain. Fountain had tried to exploit Bailey's lack of fidelity to the New Deal, stressing his votes against farm legislation in particular and his opposition to most New Deal measures. Fountain charged that Bailey "had no time to look after the interests of the farmers, but he has had plenty of time to devote to the interests of the power trust." But Fountain was a shadow of the man who had given Ehringhaus such a fright four years earlier. He had not fully recovered from a serious illness, and his campaign had neither finance nor publicity. Once Bailey had been safely returned to the Senate, he immediately moved into open opposition to the New Deal, and, not up for reelection until 1942, he could afford to be selective in the constituency pressures to which he chose to respond.[46]

Tobacco growers were therefore sufficiently in favor of Supreme Court reform, as a preliminary to crop control, to enable congressmen already disposed to reform to support the President. Their degree of commitment to the issue was not, however, as intense as their degree of support for measures that directly affected them like the Kerr-Smith Act. The growers could not muster enough support to force tobacco congressmen who opposed reform to change their minds and support Roosevelt. As in the nation, so in North Carolina, Roosevelt was not able to build up enough constituency pressure under opposition or doubtful congressmen to secure passage of his plan. The growers, like the New Deal, would have to rely not on changes in the number of judges, but on the changes in the nature of Supreme Court decisions to secure production control.

The Agricultural Adjustment Act of 1938

In February 1938 Congress finally passed a permanent substitute for the farm legislation that had been invalidated by Hoosac Mills. The second Agricultural Adjustment Act aspired to Henry Wallace's vision of the "Ever Normal Granary," where the storing of surpluses in good crop years would ensure adequate supplies in poor years and guarantee the farmer a satisfactory and stable income. In practice the act boiled down to a series of supply-control and income-supplementing devices. The existing conservation program was continued. Loans could be made on stored commodities. These were mandatory on corn, wheat, and cotton if prices were below a certain percentage of parity, but they were available for use on other commodities. If supplies were excessive, marketing quotas could be imposed and growers taxed on the sale of their excess production. In addition to the soil conservation payments, direct parity payments could be made to producers to bring their incomes up to parity.

Of these devices the one that mattered for tobacco growers was the provision of compulsory control through marketing quotas. They had to wait a long time for it. Whereas the 1933 Farm Act had passed in a matter of weeks, almost a year passed between the introduction of the legislation that eventually became the 1938 act and its passage. Several factors made the policy-making process in 1938 different from 1933 and caused the delay: lack of unity among the farm organizations, the reluctance of congressional farm politicians to defer to the Department of Agriculture, and the absence of an economic emergency.[47]

The Farm Bureau was primarily interested in strict production control that would guarantee parity prices in the marketplace through scarcity. It felt that Wallace's Ever Normal Granary with its stored surpluses might have a depressing effect on the market. Wallace, on the other hand, wanted only moderate production controls. The rigid controls envisaged by the Farm Bureau, he felt, were neither feasible nor economically desirable. He also feared that statutory commodity loans might be used by producer pressure groups to support prices at an unreasonably high level. In discussions in January 1937, however, the Farm Bureau and Wallace compromised. In return for bureau support of the Ever Normal Granary, Wallace would support potentially strict production controls. Despite efforts at a conference of national farm leaders in February 1937, the Farm Bureau was unable to line up other farm organizations behind the proposals, which it drafted with officials of the department, and it had to present these as its own when they were introduced in Congress in May 1937.[48]

Congressional leaders showed no enthusiasm for the Farm Bureau proposals. Some members of the Senate Agriculture Committee supported them, but chairman Ellison D. Smith felt that if any legislation was needed it was about time that Congress did its own drafting. In any case, he felt that the fear of surpluses in 1937 was exaggerated, and before any legislation he wanted to hold hearings around the country to get the views of real farmers. He was tired of hearing from the "same old farmers" whom he had seen around Washington for the past thirty years. He proposed to listen instead to "one-gallus men. Anybody with a white collar on won't be admitted to these hearings." House Agriculture chairman, Marvin Jones, also saw no need for urgent action. He felt there existed good legislation on the statute book already. He disliked the element of compulsion in the Farm Bureau bill. It would lead to "a million law suits in the cotton South and require a regiment of constabularies to handle them." He resented the attempts by the Farm Bureau to stir up opposition to him in his own district, and in the end he introduced his own bill. This measure provided for the Ever Normal Granary, but the marketing quotas it included could not be enforced by taxation but merely by the withdrawal of soil conservation payments.[49]

Congress could afford to delay, because there was no strong pressure from farmers to act. There was no economic emergency. Bad weather had restricted production in 1936 and led to good prices. Excessive supplies were not expected in 1937. As the summer went on, however, it became clear that the stimulus of good prices, the absence of effective controls, and the good weather were leading to renewed overproduction. This did not lead to demands for general farm legislation, but for aid for specific commodities. In August, congressional spokesmen for corn, wheat, and especially cotton called on the President for Commodity Credit Corporation loans on those commodities. Roosevelt refused to lend money on those crops until he received assurances that Congress would pass comprehensive farm legislation at its next session.[50]

The President attempted to speed up the enactment of such legislation by calling a special session in November 1937, but it was not until February 1938 in the regular session that the Farm Act was finally passed. The House Agriculture Committee was extremely reluctant to sanction compulsory controls, but Wallace felt they were essential to prevent the piling up of surpluses in government hands, as had occurred under the Farm Board. Marvin Jones and his committee eventually went along with controls, because the cost of financing an alternative voluntary program was prohibitive. On the other hand, Wallace was unhappy with the rigidity of the controls proposed by the Farm Bureau. The supply level at which quotas would be proclaimed was too low. He wanted quotas only to go into effect when supplies had reached such a high level that growers were clamoring for controls, which would increase the chances of compliance. Similarly, he wanted the loan rates lowered and the provision for parity payments made less generous. The compromises that were eventually reached maintained compulsion and kept the loan and supply levels nearer to the Farm Bureau's ideals than to Wallace's.[51]

The delay was particularly frustrating for tobacco congressmen, because virtually none of the disputes concerned tobacco. From the start, sponsors of farm legislation had recognized that tobacco was a special case and indicated that they would acquiesce in whatever provisions the tobacco congressmen agreed on. When the Farm Bureau bill was first considered, J. E. Winslow was assured by other farm leaders that they would accept any changes proposed by the tobacco growers. Similarly, Marvin Jones promised Harold Cooley that he would substitute for the tobacco section of his bill any measure suggested by the tobacco congressmen. When it became clear that no bill was going to emerge in the summer of 1937 Cooley called together a subcommittee of members from the tobacco districts to draft their own provisions for tobacco. The House Agriculture Committee accepted their recommendations of compulsory control for tobacco, even when it was rejecting controls for other crops, on the simple grounds of "the wide support of the principle [of compulsion] in the tobacco belt." It was these proposals which, with minor changes, became the tobacco title of the 1938 act. As Lindsay Warren sadly recognized, "There is more sentiment in our state for crop control than in any other state in the union, but I regret to observe that there is not much sentiment for it elsewhere." At various stages both Warren and Cooley expected to wind up with a voluntary control bill. In the end, Warren was gloomy about the prospects of any compulsory control legislation in the future: "The debate and votes make me think that this will be the last control bill ever to be passed by Congress. Except for the united front of the few members from the tobacco section the bill itself would have failed. A deep resentment has grown up against crop control in every section of the country.''[52]

The tobacco representatives were in no doubt that their support of compulsory control reflected the wishes of their tobacco-growing constituents. "We know what the tobacco people want," asserted Graham Barden. Warren believed that the tobacco provisions of the new act met with "the overwhelming approval of the tobacco farmers of the country." From the start, the attitude of Congress and the Department of Agriculture had been "that we did not wish to force anything upon the farmers and we wished the plan to come from them so that it could be shown that they were behind it."[53]

This perception by the congressmen is in one sense itself evidence of the growers' wishes. On the other hand, there is little evidence of the insistent and spontaneous demands for crop control that had characterized the tobacco program hitherto. The emergency no longer existed. Prices in 1936 had been a satisfactory 22.2¢ per pound, and in 1937 the situation was even better. A bumper crop of 866 million pounds was sold at an average of 23.0¢ a pound, bringing in a total income from the flue-cured crop of $199.2 million, the second-highest figure in history. Peculiar factors contributed to these good prices. Blue mold and rain had, to a certain extent, exercised a natural crop control, especially in 1936. The willingness of buyers in 1937 to pay such good prices for a good crop is partially explained by their expectation that the 1938 crop would be controlled and therefore smaller. It was also true that the county agents were certain that the growers planned to plant their largest crop ever, "to shoot the works," in 1938 if there was no control. They also expected a sharp decline in soil conservation compliance in the absence of control. Production in Florida had doubled since Hoosac Mills. Nevertheless, these were theoretical considerations. As an immediate practical concern, good prices did little to create a feeling of alarm and emergency.[54]

The only two demonstrations by growers in support of the legislation were carefully stage-managed. In July 1937 the Pitt County Farm Bureau organized a mass meeting in Greenville to demand enactment of the Ever Normal Granary bill. The Farm Bureau circulated petitions throughout eastern North Carolina in support of compulsory control. They were sent to the congressmen, the Department of Agriculture, and the President. This was part of a national series of meetings organized by the Farm Bureau to dispel reports that farmers did not want control legislation. Meetings in other parts of the country did not generate much enthusiasm and appear to have been attended only by county committeemen. The other demonstration in North Carolina occurred in Winston-Salem in October, when the Senate Agriculture Committee arrived to hold the regional hearings that Senator Smith had been so keen on. The state Farm Bureau, the Extension Service, and the Growers' Advisory Committee coordinated their evidence in favor of control. When Smith asked the audience whether they wanted compulsory control, they answered with a thunderous "yes."[55]

Senator Bailey, however, was by no means convinced that all growers favored control. As he told one anti–New Dealer, "My mail indicates that there is a tremendous groundswell against control and that it comes from the small farmers." The message of these letters was that only a small privileged minority of farmers wanted control legislation. "There is only an organized minority like Winslow and others who plant something like a thousand acres of tobacco who want the small man controlled." "Those asking for control are a hand-picked lot. The majority of farmers do not want it." But these large farmers had political influence: "The congressmen of those districts in which these large growers live, I am afraid, are being given too much power and too much consideration in the passage of this bill. It is more in their interest, politically, to pass a bill that will be favorable to the larger growers of tobacco and those who have been growing it for a number of years."[56]

Bailey attempted to protect the small farmers by introducing an amendment that a grower whose ten-year production was an average 15,000 pounds or less could not be reduced by more than 10 percent of his base, and that a grower whose base was less than 10,000 pounds could not be reduced by more than 5 percent. These amendments appalled the tobacco congressmen, who were convinced that they would wreck the control program, but they were supported with amusing candor by Robert Reynolds in one of his rare interventions in matters affecting tobacco farmers. The jovial senator from Asheville, who was rarely on the same side as Bailey before 1938, pointed out that senators "are all now, and more so than ever, interested in the little man, because little men have the vote; and the closer we come to the primaries of June 1938 the more intensely interested will we become and continue to be interested in the little man." Bailey's amendment was narrowly defeated, and Cooley, warehouseman Bill Fenner, and Con Lanier worked on Reynolds to make sure that he would oppose any similar change if it came up again.[57]

Bailey was preparing to vote against the Farm Act. It was unconstitutional, since it sought "absolute control over every farm." It would cost North Carolina tobacco growers, he estimated, $25 million, because they would have to grow less and it would lose them their export market. It also discriminated against tenant and small farmers by freezing agriculture. "Once a tenant farmer, always a tenant farmer under this bill. Once off the land never again back on to it." The bill said "to the one class of farmers, 'you shall always have $10,000'; but to this little fellow over here it will be said 'you will never have more than $480 a year.' " In 1934 and 1935, of course, Bailey had voted for similar bills, despite his own convictions, because he thought the bills were what the farmers wanted and he wanted their support in 1936. In 1938 he could afford to vote his own conscience. Perhaps growers did not want control. Even if they did, the 1942 elections were a long way away.[58]

The tobacco title of the 1938 act finally provided for the Secretary of Agriculture to proclaim a marketing quota on 15 November, when the total supply of any kind of tobacco—the carry-over of stocks and the estimated production for the year—exceeded the reserve supply level—a normal year's supply, a normal year's carry-over, and 5 percent of the total. This marketing quota would go into effect if it was approved by two-thirds of the growers voting in a referendum within thirty days. The basis of a state's marketing quota would be its total production in the previous five years, but no state could be reduced below 75 percent of its 1937 production—a concession to Georgia and Florida growers. To protect the small grower, no grower with a base production of under 3,200 pounds would be reduced below his average production of the past three years—with allowances made for acres diverted under AAA programs. Once the quota was imposed, a 50-percent tax would be levied on the sale of tobacco in excess of an individual's quota.[59]

Just over two years after the Hoosac Mills decision had struck down the first Agricultural Adjustment Act, the tobacco growers had secured compulsory crop control again if they wanted it. They would soon have the chance of seeing whether they liked it or not.

Chapter 6

Compulsory Control: Victory and Defeat

The confidence of tobacco congressmen that their constituents wanted compulsory control was amply and rapidly justified when the flue-cured growers voted overwhelmingly in favor of control in a referendum in March 1938. Yet in December of the same year these farmers, who had been uniquely anxious for compulsion, voted against the imposition of marketing quotas for 1939. The triumph and failure of compulsory control in 1938 raises important questions about the democratic nature of the tobacco program and about the type of farmer who benefited from the AAA.

The March Referendum

The late passage of the 1938 Farm Act had already created difficulties for any farm program in 1938. Preparations on the farms for the 1938 crops were well under way but, as a Jones County farmer complained on 1 February, "Right now, there's not a farmer in North Carolina who knows what he can plant and from the looks of matters we won't know till planting time and possibly afterwards. A Big Mess is what I'd call it." Thus, the 1938 program started with handicaps from which it never fully recovered. Normally under the act the Secretary of Agriculture would have to proclaim a national marketing quota in the November preceding the quota's operation. For the marketing year 1938–39, the secretary had to proclaim the quota within fifteen days of enactment of the legislation and to hold the referendum within forty-five days of enactment. Wallace immediately proclaimed a marketing quota for the 1938 flue-cured crop of 705 million pounds, in contrast to the 1937 crop of 850 million pounds. The referendum on this quota was to be held on 12 March.[1]

The pressing need to know what was in store for them probably accounted for the presence of over four thousand growers at an over-flow meeting in Raleigh's Memorial Auditorium on 18 February to hear Hutson explain the details of the new program. Hutson explained that a quota was necessary, since, if the growers raised as much in 1938 as they did in 1937, supplies would be nearly as excessive as those of 1931 and 1932.

What the growers wanted to hear was simply how the program would work. What was of immediate concern to them was Hutson's explanation of how acreage allotments would be calculated. Theoretically these acreage allotments, which were being made under the existing conservation program, had nothing to do with the compulsory control program, which relied not on control of what the grower planted but what he sold. But the AAA realized that they could not calculate marketing quotas in time for growers to know how much to plant. Instead, they had to rely on the allotments that would be made under the acreage conservation program, which they hoped to have in the farmers' hands by planting time. These however could only "serve as a guide" to the growers. With normal yields they ought to result in production in line with the eventual quotas. But this was not necessarily so, and the discrepancies would cause considerable difficulty to the AAA in implementing production control.[2]

Tom Bost of the Greensboro *Daily News* reported that this meeting "outdistanced all its predecessors . . . they [the farmers] went away the best-pleased crowd that Raleigh has seen indoors or out." But it was already clear that persuading the growers to vote for control would be no easy matter. Even before the act had passed, Con Lanier had spoken in Kinston, Wilson, and Ayden to explain the bill. He found that there was "considerable opposition to the bill even here in Eastern Carolina and it is going to take a lot of work to carry the referendum with a 2:1 vote." Hutson himself recognized that there were some growers who were asking "why we need any new legislation since 1937 was such a good year for flue-cured producers." Naturally the farmers' enthusiasm had changed since 1932. "Then they were enthusiastic for production adjustment and improvement of prices.

Today, many of them apparently are enthusiastic for more production.''
Given this feeling of complacency it was clear that an extensive campaign would be needed to persuade the growers to approve a new
program.[3]

E. Y. Floyd, state director of the AAA, had early seen the need
for this. In October 1937 he had written to Washington officials to urge
an early and thorough educational campaign to put over the 1938
plans. Yet his awareness then of what was needed indicated the real
difficulties that would face the 1938 control campaign. In October,
Floyd had envisaged that the farmers would know their quotas by 15
January at the latest. They were far more likely to approve a program if
they knew exactly what was required of them. In February 1938 the
task facing Floyd was to sell compulsory control to farmers who would
not have their acreage allotments until after the referendum and their
marketing quotas until just before the markets opened.[4]

The basic campaign he mapped out involved mass meetings in
each county, followed up by township and community meetings. Between 1 March and 11 March mass meetings were held in each of the
eighty-one tobacco and cotton counties. Five AAA field supervisors
toured the state to speak at these. After this, local county agents,
county and community committeemen, vocational agriculture teach-
ers, and other Extension Service employees took over the task of
explaining the program to the farmers at the township meetings. Over
four thousand people took part in the campaign.[5]

There was intense interest in these meetings. In counties where
the mass meetings were held in large auditoriums like those in Greenville, Kenansville, Guilford, Lillington, and Rockingham, between
fifteen hundred and three thousand growers attended. More often, five
hundred or more growers would crowd into a tiny courthouse. This
usually meant standing room only; often the crowd flowed outside,
where loudspeakers had to be hastily rigged up to let them hear what
was going on; sometimes two meetings were needed to accommodate
the numbers. Attendance at the township meetings was equally impressive. An estimated fifty-six hundred growers, for example, turned up
at township meetings in Johnston County. Usually the AAA official
gave a detailed explanation of the bill and then let local farmers and
farm leaders give ''pep'' talks in favor of control. The questions asked
by the farmers were invariably practical ones about the methods of
calculating allotments and quotas, so that they might have some idea
of how much they would be expected to cut back.[6]

The Extension Service was not left to fight the battle on its own. Harold Cooley, the man most responsible for the tobacco provisions of the 1938 act, came down from Washington and spoke at mass meetings on most of the days during the campaign. Senator John Bankhead also came down to speak on cotton at Shelby and Charlotte. Senator James P. Pope of Idaho, sponsor of the 1938 act, came to speak in Ahoskie on the day before polling. Senator Reynolds and the tobacco congressmen sent messages of support. The Farm Bureau organized its own meetings and sent representatives to bolster the AAA meetings. The state Grange, the commissioner of Agriculture, the state Board of Agriculture, and the governor all endorsed control. The AAA fed informational material for the farm pages of the newspapers, and of the major state and local newspapers only the skeptical Greensboro *Daily News* did not favor control.[7]

Perhaps the most notable feature of the campaign was the active role taken by the warehousemen and business interests. Warehousemen from the Carolinas and Virginia met in Raleigh on 26 February to hear Claude Hall and Winslow appeal to them, on behalf of the growers, for their support in the control election. As Con Lanier explained to his warehouse friends, "you live where the tobacco growers live and it is up to you to help. It would be a miracle if the Farm Bureau covers the whole belt in two weeks. You can." The warehousemen responded by passing resolutions in favor of control and paying for radio time for Lanier to speak in the campaign. Lanier himself spoke twice a day at meetings, and two leading warehousemen, B. B. Sugg of Greenville and Bill Fenner of Rocky Mount, toured the Eastern Belt exhorting the growers to vote for control. Fenner afterwards stated his motives bluntly. "I was working for Bill Fenner because the more the farmer gets for his tobacco the more I get for selling it from the warehouse."[8]

The warehousemen thus linked farmer prosperity with their own. So did Frank Spruill, president of the North Carolina Bankers' Association. Although he could not commit his relatively anti-Roosevelt organization to support control, he personally wrote to its members to ask them to influence farmers to vote for control. Spruill made it clear how he influenced farmers in his Rocky Mount bank. When a farmer came in for a loan, he was asked how he intended to vote in the control election. If he indicated that he would oppose control, he received no loan. Spruill spoke on the North Carolina State College radio hour the day before the election urging a favorable control vote. E. Y. Floyd was also not above utilizing economic pressure. He asked the AAA to ensure that compliance checks under the conservation program should first be sent to the heavy tobacco and cotton counties rather than the smaller counties, before the 12 March vote.[9]

The basic argument these advocates of control used was the simple necessity of adjusting supply to demand; the absence of control would lead to overproduction, especially by new growers, and low prices. These would, as Governor Hoey pointed out, "spell financial ruin for the farmer, and mean adverse conditions for all business." Cooley told the growers that, if they voted against control, Hoovercarts would return to North Carolina; there would be a business standstill, and a tailspin and depression such as they had never known before. He contrasted conditions in 1931 and 1932 with 1938, when North Carolina farmers were "living in the very agricultural paradise of America." "You are buying new cars and new clothes and you can keep on buying them as long as we maintain a stable price for the crops you grow."[10]

Most of the other arguments used by supporters of control were defensive, however. It was emphasized that control was only for a year and that there would have to be another referendum before control could be extended. If control was turned down this first time the farmers would never be able to have control again, for "if growers go to Congress after voting against control they will be told to go to hell." After all, Congress had given the growers what they wanted. Supporters were also at pains to point out that the new act avoided the pitfalls of the old; they cited the elections of committees, the provision of review and appeals committees, and the protection of the small farmer. Indeed, Con Lanier claimed that it was the large farmer who had to bear the brunt of the reduction. Finally, control provided excellent opportunities for crop diversification.[11]

Debate among the growers in response to these arguments was intense. "Control advocates and opponents have clashed at filling stations, street corners and mass meetings for the past two weeks in a battle packed with emotion and drama," reported Jack Riley, who was sent by the *News and Observer* to cover the control campaign. The outcome was by no means certain. Jonathan Daniels heard "pessimistic reports" about the vote, and Dean Schaub admitted that there was "plenty of trouble in some areas."[12]

At most meetings no opposition was reported; rather there seemed to be enthusiastic approval. At some, however, there were dissenting voices. A large grower at Fuquay Springs complained that large reductions would hit his tenants. His tenants dutifully agreed. At a meeting in Hoke County a renter feared that the referendum would be like all the others; tenants would be threatened with removal by their landlords if they did not vote for control. In Franklin one grower complained about the lack of available copies of the bill and denounced it as a ''mulatto brother'' of the old AAA. But this sort of opposition was individual and isolated.[13]

At the mass meeting in Robeson County, however, there was considerable skepticism about the act. In Sampson County a clear majority of the 2,000 growers at the meeting were opposed to control. Some of this opposition seemed to be organized, especially in Sampson, Johnston, and Wake counties. In Wake a Raleigh wholesale merchant planned to hire the Memorial Auditorium and invite Senator Bailey to speak against control, but Bailey refused, insisting that this was a matter purely for the farmers. In Johnston County on 1 March, B. T. Starling chaired a meeting of 250 growers in opposition to the Farm Act, while on 9 March S. H. Hobbs, Sr., who had denounced control at the Sampson County mass meeting, repeated his attacks at a meeting of 800 farmers in Smithfield.[14]

Starling and Hobbs were old-time foes of the AAA. In 1934 Starling had complained that his landlord had cheated him of his share of the equalization fee with the connivance of the county agent, who had then unfairly cut his cotton acreage. The same agent had willfully denied him a fair tax-exempt allotment under the Kerr-Smith Act. Starling claimed that he had been given tax-exempt warrants on only half the tobacco he grew on a farm he had just acquired that did not have a tobacco base. Other nonsigners, he claimed, had been able to sell tax-free as much tobacco as they could produce. He had taken his complaints to Dean Schaub, John Kerr, Senator Bailey, and the AAA in Washington but without success. The county agent had retorted that Starling had refused to designate his landlord as a trustee to receive the equalization payments, he had failed on three occasions to comply with his cotton contract, and he had been given all the tax-exempt allowance that the county committee was allowed to give under the law. Starling, he complained, was the only one of the four thousand contract signers in the county that no one had been able to satisfy at least in some measure.[15]

S. H. Hobbs, Sr., was a local politician from Sampson who had run for Congress in 1930 and on a number of occasions for the state Senate. His hostility to the AAA dated back to the passage of the original act in 1933 when he had threatened to call a mass meeting to protest the compulsory features of the bill. In January 1936 he had organized an effort to remove the local county agent for alleged favoritism in making allotments. He dismissed the movement for a tobacco compact that spring as simply the "clamoring [of] just the big farmers." The doctrines of North Carolina State College officials were "socialistic." In 1937 Senator Bailey had encouraged him to testify against the new farm bill at Senator Smith's Winston-Salem hearings. Hobbs charged that the meeting was stacked with Farm Bureau mouthpieces, that compulsory control was unconstitutional, and that the old AAA had been unfair to small farmers. Afterward, he complained that the *News and Observer* had given a garbled account of the meeting, which was not surprising since the Daniels' family was "Bolshevik."[16]

The background of the two leading opponents of control indicated what sort of arguments they and their followers would use against compulsory control. First, the new Farm Act was not merely unconstitutional, it was "undemocratic and unAmerican." Whatever economic good it would do, it would result in the loss of individual freedom. For Hobbs, "a Hoovercart looks better . . . than the dead carcass of personal liberty"—a point which he supported with lengthy quotations from Macaulay's *History of England*. A Lumberton Republican vowed that "if I perish to death I don't want a government man coming to tell me what to do and what not to do." If control was voted this one time, warned Hobbs, Wallace would never hold another referendum.[17]

Second, opponents of control expressed their hatred of the administration of the old AAA by the Extension Service and the county committees. These would still be in charge of the new program. Their tactics in the past had been, according to Johnston County farmers, "underhanded, undermining and tended to penalize and punish the small farmers for whom help was necessary and assist the big farmer of influence." S. H. Hobbs, Sr., also exploited the dirt farmers' distrust of theorists and extension officials who "would not know a milk cow from a buffalo. . . . The only way to keep the county agent off your farm is to give him hell." As for the economics of the new control, opponents argued that it would merely stimulate foreign production of tobacco and would harm tenants and small farmers. The

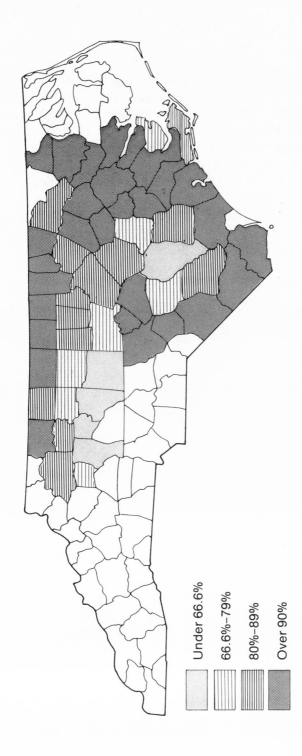

Distribution of votes in referendum on imposition of quotas for flue-cured
tobacco, March 1938

Under 66.6%

66.6%–79%

80%–89%

Over 90%

opposition was a mixture of small-farmer resentment of the establishment and straightforward conservatism, illustrated by the farmer who complained that control would not be needed if there was "honest-to-goodness enforcement of the antitrust laws. Half of the officials of the large tobacco companies should be in jail."[18]

Despite this opposition, control was approved easily. With an 85 percent turn out over the whole flue-cured belt, 86.2 percent of the voting growers favored the imposition of quotas. In North Carolina 89.6 percent voted in favor. In the counties in the heart of the Eastern Belt—the large grower counties of Edgecombe, Lenoir, Wilson, Pitt, and Greene—opponents could muster no more than a total of 500 votes. Only in Iredell, Davie, Davidson, Randolph, and Sampson did control fail to get two-thirds support, although even there it secured a simple majority. Of these counties all but Sampson were unimportant tobacco counties, and their combined anticontrol vote only reached 1,445. Large minorities of over 1,000 growers voted against control in both Johnston and Wayne, but in Sampson 2,113 growers voted against control.[19]

It was significant that Sampson should be a center of opposition. It was an old Populist stronghold, the home of former Populist Senator Marion Butler, and it had since been an area of Republican strength, often electing Republicans to local office. This suggested the possibility of an ideological objection to the principle of control. There had also been local opposition to the Extension Service. The county commissioners had not funded a county agent from 1922 to 1933. An emergency agent had to be appointed in 1933 with AAA funds. But whereas other counties willingly contributed to keep emergency agents once AAA funds ceased, Sampson county commissioners did so only reluctantly. They saw no reason why they should pay for a county agent who would be administering a federal program. In 1935 the county failed to get an assistant agent, because the county commissioners would not pay his traveling expenses. In 1936 Hobbs and others attempted to remove the county agent. There was also a history of dissatisfaction with the AAA. The county agent reported in 1935 that there was a "lot of antagonism" toward the program—and that was a very rare report in North Carolina at that time. At the heart of the trouble seemed to be intense discontent with the county's cotton allotment under the Bankhead Act. At the same time a large number of tobacco tenants were moving to farms with no tobacco base. In 1937 it was the Sampson representative in the General Assembly who pressed the amendments to the tobacco compact bill protecting small farmers and establishing a complaints procedure. In both 1936 and 1937 scarcely more than half the farmers participated in the acreage conservation program. Opposition to compulsory control was a natural step for some Sampson farmers to take.[20]

A Wilson leaf dealer and prominent member of the United States Tobacco Association ascribed the victory of control to the "Hitler tactics" of the people in Raleigh who had "jammed this program down the farmers' throats." Senator Bailey was also contemptuous of this effort in mass democracy, which he described as "a perfect model of fascism." The people in Raleigh, however, did not see their own behavior in this light. On the contrary, Frank Jeter, the extension editor, told a visitor from Washington that he had been privileged to witness "democracy in action."[21]

There could be little doubt that the "educational" campaign by the Extension Service and the AAA was a thinly veiled propaganda drive. AAA administrator Howard Tolley might remind every farmer that he was not recommending to anyone how they should mark their ballot, and Dean Schaub might protest that the campaign meetings were only designed to inform, but the actions and speeches of their agents belied this. No farmer could have been left in any doubt as to the result the AAA and the Extension Service wanted. As one small example, one county agent mailed every farmer notice of the ballot; the same notice featured a cartoon with a figure labeled "prices" bent double under a weight labeled "carry-over." The Extension Service interpreted the favorable vote as a tribute to its own campaign. Frank Jeter's *Extension Farm News* positively gloated that, as a result of the vote, "some of those who have had harsh things to say about the leaders of the Extension Service will begin to think that perhaps these leaders are not so impotent after all . . . the Extension Service has proved that it has the power to organize, conduct and conclude any reasonable effort with a maximum of results."[22]

The campaign waged by the Extension Service was in fact no different from the campaigns they had waged to sign growers up in the fall of 1933. Such campaigns had been just as much propaganda drives as the 1938 campaign. In 1933, however, few farmers had to be persuaded; they were only too eager to sign up. In 1938 no such emergency or enthusiasm existed. The AAA and the Extension Service had to fight to overcome the doubts of those who were satisfied with good prices. The image was therefore of necessity more partisan in 1938 than earlier, although the role was the same.

Discontented Growers

That control had passed so easily, despite the appearance and expectation of strong opposition, suggested that growers who had reservations about control had, nevertheless, voted for it in the end. Whether such farmers would continue to support compulsory control would therefore depend on the way the act was administered. The actual implementation of the control program led to three major sources of dissatisfaction: the allocation of acreage allotments, the imposition of the marketing quotas, and the prices that the growers received when the markets opened.

The first signs of discontent came almost immediately, when the individual acreage allotments were made. The AAA worked night and day to try to get these allotments to the growers by planting time; for their pains, the AAA and the local committees were rewarded with a barrage of complaints. The first came from Wilson, where the county committee had to meet all day to hear protests. In Wayne two hundred growers were waiting outside the county agent's office at 9.30 A.M., the day after the allotments were issued, to complain. In Vance, over one-third of the growers filed complaints, while in Johnston at least one-fifth did. Dean Schaub was alarmed at the growers' response and the way they took out the blame on the county agents. He reported that many county committeemen were either resigning or vowing never to do the job again, and he feared that it would fuel demands by some county commissioners to end their support of county agents.[23]

Such discontent was a godsend to Starling, Hobbs, and other opponents of control. They addressed meetings of growers in Goldsboro, Greensboro, and Kinston, and in Lee County. Starling claimed that all the old inequities of the AAA had been revived by the allotments, and he sought funds to challenge the new act in the courts. In the third district the dissatisfaction with allotments was such that Charles L. Abernethy, Jr., tried to exploit it in his congressional primary against Graham Barden. He expected Barden to lose thousands of votes because of tobacco control, which he attempted in every speech to tie in with the incumbent congressman. At Goldsboro and Smithfield the farmers were "as mad as wet hens about the way they were treated in this control bill." Barden agreed that the situation in his district had been "mean" since the allotments were made, and he reported that his "neck [was] being sawed on constantly."[24]

Senator Bailey naturally capitalized on this discontent. "Every mail brings letters of violent protest," he said, and he claimed that there was even "a great deal more of protest than I thought would take place so soon." To emphasize the point, he forwarded all complaints to Secretary Wallace. As Bailey pictured it, "Mass meetings are being held all over North Carolina." The Greensboro *Daily News* commented that "opposition to acreage allotments has become so widespread as to be rapidly losing its news rating."[25]

There were a number of reasons for the outcry. The issuing of the allotments at the very time the growers were planting or even later was bound to cause resentment. This was particularly true for growers who had not complied with, or taken part in, the 1936 and 1937 acreage conservation program. For these farmers new work sheets had to be prepared, and they were likely to be startled by the amount they were expected to reduce their acreage. A sample of the complaints that arrived in Washington suggests that dissatisfaction may have been more prevalent among small growers, but in particular it suggests that growers had failed to understand that there was a difference between the acreage allotments under the conservation program and the marketing quotas to be made under the new act. This confusion could disturb both large growers, who would find that they were restricted to a certain percentage of their cropland under their allotments but not under the quotas, and small growers, whose allotted acreage might be slightly reduced, whereas their production might not be cut under the quotas if it was under 3,200 pounds. Few county agents made the distinction clear, as the Franklin agent did, that the growers could ignore the allotments as long as they kept within the poundage quotas. Even that was scant consolation, since the growers did not yet know what their quotas would be.[26]

This linking of the conservation program to the control program annoyed tobacco congressmen like Kerr and Warren. They believed that they had designed a program which was as "simple and fair as could be," but that that program had been thwarted by the administrators who, in linking control with the conservation scheme, were bound to provoke "dissatisfaction and discrimination." On the floor of the Senate, Ellison D. Smith was even more blunt. "The acreage has nothing to do with it [the poundage provision] . . . "it was a total blunder to inject acreage."[27]

Complaints about the allotments were overshadowed by a second surge of discontent when the marketing quotas were issued. This was predictable. Given that the growers did not know what their quotas would be when they planted their tobacco, it was always likely that they would find that they had produced more pounds of tobacco than they were allowed to sell. This was especially probable if they failed to perceive the distinction between allotments and quotas. To make matters worse, the officials in Washington responsible for drawing up the quotas felt that allotments under the acreage conservation program had been very laxly handled, and they intended with the marketing quotas to exert a much tighter control. Administrative problems exacerbated a bad situation. At best the AAA hoped to get individual quotas to the growers only two or three days before the markets were due to open on each belt. Despite the state office's working two shifts, however, many growers had still not received their quotas by the time they sold their first tobacco. They had to be issued temporary marketing cards instead.[28]

In some cases the AAA just gave up. The protest from Georgia growers and politicians was so great that the AAA basically gave Georgia farmers all the quota they needed. In the program as a whole, however, the AAA had already tried to ease the plight of growers who had produced more than their quota. Growers who had not produced as much as their quota allowed were permitted to transfer and sell the remainder of their quota to growers who had overproduced. But this provision in turn met with the bitter opposition of county committeemen, who claimed to represent the loyal cooperating growers. It also left an untidy impression of "trading and bargaining." A further ruling enabled growers who had produced in excess to sell their lower grades under penalty before they had in fact sold all their quota. This meant they would be taxed on their lower, rather than higher, prices. These concessions unfortunately gave some growers the strong feeling that growers who had not complied with the program were being allowed to get away without penalty, while those who had stayed in line were, in effect, penalized. Some county agents reported that this resentment against those farmers who had escaped punishment was the strongest grievance of the growers.[29]

Many growers simply did not understand how the quotas were determined. "The chief basis of complaint," claimed the Greenville *Daily Reflector*, "is that farmers are not aware of the formula by which the department figured the allotments and therefore cannot do their own figuring." A grower from McDonald said that "some of us have thought that if they [the quotas] were fixed in Raleigh the calculators came from Dix Hill [the mental hospital]." Even some county committees could not explain to the growers how the quotas were allocated, and one county agent was certain that it "would be impossible to work out a formula, which, when put in practice, would be more unjust or foolish than the tobacco formula used in 1938." Growers did not necessarily object to their own quotas as such, but they often could not understand why their neighbors were allowed so much tobacco. They were bewildered by the wide variation in quotas on adjoining and similar farms.[30]

James E. Thigpen, the man responsible for the quotas, now wryly admits the force of these complaints. He recalls that the working out of the 1938 quotas was the best technical job he ever did, but also the most impracticable. Yields per acre varied so much on individual farms that "somehow the quotas never quite fitted." E. Y. Floyd remembered the dissatisfaction with the poundage quotas so vividly that thirty years later he opposed a return to a system of poundage quotas, rather than acreage allotments, because of his memories of what those quotas did to the 1938 program.[31]

The 1938 act had laid down procedures that were designed to offset the complaints of growers about their quotas and to allay their suspicions of favoritism by the local committees. Details of everybody's allotment and quota, and the data on which they were based, were meant to be available for inspection in the county agent's office, but the AAA admitted that it had not made sufficient copies of these lists. Availability in the agent's office was also very different from the public posting of information in every township that had been envisaged by people like Clarence Poe. Nor did the provision of a complaints procedure alleviate discontent. Under the act a local review committee was to be appointed to hear complaints against allotments and quotas. This review committee was not to include any member of the committee that made the original allotment. Often, however, these review committees did not start work until November, which, as Con Lanier complained, was not in time to aid any growers, for they had usually long since sold their tobacco.[32]

Unlike the protests over allotments, the protests over quotas did not necessarily come from small growers. In fact, some of the most vociferous complaints came from Robeson County, led by the largest grower in the county. Similarly, there was widespread dissatisfaction in Pitt, not so much with individual quotas but with the county's share of the state quota, which large growers did not believe reflected the county's importance in the state's tobacco production. Nor did all growers who were dissatisfied necessarily go so far as to file complaints with the review committees—only twenty growers filed appeals in Johnston County and only fifty in Guilford.[33]

The third source of grievance was the prices the growers received when the markets opened, especially on the Eastern Belt. The whole flue-cured crop received an average of 22.2¢ a pound compared with 23.0¢ the previous year. Since the growers only sold 785.7 million pounds of tobacco, their total income from the crop was $174.4 million, a drop of $24.8 million from 1937, which was just what Senator Bailey had predicted. The New Belt growers were particularly hard hit. Their income from the 1938 crop fell by a quarter from the 1937 figure.[34]

That supporters of control were embarrassed by the low prices could be seen from the elaborate rationale they developed to explain away the poor returns. They argued that the disappointing prices were the results of the growers' vociferous complaints about allotments and quotas. As a result, the tobacco companies expected that there would be no control in 1939. There was therefore no need for the manufacturers to pay good prices in 1938 when they could buy all the tobacco they wanted in 1939. The Farm Bureau arranged mass meetings to try to convince the buyers that the growers still favored control and appealed to all growers to refrain from criticism of the program that merely lowered the prices.[35]

Opponents of control, of course, believed that the low prices triumphantly vindicated their earlier arguments. By now they had formed an organization, the North Carolina Anti-Compulsory Control Association, which aimed to collect $15,000 to fight a court case against the AAA. Its headquarters were in Sanford, home of its chairman, H. I. Ogburn, who claimed to be the largest grower in Lee County. He was

Governor Clyde R. Hoey (center, in dark suit) at the opening
of the North Carolina markets, 1938

(Division of Archives and History, Raleigh, North Carolina)

backed by an executive committee that included S. H. Hobbs, Sr., and J. M. Judd, another large grower from Wake County. Their activities however were not especially notable in September. Less than one hundred people turned up in Wilson to hear Hobbs compare the AAA to a vampire sucking the blood out of the farmer. Only seventy-five heard him in Sampson, largely, it was reported, because Hobbs had called so many mass meetings in the past. Despite this, they were able to go to court. On 16 September suit was filed in Wake County Superior Court on behalf of 851 plaintiffs for the return of penalty taxes levied under the act.[36]

Evidence of dissatisfaction with control also came in the November 1938 general elections. Governor Hoey speaking in Sampson was at pains to emphasize that the 8 November elections were entirely divorced from the forthcoming elections on crop control. Republican successes in Sampson, Johnston, and Wayne at the November polls were attributed locally to the discontent with compulsory control.[37]

The December Referendum

The crop control referendum was scheduled to take place just over a month after those November elections. In that time supporters of control planned to mount a vigorous campaign to secure a favorable vote. The Farm Bureau planned to hold from five to ten community meetings in each county. It also enlisted the support of a businessmen's advisory committee representing fertilizer companies, bankers, warehousemen, and merchants in the Eastern Belt, who agreed that compulsory control was essential not only to the growers' prosperity but to theirs as well.[38]

E. Y. Floyd, for the state AAA, also asked for the aid of North Carolina bankers and fertilizer companies, without which he did not think a successful "educational" campaign could be waged. The basis of Floyd's strategy was to secure the backing of these interests at the local level to convince the growers in the community meetings, a technique that had characterized control campaigns in the past. Another essential part of the strategy was to get the individual allotments and quotas to the growers before the referendum. The quotas were to be adapted to ensure that allotments and quotas were comparable; there was to be much less provision for the transfer of excess quotas and less room for new farmers. Floyd planned, with the aid of state AAA committeemen and field workers, to enable county agents to get the quotas to growers by 1 December. He then called on all farm agency personnel to help in local community meetings. The climax of the campaign was to be a series of district meetings addressed by a Washington official, followed by a statewide meeting addressed by Wallace. In the week before the election there would be daily radio talks by the state's farm leaders.[39]

Part of Floyd's plan worked. There was adequate explanatory material in the local press, and the quotas went out to the growers in time. Hutson came down and spoke at a meeting in each belt at Winston-Salem, Lumberton, Oxford, and Greenville. Hutson stressed the potential that existed for expansion of the flue-cured crop if control was not voted. In particular, cotton farmers, with low prices of their own, would be only too anxious to switch to high-priced tobacco. This was, if anything, the major argument used by supporters of control. North Carolina's virtual monopoly of flue-cured production would soon go, if cotton farmers in Alabama, Florida, Georgia, and South Carolina switched to tobacco when control was defeated. If such an expansion did occur, Hutson recalled the conditions of 1930 to 1932 as examples of what lay in store for the growers. Wallace repeated this warning about likely expansion in his meeting in Raleigh, which was broadcast statewide. All the evidence, he argued, showed that such an expansion could not be absorbed by the market except at materially lower prices.[40]

The state's farm leaders kept this momentum up in the last week of the campaign in a series of radio speeches. Spruill for the bankers, Sugg for the warehousemen, Winslow of the Farm Bureau, and Poe as a long-time "defender of the right of the little man to live" all endorsed control. So did the governor. Hoey presented the choice to the grower in stark terms "whether he will have the control provided under this act, or take his chances with a flooded market and starvation prices."[41]

It appeared then that the campaign at the state and district level was conducted with a fervor equal to that of the spring. It was, however, at the local level that the supporters of control totally failed to mount an effective campaign.

There is no evidence that the Farm Bureau's ambitious campaign was ever anything more than a paper creation. It did not have the resources to conduct meetings on such a scale in so many counties; in particular, it was at its weakest in those counties where opposition to control was likely to be strongest. There is almost no record of Farm Bureau–sponsored community meetings. Nor did the Farm Bureau receive much help. Although the Eastern Carolina Warehousemen's Association endorsed control, as it had done before, none of its members took to the stump as Bill Fenner and B. B. Sugg had done in the spring. Con Lanier, who had played such an active part in that campaign, took no part in the December referendum. He was upset, not only by the administration of the act, but also by the opposition in Pitt of the Farm Bureau to his political ambitions. Also, unlike the spring campaign, control was publicly backed by neither the state Grange nor the state board of agriculture nor the commissioner of agriculture.[42]

Nor in the December campaign could the AAA and the Extension Service compensate for this lack of activity. There were almost none of the county and community mass meetings that had been such an integral part of earlier campaigns. The county agents and county committees were too busy trying to get out the quotas to the growers in time for the referendum to mount the usual educational campaign. The result was clearly illustrated in Vance County. There, the county agent had called a meeting of Henderson businessmen to interest them in a campaign to put over control, in view of the large amounts of tobacco and cotton that the growers planned to plant otherwise in 1939. There was no response, so "the referendum arrived with no effort having been made by any group or persons, whose interests were most vitally affected, to apprise the farmers of the danger before them."[43]

If there was an absence of any visible local activity by the supporters of control, there was little evidence of activity by their opponents. During the campaign itself there is only evidence of one anticontrol meeting, which was held in Guilford County. The only other signs of opposition activity were advertisements placed by H. I. Ogburn, chairman of the North Carolina Anti-Compulsory Control Association, in the newspapers and letters against control in the correspondence columns. Opponents of control were asked to go to Wallace's meeting in Raleigh to support a resolution that would be offered against control, but there was no sign of them at the meeting.[44]

The most visible effort of the Anti-Compulsory Control Association had in fact been earlier, when Eugene Talmadge of Georgia came to the Memorial Auditorium to give one of his "old-time red suspender speeches" to the Association. A crowd of fifteen hundred, rather than the expected ten thousand, heard the former governor. This invitation to Talmadge gave a clear indication of the ideological orientation of the anticontrollers. Their ideas resembled those of the Farmers' Holiday Association in its later years and of the anti–New Deal Farmers' Independence Council of Dan Casement. On the one hand, there was the violent right-wing rhetoric of the defense of the individual against government encroachment and dictatorship. Compulsory control destroyed the right of free self-government and meant European-style government regimentation. On the other hand, there was the neo-Populist appeal to the small farmer against the economic and social power structure, especially as manifested by the Extension Service, the impractical theorists who knew nothing about farming. This was accompanied by an economic analysis showing that continued control would mean permanently curtailed incomes and the loss of foreign markets. It claimed that the program discriminated against small and tenant farmers and young farmers wanting to start farming. It was these small and tenant farmers whom the Anti-Compulsory Control Association called upon to vote down control in the referendum.[45]

"A rather messy administrative situation"

In the December referendum crop control was defeated. With a turnout of 77.7 percent, less than two-thirds of the voters approved the imposition of quotas for 1939. Only 56.8 percent of all the flue-cured growers who voted supported control. Only 57.3 percent did so in North Carolina. Votes against control almost quadrupled in North Carolina and alone provided over 80 percent of the votes needed to stop the control program.[46]

In the postmortems on the defeat there was near unanimity on three elements: that the vote was not a vote against the principle of control; that it was a vote against the administration of control; and that it was the small farmer who most disliked the way control had been administered and had been the most responsible for its defeat. Clarence Poe summed up this feeling in the *Progressive Farmer*: "Nine-tenths of the farmers who voted against production control on 10 December seemed mad about allotments rather than against the principle of production control itself." Had the reforms suggested by Poe and others to improve administration and protect the small farmer been put into effect more rapidly, the result might have been different, for "The No votes came almost exclusively from counties where small farmers prevail. It was a revolt of the 'little man'."[47]

That it was not a vote against the principle of control seems self-evident in view of the overwhelming vote for quotas only nine months earlier. It is extremely unlikely that many growers shared the views of the Anti-Compulsory Control Association, which was ideologically opposed to compulsion by government. There is no evidence to suggest that the association had either mass support or mass organization. Its members represented a small, but permanent and vocal, minority that had been opposed to government regulation of agriculture from the start. It represented the occasional individual rather than the bulk of tobacco growers. In this absence of an ideological and committed opposition, the defeat of control in 1938 was very different from perhaps the most famous of defeats by farmers of government programs —the defeat of the wheat controls in May 1963. In that case the negative vote followed a well-financed, intensive campaign against control by major farm organizations.[48]

There could be no doubt also that the control program had been administered unsatisfactorily in 1938. A recurring theme among the farmers interviewed for the Federal Writers' Project was that "Control had been handled in a sorry manner," that what was wrong was the "way it's run." There was almost a routine assumption that "it ain't done fair." Hutson himself later recalled that they had a "rather messy administrative situation" in the field in 1938. This was the almost inevitable result of events that had taken place even before the 1938 program was launched. The two basic causes of the administrative difficulties were the late passage of the 1938 Farm Act and the need to provide for crop control in a way that would be sustained by the courts. This need for a stronger constitutional base meant that the 1938 act provided for control of marketing rather than production, in contrast to the 1933 legislation. It thus provided for marketing quotas rather than acreage allotments. Because of the late passage of the act there was no time for the AAA to collect the information needed to calculate quotas and give them to the growers before they planted their tobacco. Instead the AAA issued, as a guideline, acreage allotments under the conservation program, the data for which was already available, in the hope that the production on these would be in line with what the quotas allowed. Many growers did not understand the distinction between these allotments and the quotas—in itself testimony to an inadequate educational and publicity campaign.[49]

Because the acreage allotments were not binding and because the growers were only informed of their quotas a few days before the markets opened, many growers produced more tobacco than they could sell without paying a penalty tax. Efforts in turn to ease this problem by allowing the transfer and sale of quotas merely aroused resentment on the part of growers who had kept within their quotas.

In part because of the desire to eradicate past inequities and injustices, the number of factors to be taken into consideration in calculating quotas and allotments made the task extremely complex. There had been an attempt to get away slightly from the "historic base." Not merely past marketings but the land, labor, and equipment currently available for tobacco were given some weight. But all this made it difficult to understand. An AAA official longed for a method of calculation that would be "simple enough so that most farmers could understand." Because growers did not understand how their particular quota had been calculated, it was easy for them to believe that county and community committees were discriminating against individual farmers or in favor of influential large farmers. Even Con Lanier, who was familiar with the intricacies of control, thought that the local administration was similar "to sovietism in Russia, where each community has a commissar who rules according to his whims." The provision of review committees and the publicity of quotas do not seem to have worked well enough to counter this basic lack of understanding. The supreme effort to avoid all these difficulties in the future by getting quotas to the growers before they voted in the December referendum backfired. The county and community committees were so busy allocating and distributing quotas in order to get them to the growers in time that they had no time to conduct a vigorous educational campaign to put control over.[50]

The third element laid bare in the electoral postmortem analyses, the dissatisfaction of the small farmer, seems to be borne out by the distribution of the votes. Of the six tobacco counties—Wilson, Pitt, Greene, Edgecombe, Hoke, and Hertford—in which over 70 percent of the farms were operated by tenants, none voted against control. Of the nineteen tobacco counties in which 50 to 69 percent of the farms were operated by tenants, only eight—Robeson, Lenoir, Nash, Bertie, Halifax, Warren, Martin, and Granville—voted for quotas. Of the remaining thirty-eight tobacco counties where less than 50 percent of the farms were tenant-operated a mere five—Washington, Wilkes, Alexander, Surry, and Yadkin—voted for control. This suggests that

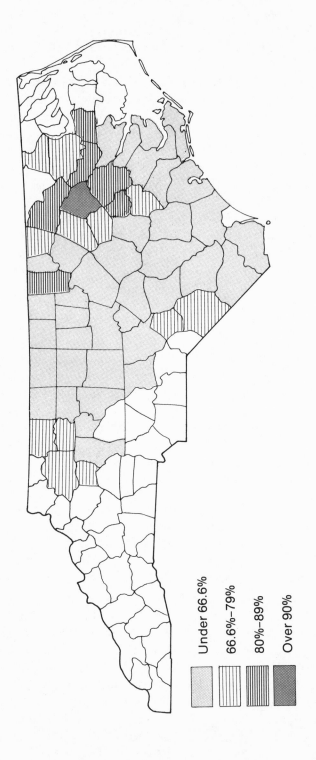

Under 66.6%

66.6%–79%

80%–89%

Over 90%

Distribution of votes in referendum on imposition of quotas for flue-cured tobacco, December 1938

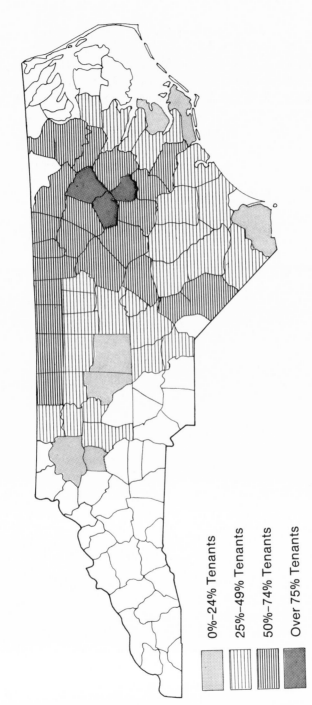

Percentage of farms operated by tenants, 1940

0%–24% Tenants

25%–49% Tenants

50%–74% Tenants

Over 75% Tenants

landlords voted for control and that their tenants supported them, either because they favored control or because they were under pressure to do so. Small independent farmers apparently opposed control. Clearly the provisions in the 1938 act designed to protect small farmers had not succeeded in removing their resentment over the fact that they had to make production cuts in the same proportion as large growers. The campaign identification of the Farm Bureau, the Extension Service, warehousemen, and creditors with the cause of compulsion could only heighten this resentment. To this might be added particular local circumstances like local Republican strength or a history of discontent with the AAA or residual distrust of the Extension Service. Sampson County had once again led the anticontrol vote.[51]

The vote against control should also be seen in a wider perspective. The tobacco growers had received good prices for five years, including two years in which there had been no significant crop control. It required a fair degree of sophistication on the part of a grower to appreciate the overall economic situation that necessitated continued restriction of production. Such an awareness was unlikely to come from the sort of campaign that had been waged in North Carolina in the spring, with its heavy emphasis on the immediate price situation. When it transpired that control in 1938 brought slightly lower prices, it is not perhaps surprising that many growers were prepared to take a chance on increased production in 1939 at continued good prices. The reactions of the tobacco growers in 1938 seemed to bear out the opinions of agricultural economists who predicted that production control, which was acceptable in an emergency situation, would become less attractive as farmers' incomes increased. They expected that growers, who were prepared to tolerate a crude control program when they needed an immediate income boost, would become increasingly irritated by imperfections and injustices in the program as prices rose. Attempts to eradicate these problems would make matters worse, because they would involve more complex programs and even more red tape, and resentments would heighten. At the same time, the benefits of compliance as against noncooperation would appear less obvious. This seemed to have happened in flue-cured tobacco in 1938. What nobody realized in December 1938 was that within a year the growers would be back in an emergency situation where the advantages of control would be once again immediately obvious.[52]

Chapter 7

War Reaches North Carolina

The defeat of compulsory control turned out to be short-lived. Even before the 1939 crop had been marketed impatient supporters of control had secured legislation that rectified some of the faults of the old program and provided for an early referendum on the restoration of quotas. Their opportunity to exploit these changes came with the outbreak of war, when the British buyers withdrew and the markets had to close. Government aid in this crisis was dependent on compulsory control, and the growers dutifully voted for its return. Not content with this, the growers' representatives moved in 1940 to ensure that compulsory controls would be a permanent feature of the tobacco program.

Trying for a Second Chance

No sooner had control been defeated in December 1938 than some growers were demanding a new referendum, because the growers had been misled and had not known what they were doing. Supporters of control wanted to make sure of success by requiring a simple majority, not a two-thirds vote, for approval of quotas. These demands were discussed by the Growers' Advisory Committee and the state Farm Bureau and presented to AAA officials and tobacco congressmen in Washington on 25 January 1939. In addition to the new referendum the growers' leaders also wanted to change the basis of the marketing quotas from poundage to acreage, thus eliminating the source of resentment and confusion that had been highlighted by the 1938 program. The quotas should also be in force for three to five years instead of one. Unabashed by their defeat, the supporters of control were trying to overturn the verdict of the polls and introduce semipermanent compulsory control.[1]

The congressmen recognized that these demands were presumptuous. The rationale for all previous special legislation for tobacco had been that the growers unanimously wanted it. Such a claim made little sense in this case after the December referendum. The unmistakable impression was, as Harold Cooley told the growers' leaders, that they were asking Congress "to change the entire philosophy of the program and the rules of the game after the vote has been taken." Hutson definitely wanted to retain the two-thirds provision, which was an essential feature of the AAA's defense of compulsory controls. The change to an acreage basis for the quotas seemed premature when the Supreme Court had yet to rule that the control of marketing under the 1938 act was constitutional, let alone the control of production. Lindsay Warren also raised an overall legislative consideration. Compulsory control had only just survived Congress in 1938. After the Republican gains in the midterm elections, compulsion was likely to be even less popular in the 1939 Congress. Any attempt to amend the 1938 act might provoke opponents to fight for outright repeal of all compulsory legislation.[2]

Despite the congressmen's frosty response they did agree to meet the growers' leaders when the Supreme Court ruled. On 17 April the Court upheld the 1938 Farm Act, and the growers returned to Washington on 26 April and 2 May for conferences with the AAA and the tobacco congressmen. Once again, the congressmen warned against any amendments unless they were absolutely necessary. In particular they warned that the Supreme Court had upheld federal control of marketing, not production. A switch to acreage quotas might "wrap the program in doubt again." The AAA, however, felt that the Court decision was broad enough to allow the acreage provision, and J. Bayard Clark suggested the final solution: they should provide both an acreage and a poundage basis to be used at the discretion of the Secretary of Agriculture. If one was shown to be unconstitutional, he could use the other.[3]

Although Warren still thought it "very doubtful if any change is going to be made in the present law," further conferences yielded other proposed amendments that would change the penalty tax, protect small growers, and provide a new referendum. Instead of the 50 percent tax on the sale of excess tobacco, there was to be a flat 10¢ per pound penalty tax. This was intended to prevent violation of the law by the purchase of low-price tobacco and the resale in its place of high-priced tobacco on which a penalty tax would otherwise have been paid. To aid small growers, there would be a 20 percent increase in allotments of flue-cured growers who produced under 3,200 pounds, provided that did not increase their allotment over 3,200 pounds. Finally, the Secretary of Agriculture could proclaim a quota at any time from the start of the marketing season to 1 December. This would enable flue-cured growers to vote on control for 1940 during the marketing of the 1939 crop, instead of waiting until after 15 November. Thus, it was hoped the buyers would be forced to pay higher prices for the 1939 crop in the knowledge that the 1940 crop would be restricted.[4]

Cooley introduced the amendments in the House on 25 May. They were called up on 6 July and passed without debate. Rep. Virgil Chapman of Kentucky simply explained that they were the product of five or six months of conferences with the growers and "represent the consensus of opinion of those interested in the tobacco program."[5]

Senator Bailey had had nothing to do with the tobacco amendments. This was not surprising, given his views on compulsory control. He felt that Roosevelt's farm policies had "utterly failed" and what was left showed "the bankruptcy of all our great plans for agriculture." He was still annoyed about the tactics of the North Carolina Farm Bureau in "using the AAA to get dues paid to the Farm Bureau Federation and the impression . . . that in order to get allotments one must pay his dues to the Bureau." He was unenthusiastic about the tobacco amendments. They still did not protect the small grower. They made it even less likely, he thought, that two-thirds of the growers would vote for quotas, and they knocked out the constitutional base of the program, since the Supreme Court would deem it to be control of production. Yet Bailey seemed resigned in his opposition. He made no effort to signify any objection to the unanimous consent passage of the amendments on 1 August.[6]

Within eight months of the growers' vote to defeat compulsory crop control, therefore, special tobacco legislation had been passed that was designed to restore control as quickly as possible, with the rationale that this was what the growers wanted.

The authority now existed for an early referendum on control to be held during the 1939 marketing season. Whether or not that authority would be used would depend on the prices the growers received for their 1939 crop and what they thought of those prices.

Ever since December 1938 supporters of control had made gloomy forecasts about a bumper flue-cured crop in 1939 and depressed prices. As the Georgia markets opened, both E. Y. Floyd and J. B. Hutson bluntly predicted 15¢ prices. Hutson explained that the acreage planted in tobacco was 21 percent up on 1938 and was likely to yield a crop of one billion pounds—the largest ever—compared to the previous peak of 865 million pounds in 1930. With the carry-over from 1938 this meant a total supply of flue-cured that was 17 percent above the normal supply level defined in the 1938 act. Demand was the same as in 1938. The effect of the crop would also be felt in the future. In order to absorb the large 1939 crop, buyers would have to purchase much less in the years to come.[7]

Such predictions annoyed anticontrollers, who believed that officials were deliberately encouraging low prices in order to secure the return of control. As one told Bailey, "the whole bunch [Floyd, Hall, Winslow, Arnold] has been mad at the growers since the defeat and have been preaching low prices, chaos and disaster . . . farmers are thoroughly indignant at Floyd for making such predictions. He is supposed to be speaking for the farmer . . . and not against him." Few of them believed the predictions. They felt that, on the contrary, manufacturers would pay good prices because they did not want to see control reestablished. In any case a large crop at an average price of 17¢ or 18¢ per pound would bring in more total receipts than a small crop at 23¢ per pound.[8]

When the Georgia markets opened, however, it seemed that supporters of control would be able to capitalize on the growers' protests about low prices to get the referendum they wanted. The North Carolina Farm Bureau called on Georgia growers to close their markets pending a referendum. On 31 July Claude Hall and Winslow went to Washington to discuss the possibility of keeping some of the 1939 crop off the market to improve prices. The next day the tobacco amendments passed Congress, and the state Grange backed a referendum. Farmers were urged to attend a mass meeting in Raleigh on 4 August.[9]

The movement, however, failed to gain strength. Only six hundred growers turned up in Raleigh to hear R. M. Evans of the AAA. The buyers persuaded Hall and Winslow that a large crop in 1939 and a restricted one in 1940 would achieve the right balance and no immediate action was necessary. The Farm Bureau merely appointed a committee in the end to watch the market situation.[10]

The reason the demand for the referendum was dropped was that farmers seemed satisfied with the prices they were getting, just as the anticontrollers predicted they would. There was no outcry when the border markets opened, and even when the New Belt opened with 16–17¢ average prices there was no outspoken dissatisfaction. The poor prices were explained away by warehousemen and buyers as the result of the poor quality of the crop. "I've never seen so many common tips in all my life" said one, while another maintained that he had seen tobacco on the floors which he did not believe grew on a tobacco stalk. Nevertheless, prices were low enough for the Farm Bureau meeting in Wilson on 31 August to renew its call to Wallace for an early referendum; but before any action could be taken, events in Europe overtook everybody in the tobacco industry.[11]

The Markets Close Again

When the war broke out in Europe the main response in North Carolina was uncertainty. On the one hand, there was speculation as to what would happen if the European buyers withdrew from the markets; on the other, there was the hope that war would, as in the past, lead to an eventual increase in prices for tobacco. The immediate consequence was that prices continued to fall.[12]

The warehousemen were already discussing moves to restrict and slow down selling in the confused market situation, when the decisive news came on 8 September that the Imperial Tobacco Company was taking its buyers off the markets. The British had stocks in hand of tobacco of 543 million pounds in July 1939, including 395 million pounds of American flue-cured leaf. By early September they had already acquired another 100 million pounds of flue-cured. Since their annual usage of American flue-cured was only 200 million pounds the British government had decided to use up the existing stocks of tobacco and safeguard its foreign exchange for necessary war supplies. The government denied exchange certificates to importers of tobacco, and Imperial therefore stopped buying on the flue-cured markets.[13]

It was impossible to overemphasize the seriousness of this move for tobacco growers. From 1934 to 1938 Britain had taken an average of 240 million pounds of flue-cured tobacco a year from the United States. This represented almost two-thirds of flue-cured exports and almost one-third of total flue-cured production. The importance of the British buyers was even greater than these figures suggested, because they bought chiefly the better grades of tobacco, which fetched the higher prices. They were responsible for almost half of the farmers' income from the flue-cured crop. This meant that with their withdrawal the tobacco growers faced what the *Progressive Farmer* called a "double-barreled" emergency. They had already produced too much tobacco, and it was selling at depressed prices. Now they found themselves having to adapt to the absence of a buyer who bought an estimated 35 percent of the better grades of North Carolina leaf.[14]

In the crisis it was the warehousemen and Hutson who took the initiative. As soon as Imperial's withdrawal was announced, the President of the United States Tobacco Association started polling members of his sales committee about closing the markets. The decision to shut them was announced the next day, 9 September, although they remained open long enough to clear the tobacco already on the warehouse floors. For the second time in six years the tobacco markets had closed in the middle of the marketing season. In contrast to 1933, the growers and the governor played no part in the decision to shut down.[15]

Meanwhile, Hutson, who had been given a few hours' warning of the withdrawal by the chairman of Imperial, had been able to assemble a meeting of one hundred farm leaders in Raleigh on 9 September. He emphasized the gravity of the situation and made it clear that the first thing to do was to decide about the size of the next year's crop. Only when that was done could the government begin to come to the aid of the growers in attempting to dispose of the surplus. Even then, the situation was so unclear that Hutson could make no promises about the effectiveness of government help.[16]

Representatives of the interested parties—the Farm Bureau, the Grange, the state Growers' Advisory Committee, bankers, warehousemen, and the Virginia and South Carolina growers—met in Washington on 13 September to arrange the details of the referendum, which all agreed was the prerequisite for any remedial action. There was disagreement as to when a referendum should be held and whether or not the markets should remain closed until the vote. This reflected the nervousness of many present about the outcome of such a vote. The machinery for a vote could be set up in three or four days, but Dean

Schaub wanted the referendum delayed for at least three weeks, with the markets closed, so that a campaign could be mounted to secure the necessary two-thirds majority. Bill Fenner for the warehousemen agreed that the markets should remain closed, but felt that the growers would vote for control immediately. Claude Hall, for the advisory committee, and Kerr Scott, North Carolina's Commissioner of Agriculture, both wanted the markets to reopen first, so that farmers could get "a taste of lower prices." Otherwise, growers, especially in the Middle and Old belts, would not be ready to vote for quotas.

The eventual decision was to hold the referendum between 30 September and 7 October, and the warehousemen decided to keep the markets closed until then. Clarence Poe and the Grange resisted a proposal to make the vote a vote for three-year control. They did not want the growers stampeded into control. Hutson regretted that individual quotas would not be known before the vote, but he promised that no one would be cut to under 80 percent of his 1939 allotment.[17]

Deciding on a referendum was but a first step. The growers had now to be persuaded to vote for control, and the government had to devise a plan to maintain prices for tobacco after the referendum.

As in the 1933 sign-up, the government was asking the growers to come out for control in return for promises that the government would act to stabilize prices, but without any detailed assurance of how the government would carry out the promise. Unlike 1933, the government had not already been working on plans when the crisis broke. In the emergency three main schemes were considered: efforts to persuade the British to return to the markets; a plan for the government to store tobacco and lend money to the growers; and a plan for the government to purchase tobacco for the British. It was a measure of the changes that had taken place in the tobacco belt since 1933 that only Josephus Daniels, writing from Mexico City, believed that the domestic tobacco companies should assume responsibility for the crisis and pay the growers enough to compensate for the British withdrawal.[18]

It was Senator Bailey who took most of the initiative in the attempt to persuade the British to return to the market. He was convinced that, once the pound had been stabilized and their credits rearranged, the British would return, because they could not afford to lose the revenue from the import duty on tobacco. He suggested that the Reconstruction Finance Corporation should provide the necessary credits for the British, and he wrote on these lines to the British Ambassador, Harry Hopkins, Morgenthau, and Jesse Jones. He received a hopeful response from the American side, especially from Roosevelt in a conference at the White House. The administration was cultivating Bailey's support for the fight over neutrality legislation, but the British government, with two years' supply of tobacco on hand, thought that tobacco was the least of its worries.[19]

The plan for a government loan on stored tobacco was most vigorously pressed by Kerr Scott, Commissioner of Agriculture, and the state Grange. Under this scheme the government would grade, redry, and store all the tobacco not wanted by the domestic manufacturers. The grower would receive a loan on the security of this tobacco, which he could repay when he sold it. Government storage would give him the chance to sell it at any time during the year when market conditions were favorable. The existing warehouses would be used. Additional redrying and storage facilities could, if necessary, be built by taxing the sale of tobacco over the next two years at ¾¢ a pound. Other schemes on similar lines varied as to the amount of tobacco the government would grade and whether or not the government would make outright purchases of tobacco. The virtues of the scheme were that there would be an immediate financial benefit to the farmer, and, in the long run, the year-round system of marketing would solve the growers' traditional marketing problems and eliminate speculators. The defects were that there was no additional buyer to compete with the domestic manufacturers; there was a danger of surpluses piling up in government hands with no way to dispose of them; and there was no provision for an eventual purchaser of the tobacco, in particular no guarantee of retaining foreign trade.[20]

The plan to which the government devoted most of its energies, and finally presented to the growers, attempted to meet some of those problems. The government planned to purchase tobacco on behalf of Imperial. As Hutson explained it in Raleigh on 25 September, the Commodity Credit Corporation would purchase the tobacco that Imperial would normally buy. The buying would be done by Imperial's team of buyers but with CCC funds, and the CCC would own the tobacco. Imperial would have the option to buy that tobacco at any time up to 1 July 1941. For that option, Imperial would pay $1.50 per hundred pounds for the services of redrying and processing at

Imperial's facilities. The government would pay any additional costs of insurance and storage. The virtue of the scheme, compared to the loans on stored tobacco, was that the growers would receive their money in the normal way with no strings attached, and the government would keep a crucial link with the export trade. What was left unsaid was what would happen if Imperial was not in a position to take up its option in 1941. The scheme depended on something being worked out by then.[21]

This was the proposal that the growers knew about when they went to vote. Not all the details had been worked out, and no agreement would actually be signed until after the referendum. Its implementation depended on how the growers would vote.

Crop Control Again

As soon as the referendum was announced, supporters of control were convinced that its successful outcome depended on the full mobilization of the resources of the government, the farm organizations, the tobacco politicians, and especially the warehousemen, bankers, and supply merchants. For once, all these groups did cooperate, and there was far more active participation by the various interested groups in the 1939 campaign than in December 1938—both in the central statewide propaganda campaign and in the grass roots activities in the counties.[22]

From Washington the Department of Agriculture mailed a letter from Wallace to each individual farmer indicating the need for control, if the government was going to maintain prices, and giving them information so that they could calculate their own quotas. Tables of statistical information and a question-and-answer sheet were sent to every county agent for use in the "educational" meetings. The message of the figures was clear: "Excess production means loss of income" ran one of the headings. The tobacco congressmen issued a statement that obviously nothing could be done for the growers unless they voted for control, although they denied that they were telling the growers how to vote. Barden, Clark, Kerr, and Cooley all managed to get back to North Carolina for the closing stages of the campaign.[23]

In the December 1938 campaign neither the state department of agriculture nor the state Grange had taken part. This time both endorsed control. Kerr Scott declared that control was "paramount to the economic stability of North Carolina agriculture." The Grange admitted that the "only immediate hope" in the emergency was control. Scott, his employees, and the master of the state Grange spoke at various control meetings. The Grange did express its concern about control as a permanent measure, and this was echoed by the Greensboro *Daily News*, a former opponent of control. The paper accepted the need for it as a condition of government aid in an emergency, but remained skeptical of its long-term implications.[24]

As in 1938 the executive committee of the state Bankers' Association, the Farm Bureau, and the Eastern Carolina Warehousemen's Association came out strongly for control. The warehousemen, in particular, painted a lurid picture of the dire effects of not voting for control. They laid plans for extensive speaking tours in the counties, especially in the "hotbeds of opposition"—Johnston and Sampson. They were all the more energetic because they felt that their own inactivity in December 1938 had led to the defeat of control.[25]

The most striking example of the businessmen's support of control was the formation of a committee headed by W. G. Clark of Tarboro and two Greenville bankers. The committee sponsored a series of thirteen widely advertised radio broadcasts to climax the statewide propaganda campaign. The speakers included Congressman Clark, Kerr Scott, Governor Hoey, J. E. Winslow for the Farm Bureau, R. Flake Shaw from the state AAA, Ralph McDonald, the defeated gubernatorial candidate in 1936, Con Lanier for the warehousemen, and Clarence Poe and Harry Caldwell of the Grange, who addressed their appeal to the small farmers.[26]

The one theme that ran through all these speeches was the reply to the charges that the government was coercing the growers into voting for control by not offering to help unless they did so. The government had no such purpose, asserted Hoey; it was merely seeking to help the grower and sincerely believed that control was the only course open to save the grower from utter ruin. "As to whether you wish to avail yourself of the aid of your government is left entirely with you." But there was, of course, only one choice possible in the way Hoey posed the alternatives. The vote would decide "whether the present tobacco crop will be sacrificed and the work of the whole season will go for naught, or whether the markets will open under conditions that will assure the farmer at least a measurably fair price for his tobacco."[27]

The final radio speech was a statewide radio hook-up of Secretary Wallace's speech to ten thousand farmers at Kinston, sponsored by the Eastern Carolina Chamber of Commerce. It was a rather philosophical account of the long-term need for economic adjustment in the wartime situation and a celebration of the democratic way of running AAA programs: "Democracy's response to the demand for adjustment and efficiency." Cooley on the same platform was far more direct; the farmers had produced "too damned much tobacco."[28]

At the local level there were two main features of the propaganda campaign for control: the township meetings and the efforts of local businessmen to convince farmers of the importance of voting for control.

The cornerstone of the campaign was the "educational" meetings arranged in every county by the county agents. County-wide meetings at the county seat addressed by state officials were followed up by five to ten meetings in each county where the county agent or his assistant would explain to the farmers gathered in the township the importance of the data sent from Washington. Unlike December 1938 it is clear that these meetings in 1939 did take place and were well attended. Over half the growers eligible to vote for example attended the meetings in Pitt and Stokes. One consequence of the 1938 defeat was that some agents were a little more cautious in "selling" the control program, leaving the advocacy of a favorable vote to the county committeemen and the local businessmen.[29]

What was striking in the local campaigns was the way in which the businessmen, merchants, and warehousemen strove to convince the growers of the necessity to vote for control. Their prosperity was as much at stake as the growers'. Merchants' associations and chambers of commerce strongly endorsed control, and their members worked hard to help the county agents' educational campaign. In both Kinston and Wilson businessmen organized mass letter-writing campaigns, putting the arguments for control to their farmer-clients. In Greenville a group of merchants, warehousemen, individual businessmen, and bankers led by the First Federal Savings and Loan Association put full-page advertisements in the local newspaper for a week before the referendum. Headed "An Appeal to the Tobacco Farmers of Pitt County and Eastern Carolina," the message was simple:

Would you refuse to be rescued?

Face Saving or Shirt Saving. Would you lose your shirt to save your face?

Restricted production or financial disaster, which will you choose?

Vote for control October 5. A vote for the financial safety of yourself and the community in which you live.

Hoovercarts or Automobiles? You must decide.

The sentiments of advertisements like these linking control to the future prosperity of the whole community were fully backed by the editorials of their fellow businessmen, the local newspaper proprietors.[30]

In the face of this propaganda barrage, opponents of control were neither as prominent nor as vociferous as in 1938. When the markets closed they promised a "right aggressive" campaign, but they appear to have had only five formal anticontrol meetings and for the rest relied on letters to the press and contacts with friendly political columnists.[31]

Much of their case was a repetition of their earlier assaults on the principle of compulsory control. At Smithfield S. H. Hobbs, Sr., spoke for forty-five minutes without mentioning the current crisis; compulsory control was "illegal, undemocratic and un-American"; county agents were "dictators." He warmed to his theme in Guilford County courthouse. Crop control was a "Hitler or Stalin form of government" and "totally unconstitutional." The anticontrollers repeated their arguments that control favored large farmers. Small farmers, according to H. I. Ogburn, would continue to receive unfair allotments, because it was impossible for the county committees not to show favoritism to the large growers.[32]

The anticontrollers had more specific charges to make concerning the current crisis. First, they argued that the closing of the markets was merely a trick on the part of the supporters of control to deceive farmers into voting for quotas. There was no crisis of overproduction, argued Ogburn, but merely a temporary dislocation caused by tobacco selling too fast. A short holiday could remedy this. Then prices would rise by two or three cents, provided that the buyers were allowed to regulate the speed of selling. Second, they argued that war would increase prices. Demand would be increased, as in World War I, and production in belligerent countries would be cut. It was a "piece of folly'' to curtail the U.S. crop when ''for the first time in many years we have a bright prospect of increased prices and increased demand.'' The problem was that ''higher-ups'' wanted control so that control, rather than economic conditions, would get the credit for this rise in prices.[33]

Third, they claimed that the government was coercing farmers into voting for control by not promising to aid them until after they voted for control. Judged by the care with which supporters of control sought to rebut this argument, it would seem to have been the most effective point that the anticontrollers made. A journalist wrote after Hoey had denied any coercive intent that hundreds of farmers would disagree with the governor: ''They considered that there never was a more obvious example of big stick wielding than the refusal to be even mildly interested in aid for this year's crop except conditional on a favorable vote.'' Their final argument was that the promise of government aid could not, in any case, be relied upon. They claimed that Imperial had rebuffed Hutson and that rebuff was the real reason why no agreement could be signed before the referendum.[34]

On 6 October two graves appeared at a crossroads in Sanford, Lee County; one headstone bore the name of local farmer, H. I. Ogburn, chairman of the Anti-Compulsory Control Association, the other that of E. L. Gavin, a local attorney who had represented the association. Instead of roses, leaves of tobacco had been placed on the graves. They signified the decisive triumph of supporters of control in the referendum. With an 83 percent turnout, 89.9 percent of the voting growers approved control. In North Carolina 90.8 percent of them had done so. The results in North Carolina were very similar to those in the first quota referendum in March 1938. Once again, the opposition could muster less than 500 votes in the large tobacco-growing counties of Edgecombe, Greene, Lenoir, Wilson, and Pitt. Only Sampson failed to provide a two-thirds majority for control, and even there the 54 percent vote for control was markedly different from the 16.1 percent cast in favor of control in December 1938. Neighboring Johnston was the only other source of a significant anticontrol vote.[35]

It is possible that this restoration of control might have taken place even if the British buyers had not been withdrawn from the markets. The amendments passed in 1939 did provide for an early referendum, and supporters of control had attempted to secure such a vote by exploiting the discontent with leaf prices in August. It was also true that the grievances that had led to the defeat of control in 1938 had to some extent been eradicated by legislative changes: the substitution of acreage for poundage in the calculation of quotas and the increased provision for small growers. However, the growers had not seemed to respond to the Farm Bureau's campaign for another referendum and, from the concern expressed by Schaub, Hall, and Kerr Scott about the outcome of a vote even *after* the markets had closed, it would seem that the result of a control election held without the withdrawal of the British buyers would have been very doubtful.

The war and the marketing holiday brought the growers face to face with low prices and also made possible the massive campaign to convince them of the need for control. In December 1938 the Farm Bureau and the Extension Service had been left to wage the battle for control on their own. In 1939 the somewhat discredited Farm Bureau was able to take a back seat. Organizations like the Grange and the state department of agriculture, which had previously been noncommittal, now actively supported control. More important, the marketing holiday prompted the business community of eastern North Carolina to wage a much more vigorous campaign for control than they had in 1938. Faced with a business standstill, they devoted far more resources to both the statewide and local campaigns. The message they had to put across was much more effective also. In 1938 the consequences of having no control were far off and debatable; in 1939 they were immediate and certain. The inevitability of low prices presented stark and compelling alternatives to the growers.

Once the growers had voted for control, the government could proceed with its agreement with the Imperial Tobacco Company and the Export Leaf Company, which Hutson signed on 9 October. This did not lead to a transformation when the markets reopened the next day. Conditions were very different from 1933. Tobacco overflowed into the streets as growers rushed to sell, and there was the danger of damaged and discolored tobacco, but the markets settled down to prices that compared with the prevailing prices before the markets closed. Prices for the whole flue-cured crop were 14.9¢ per pound, but total receipts were only a million dollars less than the year before. New Belt growers probably benefited from the agreement because their receipts rose by 13 percent over 1938, while border and Georgia-Florida growers received less than the previous year.[36]

To Make Control Permanent

The reimposition of crop control and the intervention of the government to finance the British buyers merely stabilized the tobacco situation. The long-term problems caused by the British withdrawal remained. Control of the 1940 crop together with the purchase and loan provisions for the 1939 crop had been a holding operation to sustain 1939 prices. Something would have to be done to hold up 1940 prices if the British buyers had not returned. There was then the gloomy possibility that the British might never take up their tobacco option. If this led to the permanent loss of the British market, it might mean the permanent contraction of the production of flue-cured tobacco in the United States.

It was clear that the British government intended to curtail the use of American flue-cured tobacco. In 1939 and 1940 the import duty on tobacco was raised four times. The British manufacturers would soon have to agree to reduce their use of leaf tobacco. The British also hoped to substitute Turkish leaf for American leaf. In January 1940 they announced a loan to Turkey and agreed to purchase 20 million pounds of Turkish leaf a year. This would conserve exchange and also safeguard British supplies from Turkey. British manufacturers were to increase their use of Turkish leaf in British cigarettes to 8 percent of their tobacco content by 1941.[37]

The news from London that the British intended to encourage the use of Turkish leaf was accompanied by the announcement of the specific imposition of an embargo on the import of American tobacco. This caused consternation in the ranks of the tobacco representatives. A Maryland congressman described the embargo as a "stinging blow at vast agricultural sections of this country." The master of the National Grange told Roosevelt that "the tobacco people are crushed. Whole areas are paralyzed by the action of the British." Clarence Poe reported that everyone in the tobacco area was "wholly at sea." It could scarcely have come at a worse time. Only a week earlier Hutson had told extension workers in Raleigh that the tobacco outlook was bleak in any case. Production in 1939 had been one hundred million pounds over the original estimate of one billion pounds, and allotments in 1940 would have to be cut by 35 percent, not 20 percent as planned.[38]

Tobacco congressmen went to see Secretary of State Cordell Hull to try to put State Department pressure on the British to lift the embargo, and various barter or credit schemes were put forward by which the British could purchase American leaf. But in fact the particular difficulties caused by the embargo were grossly exaggerated. In itself it did not change the existing situation. No tobacco had been imported into Britain since the exchange controls that led to the original withdrawal of the British buyers. What was new was the possibility of the British switching to Turkish leaf on a large scale. Neither a concerned congressman like John Kerr nor AAA officials in fact believed that the British could force that sort of change in consumer preference.[39]

The embargo made no difference to the AAA's plans for the 1940 crop. A referendum on marketing quotas for 1941 was to be held before the 1940 crop went to market. If the growers renewed their commitment to crop control, the AAA would negotiate another agreement with the British companies and thus support prices in 1940 as it had done in 1939.[40]

By the time the growers voted in this referendum in July 1940, the growers and their representatives had taken the opportunity to make compulsory control more permanent by securing legislative changes that made it possible for the growers to vote for control of the 1942 and 1943 crops as well as the 1941 crop. The idea of committing the growers to long-term control had arisen when the 1939 amendments were under consideration. It had occurred again at the Washington conference during the marketing holiday when the state Grange successfully opposed it. In November 1939 J. E. Winslow for the Farm Bureau stated that flue-cured tobacco ought to be under marketing quotas for five to ten years at a time. In January 1940 Claude Hall announced that he had sounded out opinion in the tobacco belt and that there was a greater demand than ever for three- to five-year control.[41]

Hall therefore pressed for an amendment that would give the grower a chance to vote for a longer period of control, and Cooley, Warren, and John Flanagan of Virginia took it up with the AAA. Hutson felt that three-year control would help stabilize prices, and in any case "if it is what the growers want I'm for it." The tobacco congressmen suggested, and representatives of the growers agreed, that the grower should be given three choices in a referendum: no control, control for one year, or control for three years. Other amendments were also agreed on: that tobacco that was being stored temporarily should be excluded from consideration when calculating the national marketing quota; that farm allotments should not be less than 10 percent below their 1940 size, as opposed to 75 percent of the 1937 level; that penalties should be collected on the first sale from the farm; and that there should be additional penalties on warehousemen who failed to keep correct sales records. The quota provisions were designed to encourage growers to plant less than they might in 1940 and to end the privileged position of new growers, especially in Florida, who could exploit their large 1937 acreages. The penalty amendments were aimed at closing loopholes in the enforcement procedures.[42]

The amendments introduced by Cooley were not due to be called up until July in the House, but Warren called them up on 20 May, persuading the House to waive the rules by unanimous consent; the amendments were agreed without debate, save for a brief statement from Warren that he wanted them passed before the referendum. This also helped Cooley, who was engaged in a primary fight in his constituency against the last-minute candidacy of an anti–New Dealer. In the Senate Bailey made no effort to obstruct them. The question of three-year control, he said, was peculiarly a question for the individual farmer.[43]

The referendum on control was held on 20 July 1940. The campaign was overshadowed in the press by controversies over the nomination of Roosevelt for a third term and by the war in Europe. The growers were, in any case, busy preparing their crops for harvest. As a result, the campaign was much quieter than any of the others since the 1938 act. The campaign basically consisted of a few major meetings addressed by leading officials and politicians and the mailing of information to the growers. In this, the campaign very much resembled the rather routine referendum campaigns that characterized the tobacco program after the war when control became almost a matter of course.

The campaign started with a statewide meeting of growers in Raleigh on 18 June, where Bill Fenner, the warehouseman, put the issue simply: "This is just a question of whether the farmers starve to death this year or whether they get relief." Dean Schaub predicted there would be 5¢ tobacco if there was no control, while Hutson hoped that a three-year program might lift prices to 15¢ or 16¢. In a number of speeches around the state Hutson predicted disaster—5¢ or 6¢ tobacco—if there was no control for 1940. He also announced the national quota for 1941 and then promised that it would be increased if the growers voted for three-year control. Governor Hoey said with surprising vehemence that the tobacco farmer had no choice, that a vote against control would be a calamity, and that it would be "unbelievable that our intelligent farmers would be willing to take a chance like that."[44]

There were some explanatory meetings in the local communities but for the most part the county agents relied on mailing notices of the referendum to the growers and on contacting them informally. Their message was unambiguous. One notice of the referendum listed the advantages of three-year control and pointed out that the governor and other business, farm, and political leaders had said that it "would be suicide to do other than vote for the three-year plan." Another quoted a leading warehouseman's prediction of 10¢ tobacco or less if there was no control.[45]

One county agent noted that there were none of the antagonisms that had previously been connected with the tobacco program, and indeed there is almost no evidence of any anticontrol propaganda. Only an earlier advertisement by supporters of Cooley's opponent in the fourth district primary hinted at any resentment against control. This stated that control had failed to aid eastern North Carolina and had been administered arbitrarily and inequitably. Cooley was held largely responsible for control and its consequences.[46]

The muted nature of the campaign perhaps accounted for the relatively low turnout of 67 percent of the eligible growers. Of the growers voting, 86.1 percent approved three-year control, 1.8 percent one-year control, and 12.1 percent opposed any control. In North Carolina 87.1 percent favored the longer period, while 11.5 percent voted against quotas altogether. Sampson still failed to provide a two-thirds majority for control, although the procontrol vote now topped 60 percent. Once again, the only other county to muster over a thousand votes against control was neighboring Johnston.[47]

Once the growers had voted, the AAA negotiated another purchase and loan agreement with the British companies and the domestic export buyers to cover the 1940 crop. These agreements were predicated on the eventual return of the British buyers; otherwise the accumulating surplus would eventually have to be dumped on a glutted market with unthinkable consequences for tobacco prices. Hutson was hoping that dwindling European stocks and three-year control in the United States would achieve the necessary supply and demand adjustment to forestall that eventuality. Prices for the 1940 crop averaged 16.4¢ per pound. Receipts for the 1940 crop were down by almost a third from 1939 and gave the growers their worst year since 1933.[48]

Within eighteen months of defeating crop control the tobacco growers had not only voted to restore control but to reestablish it on a long-term basis. This was due in part to the emergency created by the European war, in part to the success of tobacco congressmen in enacting special interest legislation. The tobacco congressmen had one more trick up their sleeves that would help the continuation of crop control for tobacco and its position of special privilege. In the fall of 1940 legislation was introduced to change the base period for calculating parity for tobacco from 1919–29 to August 1934–July 1938. This would raise the parity price of tobacco to the price level reached as the result of the success of the control program. It would be an important change, because it made parity payments on tobacco more likely, and it would also help when loans were made on stored tobacco.

Hutson sponsored the legislation, because he believed that the cost of producing tobacco had increased. Since a greater proportion of tobacco was being produced for cigarettes than for plug or chewing, plants were placed closer together, producing a thinner, lighter leaf that meant more work for less poundage (although the yields per acre had increased). Wallace accepted Hutson's explanation, but indicated his suspicion of special interest legislation sponsored by producer groups: "I think I'll go along with you if you look me straight in the eye and tell me that you think this is an honest approach to the problem. You've got to tell me that. I've got to be convinced that this is an honest approach. I don't want you to be giving in to any pressure group who may be trying to jack up the price of tobacco by some two or three cents."[49]

Whether the proposed change was an "honest approach" or an attempt to jack up tobacco prices was a moot point, but it was one that would not be subject to legislative scrutiny. Senator Alben Barkley of Kentucky introduced the amendment in the Senate on 30 September and justified it on the grounds that the Department of Agriculture wanted it in order to take into account increased growers' costs. It passed after a few minutes desultory consideration. Despite the fact that there had been no hearings on the change, that the Agriculture Committee had not considered it and had made no report, John Flanagan asked the House on 3 October for unanimous consent to suspend the rules and consider the amendment out of the regular order. There was an objection, but six days later unanimous consent was given. The amendment, however, failed to get the necessary two-thirds majority to pass under the suspension of the rules. On 18 November it was brought up again, and this time it passed without a roll-call vote.[50]

Harold Cooley may have said that the tobacco congressmen could not be expected to "change the rules of the game," but in two years they had, to a large extent, done so. They had amended the Farm Act of 1938 to allow the growers an early opportunity to reverse their anticontrol vote, to change the basis of quotas from poundage to acreage, despite the constitutional intent of the original act, to strengthen the penalty provisions and tighten up enforcement, to protect the older tobacco areas against new ones, to provide control for a possible three years instead of one, and to make the prosperous midthirties the base period for parity. They had tried hard, in other words, to ensure the final triumph of compulsory control. At the end of 1940 the prospect for tobacco growers was uncertain in view of the European situation, but their position was considerably more secure than had looked likely after the marketing referendum in December 1938. If the legislative success of the tobacco congressmen continued, the growers would have little to worry about in the future.

Chapter 8

The Price of Prosperity

Economic Consequences

The New Deal transformed the economic position of flue-cured tobacco growers by enabling them to adjust supply to demand. This remedied the greatest single weakness of the growers' marketing position, which had been the chronic tendency before 1933 to overproduce. After 1933 the AAA made it possible for growers to reduce their crops, first by promising them rental and benefit payments for voluntarily taking acreage out of production, second by taxing the sale of tobacco by noncooperating growers under the Kerr-Smith Act, and finally by taxing the tobacco sold in excess of marketing quotas laid down by the Secretary of Agriculture. This has been a permanent change, as controls have been placed on every crop since 1940.

In return for reducing production, the government in effect guaranteed the growers a minimum price for their leaf. To supplement the adjustment of supply and demand the government initially negotiated a marketing agreement with the domestic tobacco manufacturers. Later in 1939 it intervened to purchase leaf for the British buyers. This commitment has also been permanent. The government has indeed added a specific price-support program to production control. During the war the Commodity Credit Corporation acted as a shock absorber to protect growers from market fluctuations. Since 1946 the government has operated its price-support program through the Flue-Cured Tobacco Cooperative Stabilization Corporation. Funded by a nonrecourse loan from the CCC, the Stabilization Corporation buys any tobacco that fails to reach the support price, redries and stores it, and then resells the leaf whenever it can.

The tobacco farmers had therefore been given some control over their fate in the marketplace. Production control and government aid gave the farmers, who had previously struggled as individuals in a hostile market, the chance for collective action to solve their economic difficulties. They could now organize as businessmen. Whereas the tobacco growers in the 1920s had shunned a marketing cooperative and resisted appeals to restrict production, in the 1930s they acted together to control their acreage. They later supported the stabilization cooperative, sponsored an organization that would promote tobacco exports, and cooperated to fund programs for research and development. The New Deal led, as a rural sociologist noted, to a total change in the tobacco growers' value system. Their experience is an excellent illustration of Richard Kirkendall's recent assertion that the New Deal for agriculture was above all part of the "continued and accelerated evolution of a collectivist or organizational type of capitalism."[1]

The result was to increase the growers' income dramatically. Between 1934 and 1939 the North Carolina flue-cured growers received at least three times as much for their crop as they had in 1932. Even the relatively poor years of 1933 and 1940 provided the farmers with twice as much as they had made in the year preceding the New Deal. Between 1933 and 1936 the AAA gave them in addition rental and benefit payments that were almost half as much as their entire proceeds from the 1932 crop. Although the outlook at the end of the decade following the withdrawal of the British buyers was bleak, the war, in fact, soon benefited the tobacco growers by stimulating domestic demand. By 1943 the supply position of tobacco was so favorable that the Secretary of Agriculture would not have been able to proclaim marketing quotas had it not been for special congressional dispensation. The growers had indeed to worry more about the existence of wartime price ceilings than the level of price support. Since the war, stabilization has ensured the steady increase of flue-cured prices.[2]

Critics at the time doubted that production control could be applied on such a long-term basis. Agricultural economists who favored restriction as an emergency means of supply adjustment believed that as time went by control would have to become increasingly complex in order to eliminate inevitable inequities. Producers would find such regulation increasingly unacceptable, since inevitably the benefits would in time become less dramatic and obvious. In any case, they argued, control would not work, since increased yields offset acreage cuts, and artificially high prices induced by control lost export markets and stimulated foreign production. Theodore Saloutos accepts the substance of these complaints and asserts that the production control programs of the New Deal "can hardly be adjudged a success."[3]

The tobacco program seems to belie such criticism. Although the major technological advances in tobacco production, as in other crops, did not occur until after 1940, nevertheless flue-cured yields per acre did rise in the 1930s. These increases did not, however, thwart the purpose of production control, since the tobacco program restricted not only the acreage planted but the amount produced on that acreage as well. The initial 1934–35 contract laid down both acreage and poundage allotments, while the marketing quotas under the 1938 act restricted poundage rather than acreage. The decision in 1939 to move to acreage allotments, coupled with the major breakthrough in yields in the late 1950s, did threaten to overwhelm the program in the 1960s, but the reimposition of poundage quotas in 1965 ensured that production control would continue to be effective.

The loss of foreign markets as a result of control had been confidently predicted by Senator Bailey and by the local opponents of compulsion in 1938. Eisenhower's Secretary of Agriculture, Ezra Taft Benson, later claimed such fears were justified. "Even with the best quality tobacco in the world, we are pricing ourselves out of export markets . . . . The world's largest tobacco market used to be in North Carolina. Now it's in Rhodesia." In the 1930s, however, such fears had been groundless. Flue-cured exports did fall off from their 1929 level, which they never recaptured, but this fall preceded acreage reduction. After 1933 exports increased. Similarly, a threefold increase in foreign production occurred between 1929 and 1933, while the first four years of the AAA saw only a 75 percent increase abroad. Increased trade barriers and the deliberate stimulus by other governments of domestic and colonial tobacco production had a greater effect on flue-cured exports and foreign production than crop control in the United States. Since 1940 the U.S. has still been able to sell as much tobacco as in the 1930s at the steadily increasing prices demanded by the growers, even though the country's share of world flue-cured production has shrunk. Other countries have been unable to grow flue-cured tobacco of sufficiently high quality to persuade consumers that expensive American leaf is no longer necessary.[4]

This ability to maintain a foreign market and rigid production control has ensured that the price-support program for tobacco has never piled up the expensive surpluses that have bedeviled other commodities. The program has been cheap to run, since the activities of the Stabilization Corporation have been basically self-sustaining. Obligations to the CCC have been met in full, with the exception of the "discount" crops of 1955 and 1956, when the Department of Agriculture reduced its loans rates by 50 percent on these special high-yield but bland varieties. The production boom of the early 1960s threatened stabilization's operations, but poundage quotas effectively checked that danger.[5]

The continuation of effective and rigid crop control through the 1930s and afterward distinguished flue-cured tobacco from other commodities and confounded the predictions of agricultural economists that such control would be increasingly difficult to enforce. With the single exception of 1938, flue-cured growers in the 1930s participated in crop control programs with less complaint, and endorsed them with greater turnouts and majorities, than any other group of farmers. Far from becoming more burdensome and complex, the operation of production control became more routine as the years went by, so that after the war it was a familiar and noncontroversial procedure.

There are several reasons for this success. First, the principle of acreage reduction was firmly accepted by the tobacco growers' representatives before 1933. The virtues of curtailing production had been extolled time and time again during Governor Gardner's "Live at Home" campaign. What was lacking was an effective mechanism for putting restriction into practice. The Voluntary Domestic Allotment Plan therefore found a receptive audience. Second, flue-cured tobacco was grown by a relatively small number of farmers in a geographically compact area. This concentration of producers undoubtedly facilitated administration and enforcement and increased the impact of educational campaigns. Third, the immediate and tangible rewards of production control were greater for flue-cured tobacco than for other commodities. Control brought startling price rises for flue-cured tobacco. Elsewhere, control was often a quid pro quo for receiving government benefit payments without a direct effect on prices, or it was a means of eliminating large carry-overs and thus preventing prices from falling. Finally, control and government aid for tobacco were the result of a series of emergencies that confronted the growers with few alternatives. The defeat of crop control in December 1938 showed what could happen in a nonemergency situation. The result of that referendum seemed to bear out the agricultural economists' assertion that as time went on "irritation over inequities and rigidities tend to increase and the irksomeness of the necessary 'red tape' is more keenly felt, while at the same time the importance of further benefit to be derived from subsequent adjustments of less magnitude tends to shrink until many farmers feel it is not worth the effort involved." But just as in 1933 control had been introduced in an emergency, so it returned in 1939 with the crisis prompted by the withdrawal of the British buyers. Similarly, in 1946 the Stabilization Corporation was hastily launched to counteract the effect of a drastic postwar slump.[6]

Proximity to economic disaster stimulated the growers' initial commitment to control. The success of control in turn gave them a vested interest in its continuation, since its operation created for them a monopoly on the increasingly profitable growing of flue-cured leaf. Their position had improved in comparison not only with the years before the New Deal but also with other farm groups. Whereas farm prices as a whole between 1934 and 1940 averaged 70 percent of their 1920–29 level, flue-cured prices averaged 97 percent, and that would have been much higher but for the special circumstances of the 1939 and 1940 crops. When farm prices almost doubled between 1940 and 1945, flue-cured prices rose even faster. Crop control and the "historic base" method of calculating quotas and allotments froze this favorable relationship between tobacco growers and other farmers. As Clifford Hope complained in Congress, tobacco growers "already have what amounts to a monopoly . . . if you do not have a quota you can not produce unless you pay a very heavy penalty. It is not only a closed shop proposition but it is a closed union with a closed shop." Jonathan Daniels summed up this effect. It made a "vested interest of all the farmers already farming. Any newcomers to tobacco farming must squeeze into a limited 2 percent, and such newcomers are generally old growers out only because they moved away from the 'historical base' beneath them in the land."[7]

The most striking consequence was the dramatic increase in land values in the tobacco areas, especially North Carolina. The estimated value per acre of farm real estate rose twice as fast in North Carolina between 1930 and 1948 as in the nation as a whole. This rapid rise only applied to certain land in the state: land with a tobacco allotment.

Frank Jeter wrote in 1945 of a "New Way to Price Land" in the state whereby a farm of five hundred acres might sell for the same price as a twenty-acre farm on equally fertile soil. The crucial difference would be that the latter had a tobacco allotment, the former did not. One calculation suggested that a tobacco allotment enhanced the market value of a farm by \$300 to \$600 for each allotment acre.[8]

The operation of control was important for the position of tobacco farmers in relationship to the rest of agriculture, but it was also important for the structure of tobacco growing itself: for the relationships among landlords, tenants, and small farmers within flue-cured production.

The impact of the AAA on southern tenant farmers and share-croppers has been perhaps the most widely publicized of the New Deal's failings. Recent studies of the AAA's cotton program have confirmed that it discriminated in favor of the large planter at the expense of the tenant farmer. Tenants were discriminated against in the allocation of rental and benefit payments under the acreage-reduction contracts, because they received none of the rental payments and only shared in the benefit payments. They were often deprived even of this share by the landlord. Acreage reduction led many landlords to go further and evict their tenants or reduce them to the status of wage laborers.[9]

It is not easy to assess how far these criticisms were also true of the tobacco program. As in cotton, landlords received all the rental payments under the tobacco program: tenants and sharecroppers shared only in the benefit and price-equalizing payments in proportion to their share of the crop. Hutson, however, did lower the proposed rental payment from \$20.00 to \$17.50 an acre, so that higher benefit payments could be made in which tenants could share. These payments were made to the landlords, not the tenants, since it was argued that direct payments to tenants were administratively impossible. Late in 1935 Chester Davis, under pressure from the Comptroller General, did admit that it was feasible to pay individual tenants in tobacco, if not in cotton. Under the Soil Conservation and Domestic Allotment Act checks were directly mailed to the tenants.[10]

How fair landlords were in ensuring the proper distribution of government money in 1934 and 1935 depended on the awareness of tenants of their rights and the willingness of county committees to support them. If a tenant complained to Washington, he was informed of his rights and the complaint was simply referred back to the county agent for investigation, with the proviso that the tobacco section be informed of the eventual disposition of the case. Once more the tenant's fate rested in the hands of the landlord-dominated county committee. Any judgment of the operation of the program depends largely on an intuitive assessment of how fair and honest the landlords and these committees were. Two county agents who discussed the problem of payment distribution blamed ignorance and misunderstanding on both sides: on the one hand, tenants were on the whole a "low class" who automatically believed that their landlords were cheating them, and, on the other, landlords believed that they could deduct from the payments anything the tenants owed them. Farmers of both races and all tenure groups in Wilson, when questioned after the war, believed that such payments had not been fairly distributed in the first program, and today agricultural officials make no effort to hide their opinion that tenants and croppers were often deprived of payments that were rightly theirs. Nevertheless, violations in the distribution of payments did not at the time become so flagrant as to provoke noticeable tenant discontent. One survey also suggests that, despite the violations, tenants and croppers in North Carolina at least received a greater share of benefit payments on tobacco than on cotton. Whereas tenants and croppers received an average of $12 and $37 respectively as benefit payments on cotton in 1934 compared to $94 for owners, they received $29 and $58 as benefit payments on tobacco, compared to $95 for owners. The same survey found that the rates of increase in gross and net farm income between 1932 and 1934 were roughly the same for all the tenure groups.[11]

An even more important problem is to measure the extent to which the crop control program in North Carolina not merely failed to pay tenants and sharecroppers fairly, but actually displaced them from the land.

The tobacco contract for 1934 and 1935 provided that the landlord should not reduce the number of his tenants or sharecroppers because of the required acreage reduction. This, of course, did not bind the landlord to keep the same tenants nor did it prevent him from removing tenants for reasons other than cuts in acreage. Clearly, it would be difficult to enforce this provision, and once again much would depend upon how readily local committees accepted the word of their fellow landlords when checking compliance.

The first public notice that there was a problem of tenant displacement in North Carolina came in February 1934 from Capus Waynick, state director of the Federal-State Re-employment Service. Pointing to the loopholes in the contract, he maintained that his office records indicated "that the tobacco acreage reduction will have the effect of forcing a considerable number of tenant farmers to seek other employment." His Kinston office sent in immediately a list of forty-two tenants registered as having been evicted because of the acreage cuts. At the same time Lorena Hickok reported to Harry Hopkins that hundreds of tenant families were being driven into eastern North Carolina towns like Wilson because of the "practical results" of the AAA. A study for the North Carolina Emergency Relief Administration of three tobacco counties confirmed that tenants had been displaced following the signing of the acreage reduction contracts. More had been evicted in the early months of 1934 than in the whole of 1933. Of those removed, over one-quarter cited the reduction contract as the reason. A later study of three other counties provided more evidence. In early 1935 Lindsay Warren complained that thirty-nine tenants had been displaced in Pitt, while later that year a study of six mainly cotton counties in the state found that 7.3 percent of tenants on relief had been evicted in violation of their contracts. The author, from the landlord-tenant division of the AAA, was convinced also that "many violations have occurred where the tenant was not on the relief rolls." In 1938 Senator Bailey predicted that the new Farm Act would drive twenty-five to thirty thousand North Carolina farm families from the land. In April the state director of the WPA blamed the increase in unemployment on the acreage reductions. Nothing in the 1938 act protected tenants, since no contracts or government payments were actually involved in the imposition of marketing quotas. The only protection tenants had was under the soil conservation program of 1936. Over half the Wilson farmers subsequently interviewed by Robert E. Martin remembered cases of tenants being displaced because of the control scheme.[12]

Privately, the Extension Service acknowledged that displacement had taken place. Director Schaub was certain in February 1934 that a "considerable amount of chiseling of this kind" was going on. There were two reasons, however, why Schaub was reluctant to remedy the problem and publicly acknowledge its existence. First, as one of his county agents complained, it was very difficult for an agent to distinguish between those tenants who had been discharged because of acreage reduction and those who had been evicted for reasons sanctioned by the contract. Second, Schaub, backed by his national director, had no intention of letting his agents become enforcement officers. They intended to leave the matters of compliance to the county committees, despite the fact that in the cotton and tobacco programs it was the agent and not the committee who was the official representative of the AAA. Schaub's reluctance to allow his county agents to get involved reflected his unwillingness to let them challenge and question the locally influential landlords in such a delicate matter as landlord-tenant relations. In public, therefore, the Extension Service minimized the problem of tenant displacement, explained such displacement as being justified under the tobacco contract, and in the instances of acknowledged contract violations acquitted the landlords of any charges of acting in bad faith. In 1934 Schaub argued that "in most cases we have found that the tenants discharged were incompetent or unreliable and that, no doubt, some of them would have been discharged earlier." Although he regretted that some worthy tenants had been evicted, he preferred to emphasize the "almost undreamed of" benefits to the great majority of farmers. The following year an extension official argued that few violations had occurred and explained away what little displacement there had been. "It would appear that some violations have occurred if the contract is to be interpreted literally but it appears also that in most instances, the landlords have had valid reasons for making changes. . . . In many instances, the landlords ran shiftless tenants off the place and sometimes forgot to secure new ones as the contract specified."[13]

The evidence to some extent justifies Extension Service complacency. The overall figures for the state scarcely suggest a massive displacement of tenants in the 1930s, since the number of farms operated by tenants only fell by 10 percent from 137,615 to 123,476 and was almost offset by the increase in the number of owner-operated farms. This was a relatively small drop compared to the cotton states of the West South Central Division, where there was a 26 percent decrease, including a 32 percent fall in Arkansas. There is also evidence to support Calvin Hoover's contention that a considerable displacement of tenants had occurred *before* the AAA's acreage-reduction schemes were put into effect. The studies for the state relief administration by Gordon Blackwell and C. Horace Hamilton found that the greatest single cause of displacement was the low tobacco and cotton prices before the New Deal. Such survey findings were supported by the reports of local relief officials in December 1934, who argued that the real problem was not that acreage reduction by the AAA had displaced tenants in eastern North Carolina, but that crop control prevented those who had been removed before 1933 from returning to tobacco growing when prosperity was returning.[14]

The overall figures obscure two long-term trends that Blackwell and Hamilton noted: the move of Negroes from the land and the tendency of whites to replace Negroes as tenants. The surveys found that Negroes tended to be displaced before whites, and the overall figures for the 1930s show that, while there was a slight increase in the number of white tenants, the number of black tenants fell by over fifteen thousand. This could not be offset by a few hundred additional black farm owners. This emphasizes what local relief officials noted: that many tenants were displaced and replaced by other tenants. This practice was not necessarily a violation of the reduction contract, but it was a practice that liberals in the AAA's legal division tried unsuccessfully to eradicate.[15]

Despite this movement the tobacco program did not significantly alter the existing relationships between landlords and tenants. It might even be argued that the commercial success of the program held people on the land who might otherwise have moved, and who would move when employment opportunities in the cities improved in the postwar period. The major disappearance of tenants from the flue-cured areas did not occur until the late 1950s. If anything, after the early 1930s tobacco farming needed more labor than was available, not less. Such a situation is likely to be reversed only when the complete mechanization of tobacco harvesting is achieved.

The fate of the small independent farmer under the tobacco program exercised politicians far more than the plight of the tenant farmer. From the start there were protests from small farmers about the way the crop reduction program operated. It was argued that the small farmers had not been the ones responsible for overproduction. Indeed, they had often voluntarily reduced their acreage before 1933. It was therefore unfair to cut the small grower by the same percentage as the large farmer who, in any case, could easily bear acreage cuts of 30 percent, which would leave the small grower of three or four acres with too little to support his family. These small growers were the slowest to sign up in 1933; they complained to Senator Bailey throughout the 1930s that the program discriminated against them; they protested their acreage allotments in 1938, and their dissatisfaction played a prominent part in the defeat of control in that year.

Special efforts were made by the AAA to placate the small farmer. Under the original acreage-reduction contract, he was given extra benefit payments—the more under four acres his base acreage, the greater his benefit payments until he received 25 percent of the selling price of his tobacco. Under the Kerr-Smith Act 6 percent of the county's allotment could be used to give tax-exemption warrants to growers who were unable to secure an equitable base under the 1934 contract, provided that two-thirds of this went to growers producing under 1,500 pounds. In 1935 growers whose base acreage was under 3.2 acres were allowed to plant up to their base or three acres, whichever was the smaller. Under the tobacco compact bill in North Carolina growers with base acreages under three acres would not be cut. Under the 1938 act growers with base production under 3,200 pounds would be safe. In 1939 the allotments for these growers were increased by 20 percent as long as these did not then exceed 3,200 pounds.

None of these efforts went as far as the champions of the small growers wanted. In 1934 Umstead had wanted to exempt all growers planting under three acres from the Kerr-Smith Act. In 1935 Lindsay Warren had wanted all growers to be able to plant up to three acres without restriction. In the 1938 Farm Act Bailey had wanted to provide that growers producing less than 10,000 pounds should only be cut by 5 percent and those producing under 15,000 pounds by 10 percent. A year later he wanted to exempt from penalty taxes all growers who produced up to 3,500 pounds.

Bailey's views could perhaps be discounted, because he opposed the whole idea of crop control. The most enthusiastic supporter of the claims of the small grower, however, was also an enthusiastic supporter of the principle of control. From the start of the AAA, Clarence Poe, editor of the *Progressive Farmer*, championed "the right of the little man to live." He always maintained that small farmers should not be expected to reduce by as much as the large-scale commercial farmers. In particular, he objected to the idea that a grower who had balanced his farming should receive a smaller allotment than someone who planted all his acreage in tobacco. A man who grew only 20 percent of his cultivated acreage in tobacco should not be expected to cut back by as much as the large farmer, who forced his tenants to plant 80 percent of their cultivated acreage in the staple. Poe envisaged both a minimum allotment for all growers and a maximum allotment expressed as a percentage of cultivated acreage, such as the suggestion by the Grange in 1937 that no allotment under the compact should be more than 35 percent of the farmer's cultivated acreage. Such a plan would give "'equal and exact justice to all men' no matter what they did or did not do in some remote 'base period.'" This would mean the end of the "historic base" method of calculating quotas and allotments which not only froze relationships between tobacco growers and new growers, but also froze the existing relationships between large and small tobacco growers.[16]

The AAA conceded none of these points. Abandonment of the "historic base" would have penalized the very growers who most had to suffer low leaf prices during the depression. The tobacco section also claimed that the result of the basic principle of flat-rate reductions, modified only in the small adjustments noted above, was that in fact "most of the reduction in production had been taken by the large producers." Hutson quoted for Poe a survey of twenty-two flue-cured counties where allotments were expressed as a percentage of 1933 production. In this, the allotments of farmers growing under three acres were 105.9 percent of their 1933 production, while the allotments of farmers producing over 100 acres were a mere 81.7 percent. In the final analysis the AAA refused to establish minimum allotments and quotas or differential reductions, because any move to help the small farmer would penalize the tenant farmer. Hutson later explained that the AAA had won over the congressmen and senators who were pushing for minimum acreages by pointing out that "it would be extremely difficult to really favor small producers by establishing these minimums because we would cut, obviously, the larger operator. And to the extent that he was handling his operations on a cropper basis you would really hit the lowest people in the ladder, who were the share-croppers." Hutson's dilemma is illustrated by C. Horace Hamilton's survey which showed that protecting tenants and croppers did hit the small farmer. Hamilton showed that between 1932 and 1934 small farmers had to reduce their tobacco acreage by 35 percent, while tenants and croppers only cut theirs by 25 and 21 percent respectively. At the same time, of course, the small owner-operator received more in rental and benefit payments than the tenants for his reduction.[17]

Production control, the use of the "historic base," and the commercial success of the tobacco program seem therefore to have perpetuated the basic existing structure of tobacco growing; control seems to have frozen relationships between tobacco growers and other farmers, and also the relationships within the tobacco-growing community among the landlords, tenants, and small farmers. That it did so is eloquent testimony to the extent to which all the New Deal's agricultural activities in North Carolina served to secure recovery rather than reform. The New Deal succeeded much more in fulfilling its aim of rescuing the state's agriculture from depression than in planning a more efficient agriculture or achieving a more equitable agriculture.

The grand long-term plans of the agricultural economists in the AAA to produce a rational and efficient American agriculture through planning had little impact on North Carolina. The New Deal produced no startling "adjustments" in the state's agriculture. Extension Service officials had hoped that the curtailment of tobacco and cotton acreage would lead the state's farmers to carry out the aims of the "Live at Home" campaign and diversify their farming. There were some changes: the number of milk cows, beef cattle, sows, and poultry steadily increased over the decade, and the corn acreage rose by 20 percent. But the number of farms producing wheat, Irish and sweet potatoes, and commercial truck fluctuated wildly. Overall the basic structure of farming remained the same. If anything, the dependence on the staples of cotton and tobacco increased. In 1940 these two crops contributed 64 percent of the state's cash farm income compared to 56 percent in 1932.[18]

The New Deal probably did encourage better farming practices in the state and more attention to soil conservation. A notable change was the planting of lespedeza, an insignificant crop in 1929 but with the second-largest acreage in the state by 1941. Nevertheless, the Extension Service still complained that farmers were more interested in soil-diverting payments for not planting tobacco and cotton than in the payments for following soil-building practices. The new soil conservation districts in which farmers could impose conservation practices on their neighbors had a slow start, marred by a lack of interest among the farmers and by suspicion between the Extension and Soil Conservation Services. The goal of democratic planning with local farmers serving on county program planning and land-use committees was never attained. There is no evidence that such committees occupied a high place in the county agents' priorities or that the farmers themselves had any interest in them. Similarly, the New Deal prompted in North Carolina no significant retirement of submarginal land and no substantial resettlement of farmers. The number of farms and their size remained static in the 1930s. The flight from the land and the consolidation of farm units was a phenomenon mainly of the 1950s and 1960s. Postwar prosperity made more difference to the structure of North Carolina farming than did the efforts of the New Deal planners.[19]

That the overall thrust of the agricultural program in the state was toward raising farm income generally rather than redistributing that agricultural income can clearly be seen from the figures of New Deal spending. Whereas by 1939 the AAA had spent $84 million and the Farm Credit Administration had loaned $83 million in the state, poorer North Carolina farmers had only received $15 million by 1941 in rehabilitation loans under the various rural poverty programs. Even so, these rehabilitation loans to farmers on their own land were by far the most important of the reforming programs of the Emergency Relief Administration, the Resettlement Administration, and the Farm Security Administration. As elsewhere, the tenant purchase and resettlement schemes were restricted to an almost insignificant number of North Carolina farmers. By 1943 the FSA had granted loans to only 2,327 tenants to purchase their own land, despite the fact that almost one-third of the state's more than 120,000 tenants had applied for loans. The resettlement projects could at most accommodate 751 families. These projects were to come under fierce attack from Harold Cooley and others for reversing traditional government land policy, and for their alleged collectivism and excessive supervision of clients. In fact, the North Carolina projects, like those studied by Donald Holley in Louisiana, Arkansas, and Mississippi, had failed even before they had been killed off by outside critics. Individual units were often too small for clients to make enough money to hope to buy their land; it was difficult to find suitable clients especially after the start of the war; individualistic clients failed to support cooperative activities, resented supervision, and were dismayed by the lack of progress towards purchasing their own farms. Turnover was high, and by 1943 only 253 clients had been offered the chance to buy their own plots.[20]

If the New Deal did not fundamentally alter the structure of North Carolina farming in general and tobacco growing in particular, neither did it basically change the business structure of to-bacco marketing. The tobacco program altered neither the competitive situation among the tobacco manufacturers nor the auction warehouse system.

There is no evidence of any increase in competition among the Big Three cigarette manufacturers in the purchase of tobacco leaf. In 1933 the government exercised unprecedented powers over the tobacco industry, which had hitherto seemed immune from government inter-ference. But most of those powers remained unused after the manufac-turers had negotiated the marketing agreement to pay higher prices for the 1933 crop. In 1934 the AAA acquiesced in the manufacturers' refusal to sign a similar agreement for the next crop. The government made no sustained attempt to encourage competition by the indepen-dents who produced the cheaper ten-cent packs of cigarettes. The Treasury and the AAA did support proposals for a graduated reduction in the cigarette tax, which would have benefited these independents more than the Big Three, but their advocacy was only temporary and tentative. Put forward largely as a means of deflecting the pressure of the major companies for a horizontal tax reduction, the proposals were abandoned once the major companies had themselves backed down. In 1940 the government finally instituted an antitrust suit against the tobacco companies, but the conviction of the manufacturers in 1946 produced no discernible change in leaf-buying practices. Charges by growers of collusion on the part of the buyers to keep leaf prices down can still be heard in the tobacco belts.

Once leaf prices rose and the tobacco farmers recovered, the AAA had lost interest in encouraging competition among the manufac-turers. Similarly, the tobacco section virtually ignored the interests of cigarette consumers. In 1933 the consumers' counsel division had played a role in stalling the marketing agreement, but after that its influence appears to have been minimal. There is no evidence that concern for consumers played any part in policy making in the tobacco section except when the effects of the cigarette tax reduction were considered in 1934. After 1933 the consumers' counsel continued to ask the tobacco section about the likely effect of leaf price rises on cigarette prices, but these questions appear to have been submitted more for the record than to influence policy decisions.[21]

While there have been some changes in the auction warehouse system, its essentials have remained intact to the present day. The

Flanagan Act of 1935 did offer government grading on those markets where two-thirds of the growers voted for it, but control of most of the warehouse operations remained in the hands of the warehousemen themselves. Regulation of the speed of selling, for example, remained the responsibility of the local tobacco board of trade on which farmers were not represented. The opening dates of the markets were still decided by the sales committee of the United States Tobacco Association, although that body was susceptible to government pressure as in 1933, when Hutson virtually ordered the chairman of the committee to open the Border Belt markets early. The abuses of the system, however, became less important. The speed of selling penalized a grower less, once government grading gave each lot of tobacco an easily identifiable standard of quality. Pinhooking and speculating became less profitable as prices became more stable. Eventually the determination of opening dates passed into the hands of belt-wide marketing committees on which the growers had the greatest representation. In 1974 the Grower Designation Plan scrapped the belt lines and coordinated the schedules of growers, graders, buyers, and warehousemen, to enable the markets to open when and where local crops were maturing. This did not alter the fundamental nature of the auction system, however. The role of the warehouseman as the essential middleman between the grower and buyer remained.[22]

The Politics of Policy Making

The economic consequences of the tobacco program can be baldly stated: the improvement of the marketing position of the growers, tobacco's prosperity compared with the rest of agriculture, the freezing of relative positions between tobacco growers, and the lack of disruption of the business structure of the tobacco industry. Such results can only be explained by examining the way in which policy in the tobacco program was formulated and implemented, the nature and role of pressure groups, and the extent to which policy was imposed from above in Washington or created by pressure from below.

The dominant rationale of the tobacco program, as of other commodity programs, was that it was what the growers wanted. As the government proposed more and more detailed interference in the activities of the growers, so its supporters insisted that they were merely deferring to the wishes of the growers themselves. In 1933 Hutson had warned growers not to "expect us to sit in Washington, devise a plan and say here it is," and Chester Davis maintained that the AAA acted later that summer only because "riots broke out" in the tobacco belt. In 1934 the tobacco section stated that it recommended compulsory control legislation only "at the request of the tobacco growers." In the discussions of new farm legislation in 1937, Lindsay Warren was adamant that "we [tobacco congressmen and Department of Agriculture officials] wished the plan to come from them [the farmers] so that it could be shown that they were behind it." In 1940, referring to a proposed amendment, Hutson asserted, "If it is what the growers want, I'm for it."

Despite these resounding declarations, there was a sharp difference between the process of policy making in the tobacco program before the Hoosac Mills decision in 1936 and afterward. Before 1936 policy was decided under the broad authority of the Agricultural Adjustment Act, with the result that the key decisions were taken within the AAA. The tobacco section did not simply respond to growers' pressure; rather it deliberately encouraged pressure from them. It could then respond to what it had itself created and by involving the growers facilitate the implementation of the production control program. When the growers made demands that the AAA believed were too narrowly sectional, the tobacco section rejected them.

In 1933 the tobacco section had planned a long-term program of acreage reduction for flue-cured tobacco without reference to the growers, whose leaders had played no part in agitation for the Domestic Allotment Plan and the 1933 Farm Act. On the other hand, while the AAA intended to persuade growers to sign crop reduction contracts for 1934, it had no plans for the 1933 crop, once negotiations with the manufacturers to secure better prices had broken down at the end of August. It was the bold gamble of the growers at this point in persuading the governor of North Carolina to close the markets that forced the government to pledge itself for the first time to guarantee parity prices for the 1933 crop.

The AAA was thus responding to independent action by the growers and committing itself to a course of action that it had not previously intended to take. However, from the start the AAA had encouraged the growers to make their views known through a conference with leading growers at the end of July and an advisory growers' committee. The mass meetings of tobacco farmers in early August had been a direct response to invitations from Wallace and others to the growers to indicate whether they wanted any action on the 1933 crop. Once the growers had acted, the AAA was able to use their pressure to implement policies that it had already planned. The marketing holiday gave the AAA the best possible opportunity to sign up growers for the proposed reduction in 1934. The growers then left the AAA free to redeem its pledge to secure parity prices for the 1933 crop in whatever way it thought best.

The AAA also took the opportunity to encourage and formalize further pressure from the growers. Since there had previously been no effective organization of tobacco growers, the Extension Service had already moved to form an organization that could put the growers' views to the AAA. The AAA exploited this by using the inaugural meeting called by Dean Schaub to launch the sign-up campaign. It used the county delegates as county committeemen to assist the county agents in administering the program, and it recognized the officers of the new association as members of the state and regional growers' advisory committees.

Soon the county agents and the new growers' association were bringing pressure to bear on the AAA for some measure of compulsory crop control that would prevent noncooperating growers from wrecking the acreage reduction program. In the case of cotton, the AAA had bowed reluctantly to similar pressure from what it perceived to be the overwhelming majority of cotton growers. In the case of tobacco, however, the tobacco section encouraged the growers' demands and drafted the initial legislation. The tobacco section had reasons of its own for backing the Kerr-Smith Act. It did not share the growers' fears that noncooperators would plant so much that 1934 prices would collapse. It feared rather that not enough rental and benefit money could be paid to ensure that cooperating growers would receive a higher income than nonsigners. This discrepancy would jeopardize future participation in a voluntary crop control program. The tobacco section therefore favored a tax on nonsigners, and by working with the growers from the start they ensured that the tax was a moderate 25–33$\frac{1}{3}$ percent rather than the punitive 50 percent advocated by the Growers' Advisory Committee. As in 1935 with the AAA amendments, there was then pressure on the tobacco congressmen from the county agents and county committeemen prompted by local AAA officials.

That the AAA had no intention of acceding to the tobacco growers' demands if it disagreed with them was increasingly apparent in 1934 and 1935. The tobacco section refused to support the demands of the growers' leaders and the tobacco congressmen for a horizontal reduction in the cigarette tax, and the proposal collapsed. Yet it forced through compulsory government grading in the face of the opposition of North Carolina warehousemen and some tobacco congressmen who argued that the growers did not want mandatory inspection. The real determination of the AAA not to be browbeaten by a special interest was demonstrated when it rejected almost all the tobacco growers' demands for changes in the 1935 tobacco program. The AAA saw their call for a smaller crop in 1935 and emergency aid in the fall as an attempt to raise leaf prices artificially above the parity level. The growers could hold protest meetings and send delegations to Washington, but to no avail. The AAA remained firm in its contention that the growers' demands were not in the overall agricultural interest. Hutson and Wallace addressed mass meetings of farmers in North Carolina, not to listen to their arguments but simply to explain to them the decisions the AAA had already taken.

Before 1936, therefore, the AAA had used consultation with the growers more to involve them in the operation of the production control program, thereby facilitating its execution, than to defer to their wishes on matters of policy. The Growers' Advisory Committee epitomized this process. On crucial matters like the marketing agreement and the size of the 1935 crop the committee, despite the initial misgivings of its members, was soon won over to the AAA's position. What the committee offered Hutson was public support for and involvement in the tobacco section's policies and detailed, expert advice about how to implement such programs. Hutson realized that he could not know everything about tobacco, and he valued the two- or three-day, fifteen-hour-a-day discussions of "what would be practical to do." He liked men who would stand up to him, and his advisory committees were certainly more independent than present-day commodity advisory committees, which have been scrupulously screened to eliminate anyone at odds with Administration policy. Nevertheless, the Tobacco Growers' Advisory Committee of the early New Deal served more to advise the AAA than to force its hand.[23]

After 1936 the process of policy making changed, and the AAA was not nearly so powerful. The 1933 Farm Act had been an enabling act outlining various policy alternatives. The decision on which option to adopt would have to be taken within the AAA. It was into the AAA that the Growers' Advisory Committee was coopted, and it was toward the tobacco section that the growers' pressure was directed. After Hoosac Mills the restoration of crop control had to be secured from Congress, and it was therefore to Congress that the Growers' Advisory Committee and the newly formed pressure group, the North Carolina Farm Bureau, turned their attention. To achieve legislation for production control the AAA had now to play an equal or even subordinate role to those growers' groups which it had to all intents and purposes created. In 1934 the AAA handed John Kerr a draft bill for compulsory control ready for him to introduce; in 1938 the tobacco provisions of the Farm Act were the product of a subcommittee of tobacco congressmen convened by Harold Cooley. The passage of that act also furthered this trend. The 1933 Farm Act had laid down various general alternatives; the 1938 act specified clear and precise policy directions for tobacco. As a result, changes in policy would have to come from legislative, not administrative, decisions. Given the skill of the tobacco congressmen in persuading Congress to go along with what they asked for, agricultural policy became a matter of what the tobacco growers could persuade the tobacco congressmen to accept. The AAA had little choice but to acquiesce in this, especially after the defeat of crop control in late 1938 and the emergency created next year by the withdrawal of the British buyers. Drastic crop control became so essential that the AAA would cooperate with any legislation that would guarantee its continuation. In the absence therefore of a veto exercised by the AAA on behalf of the national or overall agricultural interest, the tobacco growers began to secure more and more special interest legislation.

In fact, Representative August H. Andresen of Minnesota already complained that tobacco had "had special treatment for the past seven years. . . . The Representatives of the tobacco districts have written their own tickets and have always had preferential treatment to handle the problems concerning the industry." Tobacco had been included as a basic commodity in the original Farm Act, even though its position was not central to American agriculture. It was given a special base period for the calculation of parity, an exception denied other commodities that were also dissatisfied with the 1909–14 base. Compulsory control was introduced for tobacco in 1934, despite the opposition of Secretary Wallace to the principle of compulsion and his hope that any experiment would be limited to cotton. After Hoosac Mills, tobacco was given separate legislative consideration when Congress authorized an interstate compact. From the beginning of the discussions of the 1938 Farm Act, tobacco was recognized as a special case: men who opposed compulsory control on other crops were nevertheless prepared to accept the imposition of quotas and penalty taxes on tobacco.[24]

After the defeat of quotas in 1938 the pace of special legislation quickened. To facilitate the reintroduction of control, amendments in the summer of 1939 allowed the AAA to base quotas on acreage not poundage, to change the allotments for small growers, and to allow an early referendum on control during the 1939 marketing season. In 1940 further changes gave the growers the chance to vote for three-year control, not one-year, and changed the base period for calculating parity so that the growers could permanently benefit from the high prices of the 1930s.

It was during and after World War II that the special treatment of tobacco became most marked. The war so stimulated domestic demand that under the 1938 act the supply level of flue-cured tobacco was not high enough to allow the Secretary of Agriculture to proclaim quotas for 1943. Congress however simply decreed that there could be quotas for 1943 and later extended quotas similarly from 1944 to 1947. In the 1948 and 1949 farm acts the price-support level of tobacco was higher than for other crops, and control could still be imposed irrespective of the potential supply of tobacco, provided quotas had been in force the previous year. Through the 1950s price-support levels remained fixed and mandatory for tobacco, while they were flexible and discretionary for other commodities.[25]

Why was Congress so considerate to the tobacco growers? Tobacco was heavily concentrated geographically, with the result that there were a small number of congressmen for whom tobacco growers were the single most important constituency pressure group. These congressmen, especially those in the North Carolina delegation, were extraordinarily well placed to forward the interest of the crop. Harold Cooley's seat on the House Agriculture Committee from 1934 guaranteed favorable consideration of tobacco at the outset of any legislation. He had the additional support of John Flanagan of Virginia, and they both benefited from the way chairman Marvin Jones ran their committee. The committee usually deferred to the members representing a particular commodity whenever legislation affecting that commodity came forward. Jones, who was frankly opposed to compulsory controls both in 1934 and later and was skeptical of the interstate compact in 1936, nevertheless did not prevent favorable reports coming out of his committee on such legislation. Measures for tobacco were unlikely to be held up by the Rules Committee when J. Bayard Clark sat on it, while in Lindsay Warren tobacco had the benefit of a skilled parliamentarian closely identified with the House leadership.

In the Senate, where much agricultural legislation was held up by the hostility of Agriculture Committee chairman Ellison D. Smith, tobacco was assured of support from the South Carolina senator, anxious not to alienate his tobacco-growing constituents of the Border Belt. A similar solicitude for the welfare of constituents led Alben Barkley of Kentucky to look after tobacco legislation when he became majority leader. The opposition of Senator Bailey might have been fatal, and he voted against both the 1933 and 1938 farm acts and was opposed to compulsory crop control. Bailey, however, never voted against special tobacco legislation. On general agricultural measures he could afford a stand of principle. On measures specifically for tobacco he did not feel confident enough of his political strength to oppose what he perceived to be the wishes of his constituents. He either acquiesced in those bills or actively supported them.

In both the House and Senate tobacco representatives relied on unanimous consent to bring their measures to the floor, often late in the session. Most of them provoked little debate and passed without roll-call votes. The representatives could follow this procedure because, first, there were few intracommodity disputes. Sponsors of legislation took care to ensure that the representatives of various types of tobacco were satisfied with the proposals. A crop of such limited geographical scope was, in any case, not as likely as more widely dispersed crops to produce conflicts of interest within the commodity group. Where such conflicts did arise, as over warehouse licensing and government grading, progress was slower and less sure. Second, the nature of policy making in the tobacco program enabled legislation to be presented to Congress as merely fulfilling what the growers wanted. Third, tobacco was such a relatively small crop that it did not provoke intercommodity conflicts. Representatives of other commodities and sections might not be wholly satisfied with tobacco legislation, but they rarely felt sufficiently unhappy or concerned to deny it unanimous consent.

A small group of congressmen therefore in whose constituencies tobacco growing was important was able to ensure a privileged position for their commodity by exploiting their strategic committee positions, a sympathetic leadership, their own unity, and the lack of clear opposition.

The very success of the tobacco program—the good prices and the position of special privilege the tobacco growers had won—served to make them conservative. Locally, this shift was reflected in the softening of the traditional hostility to the warehousemen and manufacturers. Nationally it meant that tobacco growers as a constituency pressure group were not going to push for a further extension of New Deal reforms.

In 1933 low leaf prices made vilification of the tobacco companies the stock-in-trade of even the most conservative North Carolina politicians. The Greensboro *Daily News* commented that summer "that when growers and buyers lie down in peace together the millenium, call it NEW DEAL or whatever you please, will really and truly have arrived." Yet by 1940 Jonathan Daniels noted that "you seldom hear it said now that millionaires in Winston-Salem are growing fat on the blood of the babies in Edgecombe County and Pitt."[26]

As early as 1934 the tobacco growers and their congressmen had lined up behind the tobacco manufacturers in their demand for a horizontal tax reduction on cigarettes. This reflected not only the growers' basic conservatism but also the skilled tactics of Clay Williams, who claimed that the tobacco companies were solely concerned with the growers' welfare, as they had been in 1933 when they had "wholeheartedly" come forward to sign the marketing agreement. Likewise the warehousemen capitalized on their "wholehearted and unanimous" cooperation with the growers in the 1933 crisis to enlist the support of the growers in opposing both federal licensing and government grading. The warehousemen continued to cooperate with the growers in the later control campaigns. Clay Williams did revive the growers' suspicions of the manufacturers when he launched his attack on the AAA amendments in 1935, but that was an isolated incident. In the 1939 crisis only old Josephus Daniels watching from the embassy in Mexico City talked in the traditional anticompany manner. His demand that the tobacco industry be taken over as a government monopoly unless the domestic manufacturers made good the loss suffered by the growers as a result of the British withdrawal found no echo in the tobacco belt.[27]

This growing conservatism of the growers was, in part, reflected in the voting behavior of the North Carolina tobacco congressmen. Before 1936 they overwhelmingly supported the New Deal. As John Kerr noted, "In my district the agricultural program has been so successful that the voters are most sympathetic with every policy proposed by the President." Given this attitude on the part of their constituents, tobacco congressmen cast only an occasional dissenting vote. Even Bailey, one of the leading conservatives in the Senate, whose bitter hostility to the New Deal was starkly revealed in his private correspondence, felt it necessary, especially in his 1936 reelection campaign, enthusiastically to affirm his loyalty and devotion to the President. After 1936, however, the limitations of agrarian liberalism were clearly shown. Even enthusiastic supporters of Roosevelt like Cooley, Kerr, Hancock, and Warren were dismayed by the increasingly northern, urban, and labor orientation of the New Deal and were reluctant to support further spending and relief legislation. The tobacco congressmen backed the efforts of one of their number, Graham Barden, on the House Labor Committee first to defeat or delay wage and hours legislation and later to restrict the power of the National Labor Relations Board. Although tobacco growers had benefited more than almost any other group from the unprecedented use of the government's coercive power in the economy, tobacco congressmen were not prepared to extend similar federal protection and aid to organized labor and the urban, or even rural, poor. A virtual closed shop and guaranteed income were acceptable for the growing of tobacco, but they were not to be tolerated for industrial labor. The economic emergency of the 1930s failed to shift traditions of individualism and business hostility to federal intervention.[28]

No better illustration of the pervasiveness of the conservatism of the farmer as businessman can be found than the attitude of the chairman of the Growers' Advisory Committee and the North Carolina Tobacco Growers' Association. Claude Hall had pushed from the start of the New Deal for more and more government control of tobacco production. In 1937 he urged growers to support the President's plan to reform the Supreme Court so that they might secure compulsory crop control. Yet when Hall appeared the next year at the "Little Business Conference" in Washington, he called for a straightforward, conservative, noninterventionist government policy as far as business was concerned: a definite statement that the President "does not intend to create any agency which might retard or compete with legitimate business,'' less talk about a third term, a check on the increase of the burden of taxation, and a clarification of labor relations.[29]

Grass Roots Democracy?

The tobacco program revealed a familiar pattern throughout the 1930s of mass meetings in the tobacco belts, delegations of growers' representatives visiting Washington, and reciprocal visits to the belts by Hutson and Wallace. Together with the more formalized structure of the Growers' Advisory Committee, local and decentralized administration by the farmers themselves, and regular referenda, this process represented an excellent example of what Henry Wallace delighted in under the name ''economic democracy.'' The extent of this grass roots democracy needs to be tested to find out how far all farmers—landlords, tenants, croppers, and small farmers— were represented in the growers' organization and on the local committees and how valid the referendum was as a test of grower sentiment.[30]

Jonathan Daniels met a Wilson farmer who was robustly skeptical about the administration of the tobacco program:

Friend, I don't know where you come from but I'll tell you tobacco's all right if you're one of these town farmers and they give you a big allotment. There's been plenty queer about that, too, if you ask me. Uncle Sam may be fair, but farm agents have pets still, and they aren't petting any little fellows . . .

Yes sir, tobacco is all right if you got a big allotment and tenants to do the work. That's dandy and sugar candy. You git up slow and take your hot bath and have a nigger fan you at breakfast. Then your chofer drives you up to Raleigh and you git up in the big meetin' in the Auditorium and say, ''Something has got to be done for us farmers. We labor and sweat and we're growin' the crop that pays more taxes to Uncle Sam than any in the world. We want justice.'' And the *News and Observer* writes it all up and says what Farmer Smith says. Probably got an editorial about it, too. Time for action. And Farmer Smith comes home and complains at supper about the tenderloin's tough. His belly's so big he can't hardly get to the table. He's a farmer all right, but I'd like to see you catch him suckering. The little farmers and the tenants get the sweat and he gets the cream.

Other critics complained that "a few agricultural leaders, including some county agents, can always work up a minority and make public sentiment seem what they wish it to be." Senator Bailey publicly complained about the sort of farmer who influenced legislation whose "hands were as soft as a Senator's. There was not a line on his face." This farmer with a one-million-pound allotment made more than $300,-000 a year from his crop. One of the leaders of the North Carolina tobacco growers was derisively dismissed as a "swivel-chair" farmer.[31]

The growers' organizations that the AAA encouraged and consulted—like North Carolina Tobacco Growers' Association, the Growers' Advisory Committee, and the North Carolina Farm Bureau—never developed any particularly representative quality. From the start the decision as to whom the AAA should consult was more a matter of selection than of election. In July 1933 the North Carolina Extension Service drew up a list of "leading growers" who were to meet Hutson and Davis. In August the first formal flue-cured Growers' Advisory Committee was selected by the state extension directors. The formation of the North Carolina Tobacco Growers' Association in September, whose executive committee members served on the state and regional advisory committees, brought a semblance of election to the process of consultation. County agents held meetings of growers to elect delegates to send to Raleigh for the organizational meeting, but the agents' reports give little indication of how many farmers attended these meetings or how formal the elections were. This Tobacco Growers' Association, in fact, never became an active organization locally. It owed its prestige and authority to the position of the Growers' Advisory Committees in the AAA, not to any grass roots organization. In February and September 1935 there were particular complaints that the association was out of touch with the farmers it was supposed to represent. Clarence Poe crystallized these complaints by calling for annual county-wide meetings to elect a state growers' committee. The committee would meet once a year to select an executive committee to represent the growers in consultations with the AAA. After 1936 the North Carolina Farm Bureau could also be scarcely said to represent all the growers. It failed to develop any local strength, it attracted few members, and its weakness was graphically illustrated by the defeat of crop control in December 1938.

The sort of growers the AAA consulted were not ordinary growers, small or tenant farmers. It was not the AAA's intention to consult them. On the contrary, Hutson recalled that the tobacco section was interested in the "outstanding man from a community and from several different communities. He might be an employee of a college of agriculture. He might be just a farmer. He might even be a farmer-lawyer. But he was a man that people respected in the area." The AAA wanted to tap the sources of influence in the tobacco belt. As Jonathan Daniels's farmer pointed out, the sort of farmer who could afford the time and money to attend mass meetings in Raleigh or committee meetings in Raleigh and Washington was not a farmer who cultivated his own land. He would be a farmer-businessman, the sort of farmer who supported the county agent and made his tenants follow the agent's advice on progressive farming practices. He was probably a local politician and a member of the board of county commissioners. (It is important to remember that this description was equally likely to apply to the 1935 *critics* of the advisory committees.) This farmer-businessman-politician was exemplified by the three North Carolina members of the Regional Growers' Advisory Committee: Claude Hall, owner of a thousand-acre farm, who had been invited to the Washington "Little Business Conference," J. E. Winslow, owner of several farms around Greenville and a mule dealer's business, and Lionel Weil of the Goldsboro family of merchants. The degree to which such men actually represented the mass of tobacco growers can be judged only from the operation and effects of the program for which they were responsible.[32]

It is difficult to specify definitively the extent to which the administration at the local level by county and community committees of farmers placed the tobacco program in the hands of the large planters. There is no study for the tobacco program of North Carolina before 1936 comparable to Henry I. Richards's analysis of county and community committees in Mississippi, Arkansas, and Louisiana under the cotton program. Richards found that large landowners dominated the county committees, and landowners comprised the bulk of the community committees. Those community committeemen who were renters had average acreages larger than the owners on the same committees. It would be surprising if North Carolina was very different. As in the cotton program, the county agent was the designated representative of the AAA in the tobacco program in 1933. He named the county and community committeemen to run the scheme in contrast to wheat and corn-hogs, where the contracting producers elected their own committeemen. It was natural that the county agent should turn to the local large planters who were often in part responsible for his salary. It was in any case traditional Extension Service philosophy to deal with the leading men in each community, since "if the leading farmers are reached first it will be an easy matter to reach all farmers through these leaders." The county agent usually had little contact with the poorer sorts of farmers in the community, and it would have been surprising if tenant farmers, small farmers, and blacks had figured prominently in the committees that he chose.[33]

There is more evidence about the committees that were elected after 1936 in North Carolina from Robert E. Martin's postwar survey of Wilson County. His findings were similar to those of Richards. One or two tenants had managed to be elected to community committees but no sharecroppers and no blacks. The county committee was made up of large landowners often with outside business interests, while smaller landowners ran the local committees. All the committeemen he interviewed were members of the Farm Bureau. Most members were reelected year after year, and turnout in the committee elections was low: an estimated average of 10.1 percent of those eligible between 1941 and 1945. It was the better-off whites who tended to vote. While 91 percent of white owners interviewed had voted in a committee election, only 24 percent of white croppers and 11 percent of black croppers had done so. "Tenants and croppers especially," he concluded, "have come to think of the election of committeemen as a function primarily of landowners."[34]

Other evidence paints a similar picture. Dean Schaub may have been concerned at election time in 1936 about undesirable farmers actively campaigning for office, but it is clear that the county agents retained considerable influence in the local administration. In contrast to some areas where the county agent had no place in the administrative setup, in North Carolina the agent was always the executive secretary to the county committee. Their reports in 1938 show that they had to spend as much time on AAA work in this capacity as they had as the AAA's designated representative in 1933.

The turnover of members on the local committees may well have been greater than Martin allowed. From the lists of committee members that survive in the county agent's reports, the turnover of membership varied from Craven and Washington in 1938, where all the community committee members were retained, to Caswell in 1939, where 80 percent of the committee was replaced. In central tobacco counties like Edgecombe and Greene between 15 percent and 40 percent of the community committeemen changed each year from 1938 to 1940. In three counties it is possible to see the shift from the early committees appointed by the county agent: in Greene only one of the twenty members of the 1933 committee was still serving in 1940, in Edgecombe ten of the thirty members from 1934 were on the committee in 1940, and in Vance only two of the twenty-six men who had served in 1934 continued to the end of the decade. This high turnover does not mean that incumbents were defeated in local elections. They may simply not have stood again. Being a local committeeman may have been a position of influence, but it was also time-consuming and could, especially in 1938, be an extremely unpleasant and unpopular job. Handling the administrative records also required some education. It was no coincidence that most of the college-educated farmers whom Martin interviewed in Wilson had served on a local committee at some time. The lists that survive also reveal at least one black community committeeman in Hertford County. While it is unlikely that tenants participated to any great extent in the committee elections, there is also no evidence that they were actively discouraged from doing so as the Southern Tenant Farmers' Union alleged in Missouri.[35]

What evidence there is therefore suggests that the local administration of the tobacco program was in predictable hands. Power gravitated to large farmers with local influence who supported and worked with the county agent and who had the time and resources to carry out such arduous duties. Tenants, sharecroppers, and blacks did not fit into that category.

It is difficult to assess how fairly these committees administered the tobacco program. There were always complaints that the committees favored other large farmers in making allotments. James E. Thigpen, who spent a large part of 1934, 1935, and 1939 working with the county committees in North Carolina straightening out their records, knew that one or two county committees had rewarded themselves with large allotments. On the whole, however, both he and Hutson, who admitted that large planters dominated the committees, felt that the administration was fair and certainly much better than trying to run the program directly from Washington. Hutson argued that the committees bent over backward to be fair to the smaller growers. That the Grange and Clarence Poe pressed for more publicity in the allotment process testifies to at least a suspicion that favoritism occurred. The vote in December 1938 also indicated dissatisfaction with the program's administration, although this was probably the result of haste and misunderstanding rather than fraud. The complaints procedure reveals little. Complaints were referred back to the county agent who was invariably supported by the Extension Service and the state office of the AAA. The review committees established under the 1938 act consisted of the same sort of farmers who sat on the county committees.[36]

The referendum was the final justification of grass roots democracy. It was, Secretary Wallace believed, "a thoroughgoing demonstration of economic democracy in agriculture." As the final test of the support for the AAA from all types of farmers, however, the referendum came under attack both in the 1930s and later. Critics argued that it distorted democracy in four ways: first, the farmers voting had by definition a vested interest in the continuation of crop control; second, growers were coerced into voting for control by the threat that government aid would not be given if control was defeated; third, landlords forced their tenants to support control; fourth, the AAA, according to Charles Hardin, had a "streamlined organization reaching down into the communities to electioneer for favorable votes."[37]

The tobacco growers who voted in referenda did have a vested interest in the continuation of control. The use of the historic base and the limited provision for new growers meant that growers already in the control program had a virtual monopoly of flue-cured growing. To vote for control was to vote to continue that monopoly position. Secretary Wallace insisted that it was reasonable to restrict the referenda to the tobacco growers. He insisted that Congress represented the national interest and the interests of other farmers and nonfarm groups. Congress then properly left the specific question of quotas to the group of farmers concerned. The referenda, he argued, "are only a step in carrying out a process which began with enactment of the law by Congress representing all groups of people . . . Congress representing the whole people has defined the conditions under which referenda of producers are in the general welfare." While it is difficult to see who could vote for tobacco quotas except the tobacco farmers, it is also true that in enacting agricultural legislation Congress did not represent the "whole people." On the contrary, Congress enacted legislation for the special interest of the tobacco growers.[38]

Opponents of control in North Carolina in 1939 complained that the government was forcing growers to vote for control by making government aid conditional on a favorable control vote. The government laid down similar conditions in 1940. The AAA could scarcely do otherwise. Conservative critics would have been even more outraged if the AAA had undertaken an open-ended commitment to give financial aid to tobacco growers on the basis of unlimited production.

Counties with high degrees of tenancy were more likely than others to support crop control. The evidence from Wilson County suggests that landlords confidently expected their tenants to vote for control. They gave them time off to vote and often provided transport to the polls. Voting was informal even when the secret ballot was mandatory under the 1938 act. Farmers often marked their ballots openly at a table. As several of them commented, "Almost everybody was voting the same way so we didn't care who saw it." Some tenants testified to landlord pressure: 43.4 percent of black and 19 percent of white tenants interviewed in Wilson felt that they had been put under some pressure to vote favorably. Explicit threats of coercion were unnecessary. The pressure often merely reflected the pattern of day-to-day living. As one black cropper recalled, "My boss stood right there and told us where to mark the ballot. There wasn't nothing else for us to do. When you live with a man, you have to do like they want us to do. Everything you have belongs to them. Most times I stayed right in the same place with the boss and he always know just about where I was and what I was doing." Nevertheless, the remarkably high turn-outs—often apparently every eligible voter in some counties—in the tobacco referenda in North Carolina cannot be explained away simply by landlord pressure.[39]

It was remarkable that blacks should vote in such large numbers at a time when they were disenfranchised effectively in local, state, and federal elections. Blacks in Wilson, and by every indication elsewhere, felt free to vote in control referenda and exercised that vote, just as they attended the biracial explanatory campaign meetings and felt free to ask questions. Whites apparently approved and welcomed this participation, because they could rely on their tenants to vote the right way and because they needed to pile up as large a majority as possible. Nevertheless, the importance the black voter assumed, the

Voting in the 1939 tobacco control referendum
(Division of Archives and History, Raleigh, North Carolina)

act of voting, and the experience of contact with the government through the farm program may have subtly loosened the ties of dependence between landlord and tenant. Tenants now had alternative sources of credit and protection. Black croppers noted that whites seemed to treat them better since the AAA, because "Tenants can now go to the government if they need something and the boss won't give it to them. They get it too. . . . Before most of us didn't know what was going on—only what the landlord said. The AAA gave us some idea about some things . . . if the landlord don't treat you right, you can go to the government, explain yourself and they will help you." The attitude of landlords to people who could vote in crucial elections had to change. "They can't slip and slide now and take it all from you. We have more say so now. We didn't have no credit. I couldn't even buy fifty cents worth of smoking tobacco—now a landlord will walk up and hold a decent conversation and talk things over and advise you. They didn't use to say a thing . . . they didn't use to care." Such changes did not alter the fundamental social order or power structure in the black belt counties, but they did give black and white tenants some more breathing space.[40]

The educational work in the referenda campaigns, wrote Howard Tolley in 1938, "should be objective and farmers should be given accurate information on all sides of the question at issue . . . they should be informed as to the disadvantages as well as the advantages of using quotas . . . [the campaign material] should present the issues in as unbiased a manner as possible." As he spoke to the tobacco farmers in March 1938 he wanted everybody to understand that "I am not recommending how anyone shall mark his ballot." Opponents of crop control in North Carolina who complained of the "Hitler tactics" of the people in Raleigh in 1938 would have had little doubt that Tolley's good intentions had not been carried out. They would have agreed instead with the Greensboro *Daily News* complaint about the "politicians and paid administrators from the highest to the lowest who have taken to the farm hustings to urge the program's approval, to stress the agricultural salvation which it alone offers, and to say little or nothing about the dangers and impositions involved."[41]

Tobacco growers in 1938 and 1939 were certainly subject to an intensive propaganda campaign in statewide, county, and community meetings, on the radio, and in the press. Some of this activity was not official; it was the work of interested bankers, warehousemen, farm organizations, and politicians. But these efforts were coordinated, directed, and encouraged by E. Y. Floyd for the AAA. The county and township meetings may have been designed as purely explanatory meetings, but they served as platforms for unashamedly procontrol speakers. The Extension Service scarcely concealed the fact that its participation in the campaign was designed to secure a favorable vote for control, and it interpreted such a vote as a tribute to its efforts. When Hutson and Wallace came down from Washington, they left the growers in no doubt as to the dire alternatives if control were defeated.

It is difficult to see how the AAA could put the case against control when it had decided on the economic necessity of marketing quotas. The case for the opposition could be, and was, put by a counterorganization: the North Carolina Anti-Compulsory Control Association. Despite the AAA's supposedly "streamlined organization," control could be, and was, defeated in December 1938. There had been no government propaganda campaigns in 1934 and 1935 when the tobacco growers had voted overwhelmingly for compulsory control under the Kerr-Smith Act and for the continuation of the tobacco program. The majorities for marketing quotas later were so decisive that they cannot simply be explained away by propaganda campaigns.

Additional testimony that the referenda were accurate in portraying the overall popularity of the tobacco program came from the politicians' perception that their constituents favored the tobacco program. After the inauguration of the program in the fall of 1933 Governor Ehringhaus, Senator Bailey, and Representative John Kerr all scrambled to claim responsibility for it or at least to deny their opponents the credit. Ehringhaus for a long time did this so successfully that it seemed he would run for the Senate against Bailey. Lindsay Warren also considered capitalizing on the success of the tobacco program to challenge the incumbent senator. Bailey was therefore careful not to go against what he considered to be the wishes of tobacco growers in favor of the Kerr-Smith Act and the 1935 AAA amendments. John Kerr similarly reacted to primary opposition by putting himself at the head of the drive for compulsory control in 1934 and the interstate tobacco compact in 1936. After 1936 all the tobacco congressmen backed the return of compulsory control on the grounds that the growers wanted it, and for the same reason they supported efforts in 1939 and 1940 to ensure that control could continue. Even Senator Bailey, who had opposed compulsory control under the 1938 Farm Act, made no effort to hinder passage of the 1939 and 1940 amendments. North Carolina politicians were in no doubt that the majority of North Carolina tobacco farmers thought they had benefited from the New Deal tobacco program.

Limited Options

It is a commonplace to emphasize the limitations of the New Deal's agricultural policy. One critique sums up the indictment: "Reflecting the political power of larger commercial farmers and accepting restrictionist economics, the [Agricultural Adjustment Act] assumed that the problem was over-production not under-consumption. . . . With benefits accruing chiefly to the larger owners, they frequently removed from production the lands of sharecroppers and tenant farmers, and 'tractored' them and hired hands off the land." It is easy to portray the New Deal's tobacco program in this context and to emphasize its basic limitations. Although it did not drive tenants and sharecroppers off the land in large numbers, it tended to freeze existing relationships between tobacco growers. It did not attempt to redistribute income among landlords, tenants, and small farmers. It created a monopoly position of special privilege for tobacco growers at the expense of other farmers. Tobacco growers receiving such aid became a conservative political force that gave little backing to efforts to extend the benefits of the New Deal to other groups in society or the rural poor. The manufacturing industry and the auction warehouse system remained unchanged.[42]

The implication of some writing, however, is that not only was New Deal agricultural policy limited, but that the New Deal could and should have adopted a more radical policy and done more for the rural poor, particularly the southern tenant farmer. It was tragic, David Conrad has concluded, "that the system [farm tenancy in the South] was not disrupted at this time for the opportunity was golden. Never in its long and cruel history had tenancy been more vulnerable." But an examination of the tobacco program suggests that such a view seriously underestimates the obstacles facing radical change. An analysis of the reasons why the New Deal farm policy was so limited—the emphasis on recovery, the restrictionist economics, the voluntary nature of crop control, local and decentralized administration, and the dependence on southern congressional support—suggests that the New Deal is being blamed for failing to take options that were never open to it.[43]

New Deal agricultural policy in general and the tobacco program in particular were limited in the first place because their aim was to achieve recovery and relief, not reform. The goal of the Agricultural Adjustment Act was to raise agricultural income, not to redistribute that income within agriculture. There was little alternative in the economic emergency of 1933. The whole discussion of farm relief by farmers, farm organizations, agricultural economists, and politicians was couched in terms of aiding those commercial farmers who were temporarily disadvantaged by economic depression. The idea that there was a "submerged third" of the rural population who were permanently disadvantaged was put forward only by a small group of rural sociologists. The supposedly radical alternatives to the Domestic Allotment plan that were canvassed in the summer of 1933 had the same basic aim of raising farm prices. The fate of the tenant farmer as a separate problem was not even considered in the passage of the Farm Act nor in the formulation of the commodity programs. Hutson recalled the essentially limited context in which the tobacco program was launched: "I don't remember that anyone came and discussed the sociological aspects of the problem of the farmers. Certainly if they did come, there were many more that were emphasizing the economic aspects of it than there were the sociological aspect. The feeling was that if the tobacco growers received a large income, the groundwork would be laid for taking care of the other problems." The failure of Hutson and his colleagues to pay more attention to these wider problems once the emergency was over is in part explained by the fact that they spent most of the 1930s coping with emergencies of one sort or another. From 1936 to early 1938 they had to try to reestablish a tobacco program that had been invalidated by the Supreme Court. In 1938 they had to try to solve the chaotic administrative problems arising from running a complex new program. In September 1939 they had to resurrect crop control (permanently, as it turned out) in yet another emergency in which the need to raise leaf prices was paramount.[44]

This need to raise leaf prices quickly also hindered the AAA in its dealings with the tobacco manufacturers in September and October 1933. The Secretary of Agriculture could have licensed the manufacturers, which would have caused striking long-term changes in the tobacco industry, perhaps even leading to some form of government monopoly. If the government had brought in a license, however, it would have had to enter the market itself and purchase the tobacco that the manufacturers were expected to buy. The AAA could not afford such a lengthy and expensive procedure when it was under constant pressure from the growers to secure an immediate agreement raising leaf prices so that the markets could reopen. This pressure was even more intense when the markets did reopen before an agreement was signed and prices were at their preclosing low level. The actual alternatives for the AAA were more apparent than real.

The desire to raise leaf prices was not in itself an unworthy aim. Paul Conkin has argued that the AAA "aided most generously the already large and prospering farmers"; but with tobacco selling at 11¢ a pound there were no prospering tobacco farmers, large or otherwise, in 1932 and 1933. The policy was of course designed to help commercial farmers, but all tobacco farmers, including tenants and small farmers, were commercial farmers. It also buttressed the existing economic structure; but to have allowed that structure to collapse in low prices would have benefited no one, least of all the tenant and small farmers, who would have been driven from the land in far greater numbers than by acreage reduction.[45]

The second limitation on New Deal agricultural policy was the decision to seek this improvement in farm prices by restricting production rather than by increasing consumption. This meant the acreage reduction that would give landlords in the South the excuse to evict tenants. Was there any alternative to restricted production? In general, the rationale of planned scarcity was that the revival of farm purchasing power would itself be a stimulus to industrial recovery and that other New Deal programs would take care of urban purchasing power. The radical alternatives of a direct subsidy or a revolutionary change in the basic system were not discussed, nor were they politically acceptable, nor would they have raised farm incomes quickly. This was even more true for tobacco than for other commodities. The only proposal to increase domestic consumption was a horizontal reduction in the federal cigarette tax suggested by the manufacturers. Such a reduction was less likely to increase demand, which was basically inelastic, than to increase manufacturers' profits. The most vociferous criticism of crop control for tobacco came not from politicians on the left concerned with underconsumption, but from Senator Bailey and the North

Carolina Anti-Compulsory Control Association on the right, who were concerned with the loss of foreign markets and the evils of regimentation and dictatorship—and even Senator Bailey had to admit that a small tobacco crop in 1933 was essential. The alternatives suggested by these critics amounted to little more than selling tobacco at rock-bottom prices in an attempt to find nonexistent new foreign markets. Such low prices would simply have caused yet more tenant displacement. For all Bailey's oft-expressed concern for the tenant farmer, he nevertheless opposed the major effort to help the tenant farmer—the Bankhead-Jones Act—when it was adequately financed in 1935 and supported it only in 1937 when it had been so curtailed that it could help tenants only marginally.

The voluntary nature of crop control was the third constraint on New Deal agricultural policy. Compulsion was rejected initially because the AAA officials were philosophically opposed to it and doubted that they could mount the necessary police action to enforce such drastic regulation. As a result of this voluntary approach, the tobacco section had to secure the cooperation of the large landlords who controlled so much of the tobacco acreage. It could not therefore afford to interfere in the delicate questions of landlord-tenant relations if it wanted to persuade farmers to embark on a new and untried program and submit to an unheard-of degree of government interference. Of greater importance in the tobacco program was that the need for cooperation meant that the AAA could not afford to help the small farmer too much. This concern accounts in large part for the continued use of the "historic base" in calculating quotas and allotments, a practice that tended to freeze the existing structure of tobacco growing. As it was, large farmers were still suspicious of the attempts made to aid the small farmer under the Kerr-Smith Act, the 1935 program, and the second Farm Act.

It has been suggested that the AAA could have safely ignored the views of the large farmers, since they were so desperate for government aid and so enthusiastically endorsed compulsion under the Bankhead and Kerr-Smith acts. Large tobacco growers, however, waxed lyrical about the benefits of compulsory control only after they saw that government regulation did not disturb existing relationships between tobacco growers. The large growers could have prevented acreage reduction, and that would have benefited no one, least of all the tenant and small farmers. The AAA was surely justified in treading warily.[46]

Linked with the restraint of voluntarism was the fourth limitation on the New Deal, the local and decentralized administration of the AAA. The use of the Extension Service and of county and community committees made up of the farmers themselves placed local administration in the hands of the existing power structure and gave at least an opportunity for discrimination against the less advantaged farmers. This recognition of the local agricultural establishment should be kept in perspective. First, the AAA was merely perpetuating existing patterns of dependence. It was no less democratic or representative than North Carolina's local and state government and general political life. Indeed, the high turnouts in control referenda and black participation suggest that democracy was more practiced in the economic field of the AAA than in the political world of the state. In other areas like the middle west, where the AAA was confronted with a less oligarchical social structure, the ideals of grass roots democracy so eloquently expounded by theorists like M. L. Wilson and Howard Tolley had more reality. Second, in the emergency of 1933 the AAA had to carry out a cotton plow-up and sign individual agreements with a million farmers in a matter of weeks. Later in September it had to sign tentative contracts with three hundred thousand tobacco farmers as quickly as possible, since the markets were shut and the farmers had no income. The AAA had no alternative in such circumstances but to use the only organization, the Extension Service, that already existed in the field. When Hutson went to Raleigh in early September to launch the sign-up campaign he had to take advantage of the meeting of county agents and growers' delegates which the North Carolina Director of Extension had already called together. In addition, the political reality confronting the AAA through the 1930s was pressure to increase the role of the Extension Service and the local administration, not to diminish it. Even if the AAA had been able to bide its time and select a field staff of its own, it is unlikely, if the experience of the Farm Security Administration is any guide, that the results would have been any different. The FSA was particularly suspicious of the grass roots democracy approach and made elaborate efforts to inculcate the values of its national administrators in its local field staff. Nevertheless, the FSA still found it impossible to recruit a competent field staff that was not excessively deferential to the local social and economic power structure.[47]

Finally, New Deal policy was limited by its dependence on southern congressional support. This restricted all New Deal policies, but it made the AAA particularly cautious in dealing with tenant displacement under the cotton program. It also made any full-scale assault on rural poverty impossible. Even the limited Bankhead-Jones Act was emasculated by Congress. The constant pressure of economy-minded southerners, with Harold Cooley often to the fore, eventually reduced the major effort of the New Deal to alleviate rural poverty—the Farm Security Administration—to little more than a glorified veterans' aid bureau. Up to 1936 it was possible to exploit southern constituency pressures—the popularity of Roosevelt, traditions of party loyalty, the economic emergency, and the region's desperate need for relief—to ensure congressional support of the New Deal. After 1936, with the increasing northern, urban orientation of the New Deal, this task became more difficult. At the very time when the New Deal began seriously to tackle the problem of rural poverty, it became difficult to secure the necessary legislation. This dependence on conservative support was not at first a problem in the tobacco program. Tobacco congressmen, on the contrary, often pressed for more generous treatment for small farmers than the AAA was willing to give. In the long run, however, the AAA had to acquiesce in the special-interest legislation for tobacco that the tobacco representatives could so easily secure in Congress. It has been suggested that with greater attention to long-term political interests the New Deal might have secured the party realignment that would have obviated the necessity for conservative southern support. James T. Patterson has convincingly demonstrated, however, that such suggestions underestimate the forces of localism in the politics of the 1930s. Such forces precluded any attempt successfully to build up liberal pro–New Deal factions in the individual states. New Deal conciliation of southern congressmen was based on a realistic assessment of the strength of congressional conservatism.[48]

Because crop control has become an accepted part of American agriculture and because the farmers who benefited from it have become such a prosperous and conservative force, it is easy to underestimate the achievement of the New Deal in successfully implementing a program of tobacco acreage reduction. In 1933 when the AAA had to confront an economic emergency there existed neither the blueprint nor the mandate nor the pressure for a revolutionary change in the system. The AAA chose instead to raise farm prices quickly and to do so by means of production control. Although tobacco growers and their leaders had for some time been fully aware of the need for crop control, they had been unable to secure it by state, cooperative, or individual efforts. Direct control of production by the AAA meant unprecedented intervention of a detailed nature by the federal government in the individual economic lives of three hundred thousand tobacco growers. This had to be achieved in a democratic society without the bureaucratic apparatus of a police state. Because of the need for speed and consent, the AAA therefore relied on local institutions and deferred to the existing power structure in the tobacco-growing areas. By an elaborate procedure of consultation, by decentralized administration, by large-scale education and propaganda campaigns, and by referenda the AAA involved the growers in the program and secured their consent. The narrow margin between success and failure was shown in 1938 when the administrative problems that arose in trying to implement a new control program quickly led the growers to reject control. It took another economic emergency to restore it.

Two points overshadow all others. The New Deal brought economic prosperity to eastern North Carolina and in doing so benefited not only the large landowners but also the overwhelming majority of tobacco growers. Second, given the strength of the obstacles it faced in the 1930s, the AAA's choice lay not between a limited tobacco program and one more radical, but between a limited program and none at all.

Notes

Abbreviations

AAA (AC) Papers   Papers of the Agricultural Adjustment Administration arranged alphabetically by correspondent.

AAA P.R.   Press Releases of the Agricultural Adjustment Administration.

AAA (SC) Papers   Papers of the Agricultural Adjustment Administration arranged by subject.

COHRC   Interview at the Columbia University Oral History Research Center.

CR   *Congressional Record*.

Governors' Papers (E)   Papers of Governor J. C. B. Ehringhaus.

Governors' Papers (G)   Papers of Governor O. Max Gardner.

Sec. Ag. Papers   Papers of the Secretary of Agriculture.

Introduction

1. There have so far been studies, not all published, of the textile industry under the National Recovery Administration, of the Works Progress Administration, and of the establishment of the relief and social security programs. The state politicians have been more generously served, with biographies of senators Josiah W. Bailey and Robert R. Reynolds, Governor O. Max Gardner, and Josephus Daniels, and an analysis of party factionalism in the depression years.

2. There were excellent studies of AAA programs sponsored by the Brookings
   Institution in the 1930s. The authors had easy access to both AAA personnel and
   AAA records, and my debt to Harold B. Rowe, *Tobacco under the AAA*, will
   become apparent in the pages that follow. These studies, however, remain
   essentially interim reports by economists. For the long-term planning goals of
   agricultural economists in the New Deal see Richard S. Kirkendall, *Social
   Scientists and Farm Politics in the Age of Roosevelt*. For the assault on rural poverty
   see Sidney Baldwin, *Poverty and Politics*, Paul E. Mertz, *New Deal Policy and
   Southern Rural Poverty*, and Donald Holley, *Uncle Sam's Farmers*. There is an
   excellent account of the AAA's first year, which should provide a model for any
   future account of the later years of New Deal farm policy, Van L. Perkins, *Crisis in
   Agriculture*. The plight of the sharecroppers, their attempts at organization and
   protest, and the response of the New Deal have been fully chronicled in David E.
   Conrad, *The Forgotten Farmers*, Louis Cantor, *Prologue to Protest*, Donald H.
   Grubbs, *Cry from the Cotton*, and numerous articles most conveniently listed in
   Holley, *Uncle Sam's Farmers*, pp. 294–95. There is a commendable effort to study
   the AAA cotton program in one state in Michael S. Holmes, *The New Deal in
   Georgia*, pp. 209–67. Robert F. Hunter, in his article "The AAA between
   Neighbors: Virginia, North Carolina, and the New Deal Farm Program," outlines
   the cotton, tobacco, peanut, and potato programs in the two states and the attitude
   of some of the local politicians. He does not analyze the process of policy making
   within the AAA or the local implementation of control programs.

Chapter 1. The Problems of Cigarette Tobacco

1. United States Department of Agriculture, *Yearbook of Agriculture, 1930*, p. 706.
   Flue-cured tobacco usually made up 50 percent of the leaf used in blended
   American cigarettes. Burley provided between 30 and 40 percent, while some
   Maryland and a little oriental leaf were also used. In the United Kingdom flue-cured
   was used on its own, since consumers preferred its sharper taste. It was rarely used
   on continental Europe in the 1930s. Expensive European cigarettes relied on the
   more aromatic Turkish leaf, while the cheaper brands used locally grown dark
   tobaccos. As a result of flue-cured tobacco's importance in cigarettes, it was
   responsible in 1933 for 54 percent of U.S. tobacco production. Burley accounted
   for 28 percent. Of the other types of tobacco—cigar filler, binder and wrapper,
   Maryland, dark air-cured, and fire-cured—fire-cured was the most important,
   accounting for 9 percent of production. United States Department of Agriculture,
   Yearbook of Agriculture, 1935, p. 452, J. H. Cyrus and W. P. Hedrick, *The
   Tobacco Story*, p. 2, J. B. Hutson, COHRC, p. 97.
2. *Yearbook of Agriculture, 1935*, p. 452. See also maps 1 and 2 in this volume.
3. United States Department of Commerce, Bureau of the Census, *Fifteenth Census
   of the United States, Agriculture*, vol. II, part 2, pp. 398–405, Benjamin F.
   Lemert, *The Tobacco Manufacturing Industry in North Carolina*, p. 67. In 1929
   tobacco was grown on 117,222 of the state's farms. Of these, 2,168 grew Burley
   in Madison County in the far west of the state. The rest grew flue-cured. In 1932

tobacco brought in $35.7 million for North Carolina farmers, cotton $27.0 million, and corn $18.8 million. There were other crops of some importance. Seventeen counties in the northeast of the state produced one-fifth of the nation's peanut crop. The state usually ranked fifteenth in potato growing, and truck farming, particularly strawberry growing, was developing in the southeastern coastal counties.

4. Guy Owen, *Journey for Joedel*, p. 68. Wightman Wells Garner, *The Production of Tobacco*, p. 209, calculates that the man-hours needed to produce an acre of tobacco were eighteen times the hours needed to produce an acre of small grains, seven times the hours needed for corn, and two and a half times those needed for cotton. The description of the growing of tobacco that follows is drawn from Nannie May Tilley, *The Bright-Tobacco Industry, 1860–1929*, pp. 37–88, S. N. Hawks, Jr., *Principles of Flue-Cured Tobacco Production*, L. T. Weeks and E. Y. Floyd, *Producing and Marketing Flue-Cured Tobacco*, pp. 7–43, and Garner, *The Production of Tobacco*, pp. 59–216. But none capture as vividly as Guy Owen's novel the pain and anguish of tobacco growing in the depression: the vulnerability of the crop, the grower's secret pride in his tobacco, the excitement of opening day at the market, and the helpless hostility of the farmers toward the buyers and pinhookers.

5. Owen, *Journey*, p. 12.

6. The calculations on man-hours taken up in the various stages of tobacco production are taken from Robert Charles Brooks, "The Development of Flue-cured Tobacco Programs, 1933–1956," p. 66.

7. For the development of the tobacco harvester and its potential consequences see the *New York Times*, 4 Oct. 1971. I am indebted to Alger Hiss for this reference. For bulk-curing see Hawks, *Principles*, pp. 207–208.

8. See map 3 in this volume. Rowe, *Tobacco under the AAA*, p. 40, Tilley, *Bright-Tobacco Industry*, p. 102, H. H. Wooten, *Credit Problems of North Carolina Cropper Farmers*, p. 40.

9. *Yearbook of Agriculture, 1935*, p. 452. The figures are for 1933.

10. Samuel T. Emory, *Bright Tobacco in the Agriculture, Industry, and Foreign Trade of North Carolina*, pp. 70–81. Jonathan Daniels, *Tar Heels*, pp. 86–91, R. Lee Covington, *Banking and Tobacco in North Carolina*, p. 50, David L. Wickens and G. W. Forster, *Farm Credit in North Carolina: Its Cost, Risk and Management*, p. 107.

11. For the rise of James B. Duke and the American Tobacco Company through the exploitation of technological advances like the Bonsack cigarette machine, aggressive marketing, and financial muscle see Robert F. Durden, *The Dukes of Durham, 1865–1929*, pp. 26–81. For the dissolution of the Trust see Durden, *The Dukes*, pp. 165–68. For the development and competitive structure of the cigarette industry after 1911 see Reavis Cox, *Competition in the American Tobacco Industry, 1911–1932*, pp. 40–48, 63–77, William H. Nicholls, *Price Policies in the Cigarette Industry*, pp. 35–103, Richard B. Tennant, *The American Cigarette Industry*, pp. 67–109.

12. Nicholls, *Price Policies*, p. 227, Bureau of the Census, *Fifteenth Census, Manufactures*, vol. III, p. 388.

13. Weeks and Floyd, *Producing Tobacco*, p. 74, Durden, *The Dukes*, pp. 79–80. British-American in fact entered the U.S. market by acquiring Brown and Williamson in 1927, Cox, *Competition in Tobacco*, p. 73.

14. Emory, *Bright Tobacco*, pp. 132–35, Nicholls, *Price Policies*, p. 227.

15. The analysis of the growers' marketing position that follows relies heavily on T. J. Woofter, Jr., *The Plight of Cigarette Tobacco*.

16. Tilley, *Bright-Tobacco Industry*, pp. 294–95, North Carolina Department of Agriculture, *Biennial Report, 1930–32*, p. 75.

17. R. Russell to Josephus Daniels, 29 Oct. 1931, Josephus Daniels Papers. Josephus Daniels to H. A. Wallace, 6 Sept. 1933, Sec. Ag. Papers.

18. Cox, *Competition in Tobacco*, pp. 141–86, Nicholls, *Price Policies*, pp. 257–97, 309–34, Tennant, *American Cigarette Industry*, pp. 316–41. Evidence of the extent of competition has always been difficult to obtain, Nicholls, *Price Policies*, p. viii, Cox, *Competition in Tobacco*, pp. 5–6.

19. For a more detailed account of the abuses of the warehouse auction system see below, ch. 4.

20. T. J. Woofter, Jr., *Plight of Cigarette Tobacco*, p. 82, Russell W. Bierman, *Flue-cured Tobacco*, pp. 87–88.

21. Joseph W. Hines, "Developments and Trends in the Export Trade in Flue-Cured Tobacco, 1939–50, with Special Emphasis on the Role of the United States Government in Grants and Loans," pp. 60–70.

22. Bierman, *Flue-cured Tobacco*, pp. 161, 163.

23. Lemert, *Tobacco Manufacturing*, p. 67, United States Department of Commerce, Bureau of the Census, *Statistical Abstract, 1934*, p. 607. Raleigh *News and Observer*, 19, 25, 26, 29 Jan. 1930, O. M. Gardner to L. C. Warren, 26 Nov. 1930, Warren Papers. Thomas Sellers Morgan, "A Step towards Altruism: Relief and Welfare in North Carolina, 1930–1938," p. 64.

24. Joseph L. Morrison, *Governor O. Max Gardner*, p. 79. Raleigh *News and Observer*, 8 Sept. 1931. Elmer L. Puryear, *Democratic Party Dissension in North Carolina, 1928–1936*, pp. 60, 73.

25. Morrison, *Gardner*, p. 79. Raleigh *News and Observer*, 1 May 1931. A. K. Robertson to I. O. Schaub, 4 Feb. 1932, R. Henniger to J. W. Bailey, 16 Jan., 6 Feb. 1932, E. W. Bushcart to R. Henniger, 19 Jan. 1932, Governors' Papers (G). *Extension Farm News*, Nov. 1931. For the lack of credit to finance the tobacco crop in Pitt County as early as the winter of 1929–30, see F. M. Wooten to F. M. Simmons, 9 Nov. 1929, Wooten to J. C. Stone, 29 Jan. 1930, Wooten Papers.

26. Rowe, *Tobacco under the AAA*, p. 84. Nicholls, *Price Policies*, p. 73. *Southern Tobacco Journal*, 19 Jan. 1933, Tennant, *American Cigarette Industry*, pp. 88–90.

27. The most comprehensive examination of the cooperative is John J. Scanlon and J. M. Tinley, *Business Analysis of the Tobacco Growers' Cooperative Association*. Tilley, *Bright-Tobacco Industry*, pp. 449–86, provides a colorful account of its struggles. It is unlikely that there will be a definitive analysis of the cooperative's failure until scholars have exploited the voluminous papers of the Tri-State Cooperative in the State Archives in Raleigh.

28. Hugh T. Lefler and Albert R. Newsome, *North Carolina*, p. 545.
29. David Leroy Corbitt, ed., *Public Papers and Letters of Oliver Max Gardner*, pp. 83–85, 269–74, Morrison, *Gardner*, pp. 75–76, 92. For a similar campaign in Georgia see Michael S. Holmes, *The New Deal in Georgia*, pp. 210–12.
30. Morrison, *Gardner*, p. 129, *Extension Farm News*, Dec. 1932.
31. Resolution, Greenville, 16 Sept. 1929, Nash, 21 Sept. 1929, Governors' Papers (G). Raleigh *News and Observer* 13, 16, 17, 19, 20, 21, 22, 25, 29 Sept., 2 Oct. 1929.
32. Raleigh *News and Observer*, 8, 15 Sept. 1929.
33. Ibid., 18 Dec. 1929, 12 Feb., 1, 18, 20 Mar. 1930. *Extension Farm News*, Feb. 1930.
34. Raleigh *News and Observer*, 24 Aug., 3, 7, 12 Sept. 1930. Corbitt, *Gardner Papers*, pp. 220–31.
35. Tobacco Carbon Statement, n.d., Josephus Daniels Papers. Memo from Tobacco Conference, 15 Sept. 1930, Minutes of Second Meeting of Interstate Tobacco Organizing Committee, Governors' Papers (G). Raleigh *News and Observer*, 17, 30 Sept. 1930. *Extension Farm News*, Sept. 1930.
36. Raleigh *News and Observer*, 18 Sept., 9, 15 Oct. 1930, 6 Feb., 13, 14 April 1931. *Progressive Farmer*, 15–31 May 1931.
37. Raleigh *News and Observer*, 30 Sept., 27 Oct. 1930.
38. Cox, *Competition in Tobacco*, p. 167, *Progressive Farmer*, 1–14 Jan. 1932. Federal Farm Board, *Second Annual Report of the Federal Farm Board for the Year Ending June 30, 1931*, p. 16.
39. L. C. Warren to J. R. Turnage, 12 Sept. 1930, Warren Papers.
40. Raleigh *News and Observer*, 3, 7, 30 Sept. 1930, 22 Mar. 1931. Corbitt, *Gardner Papers*, pp. 290–96.
41. Raleigh *News and Observer*, 21 Aug., 8 Sept. 1931.
42. Ibid., 3, 16 Sept. 1931. For Long's plan and the action of the Texas legislature see T. Harry Williams, *Huey Long*, pp. 531–33, Donald W. Whisenhunt, "Huey Long and the Texas Cotton Acreage Control Law of 1931," pp. 142–53, Robert E. Snyder, "Huey Long and the Cotton Holiday of 1931," pp. 135–60. Williams claims that calls by southern governors for acreage reduction were useless and that Long alone showed wisdom and courage. But it is not clear that Long's action was any more realistic or relevant than that of the other governors. Long showed no signs of having considered the problems of (1) how tenants and sharecroppers were going to stay on the land with no income from cotton coming in, (2) how his ban on cotton production was going to be enforced, and (3) how cotton prices would rise given the world market situation. Long's advocacy of his plan is in striking contrast to his later criticism of the practical Voluntary Domestic Allotment Plan.
43. Raleigh *News and Observer*, 25 Sept., 11, 22 Oct. 1931.
44. Ibid., 13 Nov. 1931.
45. O. M. Gardner to W. Harris, 7 Oct. 1931, J. C. B. Ehringhaus to Gardner, 19 Sept. 1931, Governors' Papers (G). Raleigh *News and Observer*, 2 Sept., 13 Nov. 1931.
46. O. M. Gardner to R. Powell, 22 Sept. 1931, Governors' Papers (G). Raleigh

News and Observer, 7 Sept. 1930, 28 Sept. 1931. For skepticism in other parts of the country about the possibility of enforcing acreage reduction see William D. Rowley, *M. L. Wilson and the Campaign for the Domestic Allotment*, p. 126.

47. V. O. Key, Jr., *Southern Politics in State and Nation*, pp. 211–15, Puryear, *Democractic Dissension*, pp. 3–20.

48. Morrison, *Gardner*, pp. 52–57, 83–91, Puryear, *Democratic Dissension*, pp. 47–91.

49. O. M. Gardner to W. Harris, 7 Sept. 1931, Governors' Papers (G). Raleigh *News and Observer*, 14 Oct. 1931. O. M. Gardner to L. C. Warren, 25 Sept. 1931, Warren Papers.

50. Josephus Daniels to M. K. Blount, 14 Oct. 1931, Daniels to J. A. Taylor, 28 Nov. 1931, Josephus Daniels Papers.

51. J. W. Bailey to J. O. Carr, 18 June 1931, Carr to Bailey, 20 June 1931, Carr Papers. Morrison, *Gardner*, pp. 105–106, Joseph L. Morrison, *Josephus Daniels*, pp. 160–61, E. David Cronon, "Josephus Daniels as a Reluctant Candidate," pp. 459–65.

52. Puryear, *Democratic Dissension*, pp. 92–120. J. C. B. Ehringhaus to E. Green, 9 Sept. 1933, Governors' Papers (E).

53. Puryear, *Democratic Dissension*, pp. 121–55, Julian McIver Pleasants, "The Senatorial Career of Robert Rice Reynolds," pp. 57–142. A. W. McLean to J. O. Carr, 21 June 1932, Carr Papers. O. M. Gardner to F. D. Roosevelt, 22 July 1932, Roosevelt Papers.

54. Gilbert C. Fite, "Farmer Opinion and the Agricultural Adjustment Act, 1933," pp. 656–73. Theodore Saloutos has commented, "That the South embraced the New Deal farm program as enthusiastically as it did was no mere accident. For years cotton and tobacco producers were nurtured on a philosophy of farm relief [acreage reduction] which the administration finally adopted and elaborated upon." *Farmer Movements in the South, 1865–1933*, p. 281.

Chapter 2. The 1933 Crisis:
A New Deal for the Growers

1. For the best account of the Agricultural Adjustment Act see Van L. Perkins, *Crisis in Agriculture*, pp. 27–78.

2. For a full account of the virtues of the Domestic Allotment plan see William D. Rowley, *M. L. Wilson and the Campaign for the Domestic Allotment*, pp. 123–41.

3. Gilbert C. Fite, *George N. Peek and the Fight for Farm Parity*, pp. 60, 111, 155, 173. Rowley, *M. L. Wilson*, pp. 69, 127, 143, 164.

4. Perkins, *Crisis*, 43–44. United States Department of Agriculture, *Agricultural Adjustment: A Report on the Agricultural Adjustment Administration, May 1933 to February 1934*, p. 6, L. J. Taber, COHRC, p. 285.

5. L. C. Warren to J. E. West, 6 Jan. 1933, Warren to W. T. Meadows, 28 Jan. 1933, Warren to R. C. Flanagan, 21 Feb. 1933, Warren Papers. J. H. Kerr to

L. C. Kinsey, 13 Dec. 1932, Kerr to K. P. Lewis, 7 Jan. 1933, Kerr Papers. There were limits to their power. The attempts by Warren, Kerr, Senator Harry Byrd (Virginia), and Senator Bailey to include peanuts as a basic commodity failed. Raleigh *News and Observer*, 31 March, 1, 20 April 1933. For a fuller discussion of the tobacco congressmen see below p. 53

6. Raleigh *News and Observer*, 1 April 1933. Perkins, *Crisis*, pp. 69–70, *CR*, vol. 77, 73rd Cong., 1st sess. (1933), pp. 745–46, 1382–83. M. Ezekiel to J. Frank, 17 April 1933, Sec. Ag. Papers. There is no strong evidence for Kerr's later claim that he was responsible for the change, J. H. Kerr to F. W. Boswell, 25 Jan. 1934, Kerr Papers.

7. I. O. Schaub, to J. W. Bailey, 22 March 1933, W. Kerr Scott, C. F. Cates, and C. Poe to Bailey, 25 March 1933, A. B. Carrington to Bailey, 22 March 1933, Bailey Papers. *Southern Tobacco Journal*, 12, 19 Jan., 13 April 1933.

8. B. B. Gossett to J. W. Bailey, 23 March 1933, W. H. Entwistle to Bailey, 21 March 1933, Bailey to W. C. Cavenaugh, 5 May 1933, Bailey Papers. Raleigh *News and Observer*, 7 May 1933.

9. J. W. Bailey to H. McRae, 31 March 1933, Bailey Papers. *CR*, vol. 77, 73rd Cong., 1st sess. (1933), pp. 1877, 1868.

10. *CR*, vol. 77, 73rd Cong., 1st sess. (1933), p. 1867. Raleigh *News and Observer*, 19 April 1933. J. W. Bailey to H. G. Winslow, 31 March 1933, Bailey Papers.

11. Raleigh *News and Observer*, 7 May 1933. J. W. Bailey to W. C. Cavenaugh, 5 May 1933, Bailey Papers.

12. Raleigh *News and Observer*, 8 May 1933. For that earlier primary see Richard L. Watson, Jr., ''A Southern Democratic Primary: Simmons vs Bailey in 1930,'' pp. 21–46, John Robert Moore, *Senator Josiah William Bailey of North Carolina*, pp. 59–76.

13. Perkins, *Crisis*, pp. 97–98.

14. Gladys L. Baker, *The County Agent*, pp. 94–95.

15. *Extension Farm News*, Sept. 1932, April, Sept. 1933. I. O. Schaub to J. H. Kerr, 25 Jan. 1932, Kerr Papers. R. Henniger to J. W. Bailey, 12 Feb. 1932, Governors' Papers (G). I. O. Schaub to C. W. Warburton, 26 Oct., 2 Nov. 1933, Extension Service Papers.

16. Raleigh *News and Observer*, 19, 21, 24, 25 June, 12 July 1933. Greensboro *Daily News*, 7, 10 July 1933. N.C. Director's Annual Report 1933, I. O. Schaub to C. W. Warburton, 1 Nov. 1933, Extension Service Papers.

17. Harold B. Rowe, *Tobacco under the AAA*, pp. 94–95. Press Release 1176–33, Sec. Ag. Papers. AAA P.R. 16–34, 3 July 1933. J. B. Hutson, COHRC, p. 105. Those taking part in the conference were John B. Hutson, Charles Gage, responsible for government grading and the *Outlook* work on tobacco in the Bureau of Agricultural Economics, W. G. Finn of the Division of Statistical and Historical Research, Paul Porter, a former Georgia newspaperman, James Dickey of the Extension Service, and E. G. Beinhardt of Virginia, who was interested in diverting surplus tobacco into tobacco by-products for noncommercial use. For the overall development of the tobacco program in 1933 see Rowe, *Tobacco under the AAA*, pp. 84–116, James C. Daniel, ''The North Carolina Tobacco Marketing

Crisis of 1933," pp. 370–82, and Perkins, *Crisis*, pp. 147–62, an excellent account that supersedes both Rowe and Daniel. An almost contemporary account of the crisis has been surprisingly ignored by historians, Joseph G. Knapp and L. R. Paramore, "Flue-cured Tobacco Developments under the AAA," pp. 325–48. Both authors had close contact with the crisis as members of North Carolina State College: one in the agricultural economics department and the other in the Extension Service. They received the assistance of two active participants in the tobacco program, G. W. Forster and E. Y. Floyd, and the article was read before publication by Hutson, J. B. Hutson to J. G. Knapp, 9 June 1934, AAA (AC) Papers.

18. J. B. Hutson, COHRC, pp. 25, 36, 72, 84, 89, 94, 104.
19. Interview with James E. Thigpen, 17 Sept. 1975. Interview with Gladys L. Baker, 17 Sept. 1975. Alger Hiss to the author, 28 Oct. 1975.
20. Perkins, *Crisis*, pp. 90–93. J. B. Hutson, COHRC, p. 132. Greensboro *Daily News*, 13 July 1933. AAA P.R. 113–34, 20 July 1933.
21. Perkins, *Crisis*, pp. 148–49.
22. Knapp and Paramore, "Developments," pp. 330–31. Raleigh *News and Observer*, 19 July 1933.
23. Charles R. Lambert, "New Deal Experiments in Production Control: The Livestock Program 1933–1935," p. 37.
24. Raleigh *News and Observer*, 26 Nov., 25 July 1933. Kinston *Daily Free Press*, 29 July 1933. Rowe, *Tobacco under the AAA*, p. 98.
25. C. C. Davis, Memorandum, 29 July 1933, AAA (SC) Papers. Raleigh *News and Observer*, 29 July, 1 Aug. 1933.
26. Raleigh *News and Observer*, 2, 6, 7, 10, 11 Aug., 26 Nov. 1933. Jonathan Daniels to the author, 10 May 1970. Greensboro *Daily News*, 4, 7, 13, 14 Aug. 1933. Greenville *Daily Reflector*, 10, 11, 14 Aug. 1933. Kinston *Daily Free Press*, 7 Aug. 1933. Goldsboro *News Argus*, 4, 5, 6 Aug. 1933.
27. The fullest collections of mass meeting resolutions can be found in the Bailey Papers and the Governors' Papers (E). Goldsboro *News Argus*, 6 Aug. 1933.
28. Greensboro *Daily News*, 9, 21 Aug. 1933. Raleigh *News and Observer*, 4, 9, 26 Aug. 1933. Goldsboro *News Argus*, 4, 5, 6 Aug. 1933.
29. Informal Tobacco Conference, 27 July 1933, AAA (AC) Papers.
30. H. A. Wallace to J. C. B. Ehringhaus, 17 Aug. 1933, Governors' Papers (E). The AAA's complacency was understandable. The unrest in the tobacco belt could be exaggerated. There were the usual, almost ritualistic, expressions of optimism about price prospects despite the knowledge that a large crop would be sold. Some growers felt that Georgia prices were satisfactory, given the low grades on that belt. There was acquiescence in the poor border prices. Few farmers signed the *News Argus* agreements. As the New Belt opening approached there were the customary promises of higher prices as market towns and individual warehouses competed for the growers' custom. Greensboro *Daily News*, 4 Aug. 1933. Kinston *Daily Free Press*, 1, 2, 5, 8, 25 Aug. 1933. Greenville *Daily Reflector*, 22 Aug. 1933.
31. C. C. Davis to I. O. Schaub, 8 Aug. 1933, J. B. Hutson to L. J. Patten, 18 Aug. 1933, AAA (SC) Papers.

32. J. B. Hutson to H. A. Wallace, 30 Aug. 1933, AAA (SC) Papers. Informal Tobacco Conference, 30 Aug. 1933, AAA (AC) Papers.
33. J. B. Hutson to C. C. Davis, 1 Sept. 1933, AAA (AC) Papers.
34. Informal Tobacco Conference, 30 Aug. 1933, AAA (AC) Papers.
35. Raleigh *News and Observer*, 28, 30 Aug., 26 Nov. 1933. Kinston *Daily Free Press*, 21 Jan. 1934. Knapp and Paramore, "Developments," p. 332. Jonathan Daniels to the author, 20 April, 10 May 1970. The single-handed efforts of Morrill ruined him physically and financially. The time merchants who benefited so much from his activities quickly forgot him and begrudged paying him the expenses he incurred.
36. Knapp and Paramore, "Developments," p. 333. Raleigh *News and Observer*, 1 Sept. 1933, Greensboro *Daily News*, 1 Sept. 1933.
37. Greensboro *Daily News*, 2 Sept. 1933. *Southern Tobacco Journal*, 21 Sept. 1933. Raleigh *News and Observer*, 2 Sept. 1933. David Leroy Corbitt, ed., *Addresses, Letters and Papers of John Christoph Blucher Ehringhaus*, pp. 70–72.
38. Raleigh *News and Observer*, 2 Sept. 1933. Greensboro *Daily News*, 2, 3 Sept. 1933. J. C. B. Ehringhaus to H. A. Wallace, 1, 2 Sept. 1933, Wallace to Ehringhaus, 1, 2 Sept. 1933, Governors' Papers (E).
39. Two tobacco congressmen from North Carolina missed the meeting. John H. Kerr, whose second district lay in the heart of the New Belt, had not gone to Washington because he understood that the growers did not want to be accompanied by politicians. Charles L. Abernethy, from the southeastern third district, was too ill to attend and had not recovered sufficiently to pay any attention to the tobacco program before he was defeated by Graham A. Barden in 1934.
40. Raleigh *News and Observer*, 5, 6 Sept. 1933. Greensboro *Daily News*, 5 Sept. 1933.
41. Raleigh *News and Observer*, 7 Sept. 1933. Knapp and Paramore, "Developments," p. 333.
42. Raleigh *News and Observer*, 7, 10 Sept. 1933. Goldsboro *News Argus*, 8 Sept. 1933.
43. Edgecombe, Johnston, Duplin, Nash, Rockingham County Agents' Reports 1933, Extension Service Papers. Greenville *Daily Reflector*, 9 Sept. 1933.
44. Columbus, Duplin, Granville County Agents' Reports 1933, Extension Service Papers. Greenville *Daily Reflector*, 9 Sept. 1933. Goldsboro *News Argus*, 11 Sept. 1933. Greensboro *Daily News*, 12 Sept. 1933. AAA P.R. 614–34, 14 Sept. 1933.
45. J. E. Forrest to J. C. B. Ehringhaus, 12 Sept. 1933, Governors' Papers (E). Greensboro *Daily News*, 12 Sept. 1933. AAA P.R. 587–34, 11 Sept.; 614–34, 14 Sept.; 628–34, 16 Sept. 1933.
46. Raleigh *News and Observer*, 14 Sept. 1933. Greensboro *Daily News*, 13, 14 Sept. 1933. Granville, Yadkin County Agents' Reports 1933, Extension Service Papers.
47. Raleigh *News and Observer*, 18, 19 Sept. 1933. AAA P.R. 747–34, 30 Sept. 1933.
48. Raleigh *News and Observer*, 9, 10, 14, 17, 18 Sept. 1933. J. H. Kerr to J. B. Hutson, 7 Sept. 1933, V. Christgau to G. Peek and H. A. Wallace, 14 Sept. 1933, AAA (AC) Papers. Davis Warehouse to J. C. B. Ehringhaus, 16 Sept. 1933,

Ehringhaus to H. J. McKeel, 20 Sept. 1933, Governors' Papers (E).

49. Knapp and Paramore, "Developments," pp. 335–36. AAA P.R. 640–34, 18 Sept. 1933.

50. Raleigh *News and Observer*, 22 Sept. 1933. Formal Hearing, 22 Sept. 1933, Sec. Ag. Papers.

51. Formal Hearing, 22 Sept. 1933, Sec. Ag. Papers.

52. Greensboro *Daily News*, 23 Sept. 1933.

53. Elmo L. Jackson, *The Pricing of Cigarette Tobaccos*, p. 130. Russell Lord made the point about the competitive advantage to the Big Three of increased leaf prices in *The Wallaces of Iowa*, p. 398.

54. Greensboro *Daily News*, 28 Sept. 1933. Perkins, *Crisis*, p. 153. C. C. Davis to G. Peek, 29 Sept. 1933, AAA (SC) Papers. J. B. Hutson to W. Westervelt and C. C. Davis, 27 Sept. 1933, AAA (AC) Papers.

55. J. B. Hutson to W. Westervelt and C. C. Davis, 27 Sept. 1933, Sec. Ag. Papers.

56. Greensboro *Daily News*, 28 Sept., 1 Oct. 1933, J. B. Hutson to W. Westervelt and C. C. Davis, 27 Sept. 1933, H. A. Wallace to F. D. Roosevelt, 28 Sept. 1933, Sec. Ag. Papers. N. Weyl, Memorandum, 29 Sept. 1933, G. Jackson to J. B. Hutson, 30 Sept. 1933, AAA (SC) Papers. Hutson had originally been unwilling to use the license because of its likely disruptive effect on the export trade, but the legal division ruled that he could exclude export buyers from a general license, and this ruling made Hutson less willing to give in to the manufacturers.

57. For an excellent analysis of the issues at stake both in the general dispute and in the particular tobacco dispute see Perkins, *Crisis*, pp. 94–96, 137–39, 154–58. Peek, *Why Quit Our Own*, pp. 146–47. Hutson did not have the difficulties that Peek, and later Chester Davis, had in dealing with the reformers in the legal division, although occasionally Jerome Frank exasperated him and he did find Lee Pressman willfully obstructive. Hutson's assistant, Con Lanier, however, shared Peek's belief that Frank's protégés were intent on socializing American agriculture. Lanier considered Frank an "arrogant son-of-a-bitch" who "didn't know a pig from a cow." Frank's assistants wanted the government to take over business and change the whole system. Lanier dismissed them as "dumb bastards," but admitted that Alger Hiss was a "slick artist." J. B. Hutson, COHRC, pp. 176–77. J. Con Lanier, Interview.

58. J. B. Hutson to C. C. Davis and W. Westervelt, 29 Sept. 1933, AAA (AC) Papers. Raleigh *News and Observer*, 3 Oct. 1933. Greensboro *Daily News*, 3, 4, 6, 7 Oct. 1933.

59. F. Hancock to J. B. Hutson, 23 Sept. 1933, Hancock to C. C. Davis, 4 Oct. 1933, AAA (AC) Papers. Greensboro *Daily News*, 28, 29 Sept. 1933. Goldsboro *News Argus*, 6 Oct. 1933. C. Hall to J. B. Hutson, 5 Oct. 1933, AAA (SC) Papers. Knapp and Paramore, "Developments," p. 339.

60. L. Weil to J. C. B. Ehringhaus, 10 Oct. 1933, Governors' Papers (E). C. Bolton-Smith to J. Frank, 5 Oct. 1933, J. Frank to J. B. Hutson, 9 Oct. 1933, AAA (SC) Papers.

61. J. Frank to P. Appleby, 10 Oct. 1933, C. Bolton-Smith to J. B. Hutson, 10 Oct. 1933, Frank to Hutson, 16 Oct. 1933, AAA (SC) Papers. Raleigh *News and Observer*, 11 Oct. 1933. J. B. Hutson, COHRC, pp. 147–48. Perkins, *Crisis*, p.

157, clearly doubts Peek's version, *Why Quit Our Own*, p. 149, that Roosevelt overruled Wallace and Frank. Perkins argues, "As Wallace had gained almost everything he sought, it is difficult to understand why it was necessary, as Peek asserted, for the President to overrule Wallace, thus forcing him to sign the agreement." It is certainly true that the decision to revive the license scarcely suggests that Roosevelt overruled Wallace at the 8 October meeting. But it is equally true that Wallace's determination to go ahead with the license after the 9 October meeting indicates that he did not think that he had gained everything that he had sought, and Hutson's memory in his Columbia oral history interview of the President's order stopping work on the license the next day is quite clear. Hutson's interview was not apparently available to Perkins.

62. The full text of the agreement is printed in Rowe, *Tobacco under the AAA*, pp. 263–72. The agreement paved the way for similar agreements for Burley, fire-cured, dark air-cured, and cigar leaf tobacco. A more rigorous agreement regulating closely the handling of tobacco was signed with the Connecticut Valley Shade Growers' Association. Perkins, *Crisis*, p. 159. Rowe, *Tobacco under the AAA*, pp. 129–30.

63. J. C. B. Ehringhaus to C. C. Davis, 26 Sept. 1933, J. Y. Joyner to Ehringhaus, 27 Sept. 1933, Governors' Papers (E). L. B. Gunter to H. A. Wallace, 11 Oct. 1933, AAA (SC) Papers. Raleigh *News and Observer*, 26, 29 Sept. 1933. Greensboro *Daily News*, 26 Sept. 1933.

64. J. C. B. Ehringhaus to H. G. Connor, 30 Sept. 1933, Ehringhaus to F. D. Roosevelt, 2, 6 Oct. 1933, Governors' Papers (E). C. C. Davis to J. B. Hutson, 27, 28 Sept. 1933, AAA (AC) Papers.

65. Raleigh *News and Observer*, 15, 16 Oct. 1933. Lanier and Hancock had quarreled at the 5 September conference over the reopening dates for the markets. Lanier's friend Lindsay Warren, who had been involved on that occasion, was seen by Hancock as the man behind Lanier's October outburst. F. Hancock to L. C. Warren, 16 Oct. 1933, Warren to J. C. Lanier 16, 27 Oct. 1933, Warren Papers.

66. J. C. Lanier, Memorandum, 18 Oct. 1933, Sec. Ag. Papers. J. C. Lanier to L. C. Warren, 16 Nov. 1933, Warren Papers. J. W. Bailey to M. H. McIntyre, 20 Dec. 1933, Bailey Papers. Greensboro *Daily News*, 12 Dec. 1933. Raleigh *News and Observer*, 3, 7, 10, 17 Dec. 1933.

67. Kinston *Daily Free Press*, 24 Oct. 1933. AAA P.R. 1393–34, 15 Dec. 1933. L. T. Weeks and E. Y. Floyd, *Producing and Marketing Flue-Cured Tobacco*, p. 73. Russell W. Bierman, *Flue-cured Tobacco*, p. 163. Cash receipts from the sale of the flue-cured crop rose 160 percent in 1933, wheat increased by 60 percent, cotton by 50 percent, and corn by 24 percent. United States Department of Commerce, Bureau of the Census, *Statistical Abstract, 1935*.

68. J. C. B. Ehringhaus to G. A. Barden, 21 Oct. 1933, Barden to Ehringhaus, 4 Nov. 1933, Governors' Papers (E). J. W. Bailey to T. Page, 10 Nov. 1933, J. C. Lanier to Bailey, 16 Nov. 1933, Page to Bailey, 28 Nov. 1933, Bailey Papers. Greensboro *Daily News*, 28 Nov. 1933. J. H. Kerr to J. B. Hutson, 23 Dec. 1933, AAA (AC) Papers. J. H. Kerr to J. B. Hutson, 8 Jan. 1934, Hutson to Kerr, 12 Jan. 1934, Kerr Papers.

69. E. M. Green to J. C. B. Ehringhaus, 2 Sept. 1933, J. Perkins to Ehringhaus, 3

Oct. 1933, B. B. Sugg to Ehringhaus, 30 Nov. 1933, Governors' Papers (E). Raleigh *News and Observer*, 11 Nov., 17 Dec. 1933. Greensboro *Daily News*, 28 Nov., 25 Dec. 1933. Goldsboro *News Argus*, 21 Dec. 1933. Jonathan Daniels to Josephus Daniels, 14 Jan. 1934, Jonathan Daniels Papers. By relying on the local press and the governor's own papers, Daniel, "Marketing Crisis," p. 371, has managed to portray a rather misleading picture of Ehringhaus as "one of the foremost leaders" in a "New Deal era characterized by bold action."

70. J. W. Bailey to M. G. Mann, 24 June 1936, Bailey to C. Poe, 26 Feb. 1934, Bailey to F. D. Roosevelt, 31 Aug. 1933, Bailey Papers. Raleigh *News and Observer*, 23 Dec. 1933.

71. J. H. Kerr to J. Y. Joyner, 19 Feb. 1934, Kerr to Ruth Burke, 12 Feb. 1934, Kerr Papers.

72. S. C. Williams to R. G. Tugwell, 21 May 1934, Williams to F. D. Roosevelt, 23 May 1934, AAA (AC) Papers. L. C. Warren to H. A. Wallace, C. C. Davis, and J. B. Hutson, 8 Mar. 1934, Warren Papers.

73. J. B. Hutson, COHRC, p. 140.

74. Lambert, "New Deal Experiments," pp. 38–40.

75. A. L. Skipworth to J. Hutcheson, 13 Sept. 1933, J. B. Hutson to L. J. Patten, 18 Aug. 1933, N. Weyl, Memorandum, 29 Sept. 1933, Hutson to C. C. Davis and W. Westervelt, 23 Oct. 1933, AAA (SC) Papers. Informal Tobacco Conferences 27 July 1933, 30 Aug. 1933, A. B. Carrington to J. C. Lanier, 25 Aug. 1933, AAA (AC) Papers.

76. See the discussion by Perkins, *Crisis*, p. 158.

77. Greenville *Daily Reflector*, 28 Oct. 1933.

Chapter 3. Compulsory Crop Control

1. AAA P.R. 1052–34, 10 Nov. 1933; 1125–34, 18 Nov. 1933. For the fullest discussion of the contract see Joseph G. Knapp and L. R. Paramore, "Flue-cured Tobacco Developments under the AAA," pp. 340–47.

2. The price-equalization payment was 20 percent of the price of leaf sold before the markets closed and 10 percent of the price of leaf sold between the reopening of the markets and 7 October, when prices started to rise (or in the case of the Border Belt, 28 October). Nearly $4.5 million was paid out, and the calculation of the payments proved an unexpectedly large administrative task. I. O. Schaub to C. W. Warburton, 8 Jan. 1934, Extension Service Papers.

3. Knapp and Paramore, "Developments," pp. 340–42, 348. R. G. Tugwell to J. W. Bailey, 25 April 1934, H. A. Wallace to Bailey, 2 March 1934, Bailey Papers. The growers were allowed to choose among (1) the average of acreage and production 1931–33, (2) 85 percent of any two of those years, (3) 80 percent of 1933, and (4) 70 percent of 1931 and 1932.

4. David E. Conrad, *The Forgotten Farmers*, pp. 54–60. J. A. Dickey to J. B. Hutson, 7 Nov. 1933, AAA (SC) Papers.

5. J. B. Hutson to M. Harris, 28 Nov. 1933, AAA (SC) Papers. J. C. Lanier,

Memorandum, 18 Oct. 1933, Sec. Ag. Papers. Greensboro *Daily News*, 13 Nov. 1933. AAA P.R. 1200–34, 25 Nov. 1933.

6. J. E. Thigpen to J. B. Hutson, 4 Dec. 1933, AAA (AC) Papers. Raleigh *News and Observer*, 24 Dec. 1933.

7. J. E. Thigpen to J. B. Hutson, 4 Dec. 1933, AAA (AC) Papers.

8. Raleigh *News and Observer*, 24 Dec. 1933, 7 Jan. 1934. C. Poe to C. C. Davis, M. Ezekiel, J. Frank, 26 Dec. 1933, AAA (AC) Papers.

9. Raleigh *News and Observer*, 12 Jan., 9, 11, 15, 18, 19 Feb. 1934. C. Hall to C. C. Davis, 11 Jan. 1934, AAA (AC) Papers. Kinston *Daily Free Press*, 20 Feb. 1934. Greenville *Daily Reflector*, 14 Feb. 1934. Greensboro *Daily News*, 17 Feb. 1934. I. O. Schaub to C. W. Warburton, 29 Jan. 1934, Extension Service Papers.

10. Raleigh *News and Observer*, 9 Jan. 1934. AAA P.R. 2005–34, 5 March 1934. The flue-cured growers signed up more of their acreage—an estimated 97.6 percent—than any other type of tobacco. In comparison, cotton growers signed up 85.6 percent of their base acreage and wheat growers 75 percent. Harold B. Rowe, *Tobacco under the AAA*, p. 159, Henry I. Richards, *Cotton and the AAA*, p. 119, Joseph S. Davis, *Wheat and the AAA*, pp. 97–98.

11. C. Sheffield to L. C. Warren, 27 Jan. 1934, Warren Papers. C. Poe to J. W. Bailey, 28 Feb. 1934, Bailey Papers. I. O. Schaub to C. W. Warburton, 5 Feb. 1934, Extension Service Papers.

12. C. W. Warburton to I. O. Schaub, 31 Jan. 1934, Extension Service Papers.

13. Van L. Perkins, *Crisis in Agriculture*, p. 178. H. A. Wallace, *America Must Choose*, p. 9, H. A. Wallace, *New Frontiers*, pp. 56–58.

14. M. Ezekiel, COHRC, p. 50. AAA P.R. 1706–34, 26 Jan. 1934, 1807–34, 7 Feb. 1934. This referendum was something of a self-fulfilling prophecy. The questionnaires were not sent to all cotton growers. They were sent to 30,000 crop reporters, 6,000 local committeemen, and 6,000 county agents who were asked what percentage of farmers in their community approved compulsory control and would cooperate in its enforcement. The tobacco section rejected a proposal of Schaub to poll all tobacco growers about compulsory control on the grounds that naturally the cooperating growers would favor it. C. W. Warburton to I. O. Schaub, 31 Jan. 1934, Extension Service Papers.

15. AAA P.R. 1706–34, 26 Jan. 1934; 1835–34, 13 Feb. 1934; 2390–34, 21 April 1934. Roosevelt quoted in Michael Wayne Schuyler, "Agricultural Relief Activities of the Federal Government in the Middle West, 1933–1936," p. 166.

16. Raleigh *News and Observer*, 12 Nov. 1933. Goldsboro *News Argus*, 10 Jan. 1934.

17. J. B. Hutson to C. Poe, 3 Feb. 1934, AAA (SC) Papers. House *Reports*, 73rd Cong., 2nd sess., no. 1745, pp. 6–7.

18. House *Reports*, 73rd Cong., 2nd sess., no. 1745, p. 7. Examples of lawlessness and night riding against nonsigners were more prevalent in cotton than tobacco. But the hostility of cooperating growers toward nonsigners was much greater in both cotton and tobacco than in other crops like wheat. The probable explanation is that in cotton and tobacco the acreage reduction was crucial to the rise in prices and incomes. In wheat, where the acreage cuts for individual farmers were relatively small, the rise in income was expected from government payments that nonsigners would not receive in any case. Richards, *Cotton and the AAA*, p. 83.

19. House *Reports*, 73rd Cong., 2nd sess., no. 1745, p. 6. J. B. Hutson, COHRC, p. 146.
20. H. A. Wallace to J. W. Bailey, 16 May 1934, Bailey Papers.
21. J. E. Thigpen to J. B. Hutson, 4 Dec. 1933, AAA (AC) Papers. Raleigh *News and Observer*, 21, 23 Feb. 1934.
22. *The State*, 17 Feb. 1934. Raleigh *News and Observer*, 21 Jan. 1934. J. H. Kerr to Ruth Burke, 12 Feb. 1934, Kerr to C. W. Lassiter, 1 March 1934, Kerr Papers.
23. J. H. Kerr to J. E. Daniel, 26 Jan. 1934, Kerr to J. H. Matthews, 25 Jan. 1934, Kerr Papers. Kinston *Daily Free Press*, 11 Feb. 1934.
24. J. H. Kerr to J. B. Hutson, 10 Feb. 1934, Kerr to G. T. Parker, 24 April 1934, Clipping, 20 May 1934, Kerr Papers. J. Miller to J. B. Hutson, 2 Sept. 1933, AAA (SC) Papers.
25. Raleigh *News and Observer*, 1, 3 March 1934. House *Reports*, 73rd Cong., 2nd sess., no. 1745, p. 6.
26. Raleigh *News and Observer*, 12 March, 15 April 1934.
27. Ibid., 17, 27 April 1934. Greensboro *Daily News*, 7 June 1934. M. Jones, COHRC, p. 681. For a general assessment of Jones's relations with the New Deal see Irvin May, Jr., "Marvin Jones: Agrarian and Politician," pp. 421–40.
28. Raleigh *News and Observer*, 5, 9, 19, 24 May 1934. Greensboro *Daily News*, 17 April 1934.
29. Raleigh *News and Observer*, 21 Feb., 26 April 1934. W. B. Umstead to J. B. Hutson, n.d., AAA (AC) Papers.
30. Raleigh *News and Observer*, 11 May 1934. C. Hall to all members, N.C. State Tobacco Advisory Board, 31 May 1934, AAA (AC) Papers. L. C. Warren to J. B. Patrick, 7 June 1934, Warren Papers. Greensboro *Daily News*, 7 June 1934.
31. J. B. Hutson to all county agents, 31 May 1934, AAA (AC) Papers.
32. J. W. Bailey to C. Poe, 26 Feb. 1934, H. W. Barnes to Bailey, 5 May 1934, A. F. Scott to Bailey, 21 May 1934, G. M. Miller to Bailey, 17 June 1934, Bailey Papers.
33. J. B. Hutson to all county agents, 31 May 1934, AAA (AC) Papers. *CR*, vol. 78, 73rd Cong., 2nd sess., (1934), pp. 12364–65.
34. Raleigh *News and Observer*, 14, 17 April 1934. J. C. B. Ehringhaus to Governor Peery et al., 13 April 1934, Governors' Papers (E). H. A. Patten to I. O. Schaub, 23 March 1934, Barden Papers. The governor's intervention angered some of the congressional delegation, especially Kerr. They were determined that Ehringhaus should not preempt the political credit for the tobacco growers' fight in the way that he had in 1933.
35. Kinston *Daily Free Press*, 7, 28 March 1934, Goldsboro *News Argus*, 6 March 1934. H. A. Patten to I. O. Schaub, 23 March 1934, Barden Papers. Greenville *Daily Reflector*, 24 March 1934. A Lenoir farmer complained that his county agent had called a special meeting of the local growers to sign a telegram protesting Bailey's opposition to the Bankhead Act, J. L. Jones to J. W. Bailey, 2 April 1934, Bailey Papers.
36. *CR*, vol. 78, 73rd Cong., 2nd sess. (1934), pp. 10645–67. Raleigh *News and Observer*, 7 June 1934.
37. J. W. Bailey to G. L. McGhee, 1 Feb. 1934, Bailey to C. Sheffield, 19 Feb. 1934,

J. Pittman to Bailey, 15 Feb. 1934, Bailey to Pittman, 19 Feb. 1934, Bailey to C. Poe, 26 Feb. 1934, Bailey Papers.

38. Raleigh *News and Observer*, 21 Feb., 3, 25 March 1934.

39. *CR*, vol. 78, 73rd Cong., 2nd sess. (1934), pp. 5420–21.

40. Written notes, Senate Memo Paper, n.d., Bailey Papers. Raleigh *News and Observer*, 27 March 1934.

41. J. W. Bailey to the Editor, 5 April 1934, Release, 18 April 1934, Bailey Papers.

42. J. W. Bailey to D. M. Springle, 23 April, 1 May 1934, Bailey Papers.

43. Raleigh *News and Observer*, 16, 17 June 1934.

44. J. W. Bailey to G. M. Miller, 20 June 1934, Bailey Papers. *CR*, vol. 78, 73rd Cong., 2nd sess. (1934), p. 5421.

45. J. W. Bailey to G. M. Miller, 20 June 1934, Bailey to R. T. Cox, 24 Sept. 1934, Bailey Papers.

46. Raleigh *News and Observer*, 18 June 1934. *CR*, vol. 78, 73rd Cong., 2nd sess. (1934), pp. 12364–65.

47. Raleigh *News and Observer*, 4 July 1934. Rowe, *Tobacco under the AAA*, p. 176.

48. U.S. *Statutes at Large*, vol. 48, 73rd Cong., 2nd sess. (1934), pp. 1276–81. The Bankhead Act for cotton differed from the tobacco measure by (1) providing for a 50 percent tax rate, (2) requiring the approval of two-thirds of the people who controlled the crop, (3) allowing the exchange of tax-exempt certificates, and (4) providing a state 10 percent reserve allotment for special cases.

49. Rowe, *Tobacco under the AAA*, pp. 160–63. Gladys L. Baker, *The County Agent*, pp. 72–74.

50. Other types of tobacco did have production control associations, but Rowe argues that even in these the county agent had more responsibility than in other AAA commodity programs. Rowe, *Tobacco under the AAA*, p. 162.

51. J. E. Thigpen to J. B. Hutson, 4 Dec. 1933, AAA (AC) Papers. Knapp and Paramore, "Developments," pp. 345–47. Rowe, *Tobacco under the AAA*, pp. 167–68.

52. Caswell, Wake, Orange, Vance, Halifax County Agents' Reports 1934, Extension Service Papers. Posting information was common in other programs, for example wheat, Davis, *Wheat and the AAA*, p. 90.

53. I. O. Schaub to C. W. Warburton, 16 Oct. 1933, 11, 23 Jan. 1934. Extension Service Papers.

54. Interview with F. Sloan and G. Capel, 2 Aug. 1974. I. O. Schaub to C. W. Warburton, 3 Jan. 1934, Extension Service Papers.

55. I. O. Schaub to C. W. Warburton, 4 June 1934, Extension Service Papers. Martin, Nash, Pitt, Wake, Vance County Agents' Reports 1934, Extension Service Papers. Richards, *Cotton and the AAA*, pp. 124–34. Davis, *Wheat and the AAA*, p. 129.

56. I. O. Schaub to C. W. Warburton, 26 June 1934, Extension Service Papers.

57. Halifax, Franklin, Nash, Edgecombe County Agents' Reports 1934, Extension Service Papers.

58. Rowe, *Tobacco under the AAA*, pp. 179–80.

59. Pitt, Martin County Agents' Reports 1934, Extension Service Papers. Rowe, *Tobacco under the AAA*, pp. 174–77.

60. C. W. Warburton to I. O. Schaub, 31 Jan. 1934, Extension Service Papers.

Edwin G. Nourse, Joseph S. Davis, and John D. Black, *Three Years of the Agricultural Adjustment Administration*, p. 141. For local problems with the Bankhead Act in Georgia see Michael S. Holmes, *The New Deal in Georgia*, pp. 228–31.

61. AAA P.R. 181–34, 24 July 1934; 178–35, 25 July 1934; 214–35, 28 July 1934. Raleigh *News and Observer*, 28 July 1934. H. A. Wallace to Josephus Daniels, 18 Aug. 1934, AAA (SC) Papers.

62. Russell W. Bierman, *Flue-cured Tobacco*, p. 163. E. T. Weeks and E. Y. Floyd, *Producing and Marketing Flue-Cured Tobacco*, p. 73. *The State*, 23 Nov. 1934, Kinston *Daily Free Press*, 9 Nov. 1934, Goldsboro *News Argus*, 28 Aug. 1934. Greenville *Daily Reflector*, 9 Oct., 16 Nov. 1934. *Southern Tobacco Journal*, Dec. 1934.

63. J. W. Mitchell, Report 1934, Extension Service Papers.

64. Raleigh *News and Observer*, 9, 20 Sept. 1934. L. C. Warren to J. E. Morris, 17 Sept. 1934, Warren Papers.

65. J. W. Bailey to H. A. Wallace, 6 Oct. 1934, Bailey to J. Ellington, 9 Nov. 1934, Bailey Papers.

66. AAA P.R. 1308–35, 3 Jan. 1935. Goldsboro *News Argus*, 17 Dec. 1934.

67. J. W. Bailey to H. McNeil, 26 Sept. 1934, Bailey to C. Sheffield, 15 Oct. 1934, Bailey Papers. N.C. Director's Report, Bertie, Wilson County Agents' Reports 1934, Extension Service Papers.

68. J. W. Bailey to editor, *South Atlantic Quarterly*, 17 Dec. 1934, Bailey to L. R. Harrill, 6 Feb. 1935, Bailey Papers.

69. Kinston *Daily Free Press*, 4 June 1934. Raleigh *News and Observer*, 22 Sept. 1935.

70. United States Department of Agriculture, *Agricultural Adjustment in 1934*, p. 138. H. A. Wallace to J. W. Bailey, 16 May 1934, Bailey Papers.

71. Edwin G. Nourse, *Marketing Agreements under the AAA*, pp. 138, 139, 146. Nourse, Davis, and Black, *Three Years*, pp. 42–43. J. B. Hutson, COHRC, pp. 197–98. James E. Thigpen has pointed out that although the congressmen believed Hutson was trying to sabotage potato control, the AAA in fact tried to construct a program for the potato growers; but it was an impossible task because of the perishability of the crop, the variations in yield, and the nature of the marketing situation. Interview with J. E. Thigpen, 22 Sept. 1976. See also Robert F. Hunter, "The AAA between Neighbors: Virginia, North Carolina, and the New Deal Farm Program," pp. 563–66.

Chapter 4. Divisions in the Ranks

1. Christiana M. Campbell, *The Farm Bureau and the New Deal*, pp. 138–39.

2. R. L. Doughton to H. P. Taylor, 15 Jan. 1934, Doughton Papers.

3. U.S. House of Representatives, Committee on Ways and Means, *Tobacco Taxes: Hearings before the Subcommittee of the Committee on Ways and Means*, 73rd Cong., 2nd sess. (1934), p. 308.

4. A.P. Clipping, 23 April 1934, AAA (AC) Papers.

5. Raleigh *News and Observer*, 4 March 1934. *Tobacco Taxes: Hearings*, pp. 1, 7–16, 59, 61–64, 104–42, 278–79, 315–21, 322–33, 373–84.

6. *Tobacco Taxes: Hearings*, pp. 279–90, 388.

7. House *Reports*, 73rd Cong., 2nd sess. (1934), no. 1882, p. 3.

8. N. Weyl, Memorandum, 29 Sept. 1933, AAA (SC) Papers. J. B. Hutson to H. A. Wallace, 27 April 1934, Hutson to C. C. Davis and Wallace, 28 May 1934, AAA (AC) Papers. Raleigh *News and Observer*, 22 March 1934. Roosevelt Press Conference, vol. 3, p. 290, 20 April 1934, Roosevelt Papers.

9. Raleigh *News and Observer*, 21, 25 April 1934. S. C. Williams to R. G. Tugwell, 21 May 1934, Williams to F. D. Roosevelt, 23 May 1934, AAA (AC) Papers. I have found no evidence of such a campaign in 1934.

10. Diary, Book 1, p. 46, 1 May 1934, Morgenthau Papers. J. B. Hutson to H. A. Wallace, 7 May 1934, AAA (AC) Papers.

11. Resolutions, 13 April 1934, J. C. B. Ehringhaus, C. Poe, L. Weil, and J. Y. Joyner to J. B. Hutson, 25 May 1934, Governors' Papers (E). Raleigh *News and Observer*, 19, 20 April 1934.

12. Raleigh *News and Observer*, 6 Jan. 1935. L. C. Warren to W. J. Boyd, 2 May 1935, Warren Papers. W. H. Dail to R. L. Doughton, 3 May 1935, Doughton Papers.

13. Josephus Daniels to C. Poe, 9 Jan. 1935, Josephus Daniels Papers.

14. *Progressive Farmer*, Oct. 1933.

15. See above, ch. 2.

16. Raleigh *News and Observer*, 28 Feb. 1935. H. A. Wallace to M. Jones, 24 April 1934, Sec. Ag. Papers. Robert F. Hunter, "The AAA between Neighbors: Virginia, North Carolina, and the New Deal Farm Program," p. 551, confuses this Flanagan bill of 1934 for the complete regulation of warehouses with the Flanagan bill of 1935 that simply provided for government grading.

17. J. C. Lanier to L. C. Warren, 26 Feb. 1934, Warren to W. Z. Moton, 26 Feb., 2 March 1934, Warren to Robersonville Warehousemen, 6 March 1934, Warren Papers. L. C. Warren to H. A. Wallace, C. C. Davis, and J. B. Hutson, 8 March 1934, AAA (AC) Papers. Raleigh *News and Observer*, 1 March 1934.

18. Raleigh *News and Observer*, 27 April 1934. *Southern Tobacco Journal*, March 1934.

19. AAA P.R. 9–35, 2 July 1934; 126–35, 17 July 1934. *Progressive Farmer*, Oct. 1934. *Southern Tobacco Journal*, Aug. 1934.

20. C. Hall to J. C. B. Ehringhaus, 30 April 1934, Governors' Papers (E). O. A. Glover to J. H. Kerr, 8 May 1934, Kerr Papers. J. E. Winslow to L. C. Warren, 19 May 1934, Warren to Winslow, 21 May 1934, Warren Papers.

21. Wilson Tobacco Board of Trade, 6 March 1935, Greenville Tobacco Board of Trade, 7 March 1935, Clipping, Wilson *Daily Times*, 4 March 1935, Bailey Papers. Kinston Tobacco Board of Trade, 28 Feb. 1935, Washington Tobacco Board of Trade, 9 March 1935, Warren Papers. J. B. Ficklen to G. A. Barden, 2 March 1935, Barden Papers. *Southern Tobacco Journal*, March, April, May 1935. J. D. Gold to J. H. Kerr, 15 Aug. 1935, Kerr to Gold, 16 Aug. 1935, Kerr Papers.

22. Raleigh *News and Observer*, 12, 28 Feb., 1, 8, 13 March 1935. G. A. Barden to J. C. Britt, 12 March 1935, H. A. Patten to Barden, 12 March 1935, Barden

Papers. L. V. Morrill, Jr., to L. C. Warren, 8 March 1935, Warren Papers.

23. Raleigh *News and Observer*, 21 Feb., 14 March 1935. C. Hall to J. C. B. Ehringhaus, 25 Jan. 1935, Governors' Papers (E). J. E. Winslow to L. C. Warren, 9 Feb. 1935, Warren Papers. L. Weil to G. A. Barden, 3 March 1935, C. Poe to Barden, 25 July 1935, Wayne County Committee to Barden, 7 March 1935, Barden Papers. C. Poe and E. Vanatta to Jonathan Daniels, 2 April 1935, Jonathan Daniels Papers. Granville County Grange, 2 March 1935, Robeson County Grange, 28 May 1935, Bailey Papers. None of the replies to Cooley survive.

24. Raleigh *News and Observer*, 31 March 1935.

25. R. T. Cox to J. Flanagan, 9 March 1935, Warren Papers. J. H. Lane to Jonathan Daniels, 6, 7 March 1935, Jonathan Daniels to N. C. Congressmen, 3 April 1935, G. A. Barden to Jonathan Daniels, 6 April 1935, Jonathan Daniels Papers.

26. Raleigh *News and Observer*, 22 March, 22 June 1935.

27. Raleigh *News and Observer*, 22 June 1935.

28. *CR*, vol. 79, 74th Cong., 1st sess. (1935), pp. 11803–808, 11867–72, 11879, 11886–88.

29. Ibid., pp. 11888–89, 11891. Raleigh *News and Observer*, 9, 17 Aug. 1935. J. W. Bailey to J. Thorpe, 14 Aug. 1935, Bailey Papers. J. W. Bailey to Jonathan Daniels, 8 April 1935, Jonathan Daniels Papers.

30. J. C. Lanier to H. D. Cooley, 25 June 1936, A. G. Black to Lanier, 7 July 1936, Cooley Papers.

31. Goldsboro *News Argus*, 2, 3, 22 July, 17, 18, 20 Aug. 1936.

32. Raleigh *News and Observer*, 16, 18 Aug., 18 Sept., 6, 19 Nov. 1936. F. Hancock to Jonathan Daniels, 6 Aug. 1935, Jonathan Daniels Papers. Almost forty years later Lanier admitted that he had been wrong to oppose government grading, especially as the growers could not have had the postwar price-support program without it, J. Con Lanier Interview.

33. Raleigh *News and Observer*, 18 Oct., 9 Nov. 1934. L. C. Warren to J. B. Hutson, 10 Nov. 1934, Warren Papers. J. B. Hutson to L. C. Warren, 15 Nov. 1934, AAA (AC) Papers. J. C. B. Ehringhaus to J. B. Hutson, 23 Nov. 1934, Hutson to Ehringhaus, 13 Dec. 1934, Governors' Papers (E).

34. AAA P.R. 1185–35, 12 Dec. 1934. L. C. Warren to J. B. Hutson, 24 Dec. 1934, W. B. Umstead to Hutson, n.d., AAA (AC) Papers. G. A. Barden to W. P. Anderson, 19 Jan. 1935, Barden to J. D. Brinson, 16 Feb. 1935, Barden Papers. Resolutions, N.C. Extension Agents Meeting, 10 Jan. 1935, AAA (SC) Papers. South-East District Agent, N.C. Report 1934, Columbus, Orange, Harnett County Agents' Reports 1934, Orange County Agents' Report 1935, Extension Service Papers.

35. AAA P.R. 1247–35, 22 Dec. 1934. J. B. Hutson to L. C. Warren, 26 Dec. 1934, AAA (AC) Papers. J. E. Thigpen to W. P. Singletary, 15 Jan. 1935, AAA (SC) Papers. J. B. Hutson, COHRC, pp. 142–43.

36. AAA P.R. 1623–35, 25 Feb. 1935. C. C. Davis to J. Hutcheson, 25 Feb. 1935, AAA (SC) Papers. L. C. Warren to M. V. Hollaway, 19 Jan. 1935, Warren Papers.

37. AAA P.R. 1622–35, 1623–35, 25 Feb. 1935.

38. Raleigh *News and Observer*, 21 Oct., 9 Nov. 1934. C. Hall to J. B. Hutson, 3 Nov. 1934, AAA (AC) Papers. L. V. Morrill, Jr., to L. C. Warren, 19 Nov. 1934, Warren Papers.

39. AAA P.R. 1185–35, 12 Dec. 1934.

40. Raleigh *News and Observer*, 10, 28 Jan., 7 Feb. 1935.

41. Ibid., 17 Jan. 1935. Jonathan Daniels to Josephus Daniels, 5 March 1935, Jonathan Daniels Papers.

42. Raleigh *News and Observer*, 7, 12, 14 Feb. 1935.

43. Ibid., 15, 19 Feb. 1935. J. B. Hutson to C. Hall, 14 Feb. 1935, AAA (AC) Papers. There was some bitterness at this time between the Advisory Committee and Morrill. Clarence Poe, Jonathan Daniels, and Lionel Weil were negotiating between the committee and Morrill over payment of his 1933 expenses. As Daniels remembered it, Morrill "was hard up and his efforts had enriched many farmers, time-merchants etc., who grew stingy in their memory." L. Weil to Jonathan Daniels, 21 Jan. 1935, Daniels to C. Hall, 28 March 1935, Jonathan Daniels Papers. Jonathan Daniels to the author, 10 May 1970.

44. Raleigh *News and Observer*, 26 Feb. 1935.

45. Ibid., 26 Feb. 1935. H. R. Tolley, COHRC, p. 231. Richard S. Kirkendall, *Social Scientists and Farm Politics in the Age of Roosevelt*, p. 136. Wallace had to listen to what the *News and Observer* described as a "farmer-defending" contest between Bailey and Ehringhaus as each tried to champion the farmer's cause with thoughts of the 1936 primary not far away. Bailey called for a reduction in the cigarette tax; Ehringhaus wanted to amend Bailey's resolution to guarantee that farmers received the benefit of the reduction. At one point they were both trying to use the same microphone at the same time. The governor received an easy cheer for saying the growers did not want a cooperative. References to taxation in North Carolina and New York were part of Ehringhaus's continuing battle to convince federal officials that North Carolina was contributing its fair share to relief spending.

46. Raleigh *News and Observer*, 17 March 1935.

47. J. C. B. Ehringhaus to H. A. Wallace, 18, 24, 27 March 1935, Wallace to Ehringhaus, 23 March 1935, Governors' Papers (E).

48. Raleigh *News and Observer*, 13, 18, 20 Sept. 1935. J. C. B. Ehringhaus to H. A. Wallace, 12 Sept. 1935, Ehringhaus to J. B. Patrick, 18 Sept. 1935, Ehringhaus to J. H. Blount, 16 Sept. 1935, Wallace to Ehringhaus, 18 Sept. 1935, Governors' Papers (E). H. A. Wallace to F. Hancock, 10 Sept. 1935, AAA (SC) Papers. AAA P.R. 477–36, 18 Sept. 1935.

49. Subcommittee Program, 20 Sept. 1935, Governors' Papers (E). Raleigh *News and Observer*, 22, 26 Sept. 1935.

50. J. C. B. Ehringhaus to H. G. Whitehead, 28 Sept. 1935, Governors' Papers (E). Raleigh *News and Observer*, 12, 20, 22 Sept. 1935.

51. Greensboro *Daily News*, 26 Sept. 1935. Subcommittee Program, 20 Sept. 1935, Governors' Papers (E).

52. Greensboro *Daily News*, 15, 19 Sept. 1935. Raleigh *News and Observer*, 27 Sept. 1935. L. T. Weeks and E. Y. Floyd, *Producing and Marketing Flue-Cured Tobacco*, p. 73. Russell W. Bierman, *Flue-cured Tobacco*, p. 163.

53. Raleigh *News and Observer*, 11, 16, 22, 24 April 1935. *CR*, vol. 79, 74th Cong., 1st sess. (1935), pp. 6224–25. C. Hall to L. C. Warren, 29 April 1935, Warren Papers.

54. Raleigh *News and Observer*, 14, 15 May 1935. C. Hall to J. B. Hutson, 29 April

1935, Hutson to Hall, 2 May 1935, AAA (AC) Papers. Wake County Agent Report 1935, Extension Service Papers.
55. Greensboro *Daily News*, 20, 29 June, 9 July 1935. S. C. Williams statement, 2 July 1935, Bailey Papers.
56. Raleigh *News and Observer*, 30 June 1935.
57. J. W. Bailey to L. Kitchen, 9, 19 July 1935, Bailey to C. Dowd, 20 April 1935, Bailey to E. Godney, 11 May 1935, Bailey to N. Chambliss, 29 April 1935, D. G. Campbell to Bailey, 20 July 1935, Bailey Papers. Raleigh *News and Observer*, 19 July 1935.
58. *CR*, vol. 79, 74th Cong., 1st sess. (1935), pp. 11148, 11386, 11476–77.
59. J. W. Bailey to N. Bartlett, 25 July 1935, Bailey to C. Cannon, 25 July 1935, S. C. Williams to Bailey, 16 Aug. 1935, Bailey to Williams, 17 Aug. 1935, Bailey Papers.
60. United States Department of Agriculture, AAA, *Agricultural Adjustment, 1933–1935*, pp. 200, 206. AAA P.R. 32–36, 6 July 1935.

Chapter 5. The Aftermath of Hoosac Mills

1. *CR*, vol. 80, 74th Cong., 2nd sess. (1936), p. 2570.
2. Ibid., pp. 97, 5195. Raleigh *News and Observer*, 7 Jan. 1936. Greensboro *Daily News*, 7 Jan. 1936. J. H. Kerr to Mrs. W. T. Tadlock, 6 Feb. 1936, Kerr Papers. H. D. Cooley to D. Gilliam, 20 Jan. 1936, Cooley Papers.
3. Raleigh *News and Observer*, 7, 8 Jan. 1936. Goldsboro *News Argus*, 9, 11 Jan. 1936. Greensboro *Daily News*, 9, 14 Jan. 1936.
4. H. D. Cooley to T. J. Pearsall, 24 Feb. 1936, Cooley Papers. *CR*, vol. 80, 74th Cong., 2nd sess. (1936), p. 2361. *Extension Farm News*, Feb. 1936. Raleigh *News and Observer*, 16 March 1936.
5. Richard S. Kirkendall, *Social Scientists and Farm Politics in the Age of Roosevelt*, pp. 145–48.
6. E. Y. Floyd Report, Caldwell, Chowan, Franklin, Jones, Onslow, Orange, Pamlico County Agents' Reports 1936, Extension Service Papers.
7. United States Department of Agriculture, AAA, *Agricultural Conservation, 1936*, pp. 53–59. I. O. Schaub to H. R. Tolley, 16 March 1936, AAA (AC) Papers.
8. E. Y. Floyd Report, Vance, Wilson County Agents' Reports 1936, Extension Service Papers.
9. I. O. Schaub to J. B. Hutson, 8 June 1936, Schaub to W. G. Finn, 23 June 1936, AAA (AC) Papers.
10. J. Hester to Editor, 11 June 1935, AAA (AC) Papers. Raleigh *News and Observer*, 7 Jan., 11 Feb. 1936.
11. For the history of the Social Security controversy see Thomas Sellers Morgan, "A Step towards Altruism: Relief and Welfare in North Carolina, 1930–1938," pp. 296–336. For the controversies of the 1935 legislature see Elmer L. Puryear, *Democratic Party Dissension in North Carolina, 1928–1936*, pp. 188–89.
12. Raleigh *News and Observer*, 8, 14, 15, 19, 26, 27, 28 Feb. 1936. Conference Minutes, 25 Feb. 1936, Special Committee Minutes, 26 Feb. 1936, Governors' Papers (E).

13. J. H. Blount to J. C. B. Ehringhaus, 27 Feb. 1936, H. G. Whitehead to Ehringhaus, 29 Feb. 1936, E. Y. Speed to Ehringhaus, 29 Feb. 1936, J. H. Harper to Ehringhaus, 3 March 1936, Resolutions of Martin, Wayne, Greene, Wilson, Edgecombe, and Bertie Farm Bureaus, Governors' Papers (E). Raleigh *News and Observer*, 3, 4 March 1936.

14. Raleigh *News and Observer*, 29 Feb., 2 March 1936.

15. David Leroy Corbitt, ed., *Addresses, Letters and Papers of John Christoph Blucher Ehringhaus*, pp. 212–29.

16. I. Valentine to H. D. Cooley, 2 April 1936, Cooley Papers. Raleigh *News and Observer*, 13, 20, 26, 27 March 1936. Corbitt, ed., *Addresses of Ehringhaus*, pp. 219–25. Minutes, 17 March 1936, Governor Peery to J. C. B. Ehringhaus, 24 March 1936, Governors' Papers (E).

17. Raleigh *News and Observer*, 21, 27 March, 3, 4, 9, 10 April 1936.

18. Ibid., 10 April 1936.

19. Ibid., 8, 30 April 1936.

20. Ibid., 11, 12, 16 April 1936.

21. R. T. Cox to J. C. B. Ehringhaus, 16 April 1936, Governors' Papers (E). Greenville *Daily Reflector*, 20 April 1936. Kinston *Daily Free Press*, 16, 17, 19 April 1936. Raleigh *News and Observer*, 19 April 1936.

22. Raleigh *News and Observer*, 22 April 1936.

23. Corbitt, ed., *Addresses of Ehringhaus*, pp. 238–58. His discussion of the penalties was a little misleading. He complained that the penalty for the first offense was only $10. This was true, but he did not mention that civil suit could also be brought against the grower for three times the market value of his excess tobacco.

24. Raleigh *News and Observer*, 30 April 1936. Statement, 5 May 1936, Kerr Papers. Corbitt, ed., *Addresses of Ehringhaus*, pp. 325–31. In 1936 Kerr was once again facing Oscar Dickens and won comfortably.

25. L. T. Weeks and E. Y. Floyd, *Producing and Marketing Flue-Cured Tobacco*, p. 73. J. C. B. Ehringhaus to F. Brown, 22 Sept. 1936, Ehringhaus to F. D. Roosevelt, 13 March 1936, Governors' Papers (E). Jonathan Daniels to Josephus Daniels, n.d., Jonathan Daniels Papers.

26. For Ehringhaus's struggle with Harry Hopkins over North Carolina's contribution to relief programs see Morgan, "A Step towards Altruism," pp. 106–112, 209–17. For the governor's defeat over WPA patronage and the increased recognition given to Senator Bailey and the congressional delegation see also pp. 241–51 and Ronald Ely Marcello, "The North Carolina Works Progress Administration and the Politics of Relief," pp. 59–81.

27. C. F. Cowell to J. C. B. Ehringhaus, 3 March 1936, Governors' Papers (E).

28. Raleigh *News and Observer*, 15, 16, 22 Sept. 1936.

29. Jonathan Daniels to N. T. Wells, n.d., Jonathan Daniels Papers. Raleigh *News and Observer*, 18 Jan. 1937. C. Poe to C. Cobb, 18 Dec. 1936, AAA (AC) Papers. *Progressive Farmer*, Feb. 1937.

30. Raleigh *News and Observer*, 19, 20, 21, 26, 27, 28, 30 Jan., 2, 3, 4, 6 Feb. 1937.

31. E. Rivers to C. R. Hoey, 10 Feb. 1937, Governor Hoey Papers. Raleigh *News and Observer*, 17 Feb. 1937.

32. For an analysis of the difficulties of the compact approach see William E. Leuchtenburg, *Flood Control Politics*, pp. 247–54.

33. Stuart Noblin, *The Grange in North Carolina, 1929–1954*, pp. 4, 10–18, 51.
34. Christiana M. Campbell, *The Farm Bureau and the New Deal*, pp. 95–100. Campbell has emphasized the role of tobacco in the formation of the North Carolina Farm Bureau from her study of the national Farm Bureau papers. I have reached a similar conclusion from local material.
35. Raleigh *News and Observer*, 10, 17 Feb., 6 April 1936. Greenville *Daily Reflector*, 10 Jan. 1936. Goldsboro *News Argus*, 16 Jan. 1936.
36. E. F. Arnold to J. B. Hutson, 27 May 1938, AAA (AC) Papers. Kinston *Daily Free Press*, 29 Feb. 1936. There is a list of the organized counties in Campbell, *The Farm Bureau*, p. 95.
37. Campbell, *The Farm Bureau*, p. 96. Goldsboro *News Argus*, 24 Feb., 1, 2 April 1936. Edgecombe, Moore, Johnston, Rockingham, Person, Wilson County Agents' Reports 1936, Extension Service Papers.
38. Campbell, *The Farm Bureau*, pp. 97–98. Raleigh *News and Observer*, 16 July 1940.
39. Raleigh *News and Observer*, 1 Nov. 1936. Greensboro *Daily News*, 20 Jan. 1937. Jonathan Daniels to Josephus Daniels, 4 Dec. 1936, Jonathan Daniels Papers.
40. J. G. Korner to L. C. Warren, 4 Nov. 1929, J. E. Winslow to Warren, 2 March 1936, J. C. Lanier to Warren, 7 March 1936, Warren Papers. J. W. Bailey to C. H. Robertson, 13 Feb. 1936, Bailey to C. B. Griffin, 17 Feb. 1936, Bailey Papers. Bailey in a letter to E. Y. Speed, 14 Feb. 1936, talks of a "pleasant interview" with O'Neal.
41. Raleigh *News and Observer*, 18, 26 Feb., 9, 26 March 1937. E. F. Arnold to L. C. Warren, 3 March 1937, Warren Papers.
42. Raleigh *News and Observer*, 6, 20 Feb. 1937. F. Hancock to Josephus Daniels, 21 Dec. 1936, Josephus Daniels Papers.
43. M. Dawson to J. H. Kerr, 19 Feb. 1937, Kerr to F. D. Roosevelt, 14 April 1937, Kerr Papers. Raleigh *News and Observer*, 19 Feb., 9 March 1937.
44. L. C. Warren, Memorandum, 7 Feb. 1937, Warren Papers.
45. Resolution, Directors of North Carolina Farm Bureau, 3 March 1937, Bailey Papers.
46. Goldsboro *News Argus*, 16 April 1936. Poster, 1936, Fountain Papers. For conflicting views of Bailey's relationship with the New Deal and with constituency pressure see John Robert Moore, *Senator Josiah William Bailey of North Carolina*, p. 129, and James T. Patterson, *Congressional Conservatism and the New Deal*, pp. 26–29. For Bailey's use of WPA support in his 1936 primary see Marcello, "The North Carolina WPA," pp. 122–26. Later he was bitterly to denounce the use of the WPA as a political machine.
47. There are no authoritative accounts of the 1938 Farm Act, but see Dean Albertson, *Roosevelt's Farmer*, pp. 111–17, Campbell, *The Farm Bureau*, pp. 111–14, Murray R. Benedict, *Farm Policies of the United States, 1790–1950*, pp. 375–81, Don F. Hadwiger, *Federal Wheat Commodity Programs*, pp. 137–53.
48. Hadwiger, *Federal Wheat Commodity Programs*, pp. 140–47.
49. *New York Times*, 18 May, 12 June, 21, 22, 24 July, 12 Aug. 1937.
50. Ibid., 16 May, 4 July, 1, 14 Aug. 1937.
51. Ibid., 28 Oct., 5, 13, 28 Nov., 2, 5 Dec. 1937, 12 Jan. 1938.

52. Ibid., 3 Nov. 1937. Raleigh *News and Observer*, 9 April, 20 June, 21 July, 14 Aug. 1937. L. C. Warren to W. A. Thomas, 16 June 1937, Warren to J. R. Parker, 5 Nov. 1937, Warren to J. H. Blount, 11 Dec. 1937, Warren Papers. *CR*, vol. 82, 75th Cong., 2nd sess. (1937), p. 659.

53. *CR*, vol. 82, 75th Cong., 2nd sess. (1937), pp. 867, 1192. L. C. Warren to J. C. Lanier, 25 Feb. 1937, Warren Papers.

54. Weeks and Floyd, *Producing and Marketing*, p. 73. Brunswick, Columbus, Harnett, Pitt, Wilson County Agents' Reports 1937, Extension Service Papers.

55. Raleigh *News and Observer*, 3 July, 19 Oct. 1937. E. F. Arnold to G. A. Barden, 19 July 1937, Barden Papers. E. F. Arnold to J. W. Bailey, 7, 19 July 1937, Bailey Papers. E. F. Arnold to F. D. Roosevelt, 19 July 1937, AAA (AC) Papers. *New York Times*, 20 June, 1 Aug. 1937.

56. J. W. Bailey to J. Hester, 8 Nov. 1937, C. Attwood to Bailey, 18 Nov. 1937, C. F. Cowell to Bailey, 29 Oct. 1937, J. A. Powers to Bailey, 9 Dec. 1937, Bailey Papers.

57. *CR*, vol. 82, 75th Cong., 2nd sess. (1937), p. 1156. Raleigh *News and Observer*, 15 Dec. 1937.

58. Greensboro *Daily News*, 3 Nov. 1937. *CR*, vol. 82, 75th Cong., 2nd sess. (1937), pp. 526, 1429; vol. 83, 3rd sess. (1938), p. 1847.

59. United States *Statutes at Large*, vol. 52, 75th Cong., 3rd sess. (1938), pp. 45–48

Chapter 6. Compulsory Control: Victory and Defeat

1. *Progressive Farmer*, March 1938. AAA P.R. 1285–38, 18 Feb. 1938.

2. AAA P.R. 1286–38, 18 Feb. 1938; 1262–38, 16 Feb. 1938.

3. Greensboro *Daily News*, 19 Feb. 1938. J. C. Lanier to L. C. Warren, 7 Feb. 1938, Warren Papers. AAA P.R. 1286–38, 18 Feb. 1938.

4. E. Y. Floyd to W. G. Finn, 20 Oct. 1937, AAA (AC) papers.

5. Raleigh *News and Observer*, 24 Feb., 3 March 1938.

6. The accounts of these meetings are based on a series of reports in the *News and Observer* between 1 March 1938 and 12 March 1938.

7. Ibid. F. Jeter to R. Brigham, 14 March 1938, Sec. Ag. Papers. Greensboro *Daily News*, 1 March 1938. Kinston *Daily Free Press*, 10 March 1938.

8. Raleigh *News and Observer*, 27 Feb. 1938. Greensboro *Daily News*, 27 Feb. 1938. Greenville *Daily Reflector*, 15 March 1938.

9. Greensboro *Daily News*, 27 Feb. 1938. F. Jeter to R. Brigham, 14 March 1938, Sec. Ag. Papers. E. Y. Floyd to W. G. Finn, 21 Feb. 1938, AAA (AC) Papers.

10. David Leroy Corbitt, ed., *Addresses, Letters and Papers of Clyde Roark Hoey*, p. 425. Raleigh *News and Observer*, 1, 9 March 1938.

11. Raleigh *News and Observer*, 11 March 1938. Kinston *Daily Free Press*, 9 March 1938. Greensboro *Daily News*, 27 Feb. 1938.

12. Raleigh *News and Observer*, 12 March 1938. Jonathan Daniels to J. C. Lanier, 5 March 1938, Jonathan Daniels Papers. I. O. Schaub to C. Sheffield, 4 March 1938, Extension Service Papers.

13. Raleigh *News and Observer*, 2, 3, 6 March 1938.

14. Ibid., 4, 7 March 1938. Greensboro *Daily News*, 24 Feb. 1938. Smithfield *Herald*, 1, 11 March 1938.

15. B. T. Starling to H. A. Wallace, 29 May 1934, J. H. Kerr to J. B. Hutson, 20 Sept. 1934, AAA (AC) Papers. B. T. Starling to J. W. Bailey, 23 Nov. 1934, L. C. McLendon to Bailey, 17 Dec. 1934, Bailey Papers.

16. S. H. Hobbs, Sr., to J. W. Bailey, 5 May 1933, Hobbs to Bailey, 27 Sept. 1937, Bailey to E. D. Smith, 16 Oct. 1937, Hobbs to Bailey, 20 Oct. 1937, Bailey Papers. Raleigh *News and Observer*, 7 Jan. 1936, 19 Oct. 1937. S. H. Hobbs, Sr., to J. C. B. Ehringhaus, 10 April 1936, Governors' Papers (E).

17. Raleigh *News and Observer*, 8, 11 March 1938. Greensboro *Daily News*, 6 March 1938. Lumberton *Robesonian*, 9 March 1938.

18. B. T. Starling to J. W. Bailey, 1 March 1938, Bailey Papers. Raleigh *News and Observer*, 11 March 1938. Smithfield *Herald*, 1 March 1938.

19. AAA P.R. 1483–38, 25 March 1938. See map 4. Despite the concessions to Florida and Georgia growers, they failed to vote a two-thirds majority for control. This was not very important since their total vote was under 30,000. Overall, 219,842 flue-cured growers voted for control, 35,253 voted against; 151,503 North Carolina growers voted for quotas, 17,340 opposed them.

20. H. Hubbard to J. W. Bailey, 4 June, 27 Sept. 1934, Bailey Papers. Sampson County Agent Reports 1934, 1935, 1938, 1940, Extension Service Papers. Raleigh *News and Observer*, 27 Jan., 3 Feb. 1937.

21. Raleigh *News and Observer*, 30 March 1938. *CR*, vol. 83, 75th Cong., 3rd sess. (1938), p. 6225. F. Jeter to R. Brigham, 14 March 1938, Sec. Ag. Papers.

22. AAA P.R. 1402–38, 11 March 1938. Kinston *Daily Free Press*, 28 Feb. 1938. *Extension Farm News*, March 1938. Anson County Agent Report 1938, Extension Service Papers.

23. Kinston *Daily Free Press*, 29 March 1938. I. O. Schaub to C. Warburton, 20 April 1938, Schaub to R. Brigham, 4 May 1938, Halifax, Vance County Agents' Reports 1938, Extension Service Papers. Smithfield *Herald*, 12, 29 April 1938. Goldsboro *News Argus*, 11 April 1938. Greensboro *Daily News*, 21 April 1938.

24. Kinston *Daily Free Press*, 26 April 1938. Goldsboro *News Argus*, 26 April 1938. Greensboro *Daily News*, 7 May 1938. Raleigh *News and Observer*, 20 May 1938. C. S. Hardison to C. L. Abernethy, Jr., 30 May 1938, Abernethy to C. Morrison, 11 May 1938, Abernethy to Hardison, 2 June 1938, Abernethy Papers. G. A. Barden to J. B. Hutson, 4 May 1938, AAA (AC) Papers. G. A. Barden to L. C. Warren, 12 May 1938, Warren Papers. Charles L. Abernethy, Jr., tried to recapture his father's seat in 1936, 1938, and 1940. He chose whatever issues he thought might bring him success. In 1936 this meant the Townsend Plan; in 1938 support of the New Deal and wage-hour legislation but opposition to crop control; in 1940 price-fixing for farmers and opposition to Barden's attempts to amend the wage-hour law. He came closest to victory in 1936 when he scared Barden and came just over 3,000 votes behind. His position then declined until in 1940 he was arrested a few days before the election in possession of stolen ballot papers. He lost for the final time by over 12,000 votes.

25. J. W. Bailey to E. W. Bryant, 11 May 1938, Bailey to H. A. Wallace, 29 April 1938, Bailey Papers. *CR*, vol. 83, 75th Cong., 3rd sess. (1938), p. 6225. Greensboro *Daily News*, 6 May 1938.

26. There are a batch of 266 complaints in the AAA (SC) Papers. I. O. Schaub to R. Brigham, 4 May 1938, Jones County Agent Report 1938, Extension Service Papers. J. C. Lanier to Jonathan Daniels, 16 April 1938, Jonathan Daniels Papers. Franklin *Times*, 29 April 1938.

27. L. C. Warren to H. C. Vaughan, 4 May 1938, Warren Papers. J. H. Kerr to G. Capehart, 6 May 1938, Kerr Papers. *CR*, vol. 83, 75th Cong., 3rd sess. (1938), p. 6159.

28. J. E. Thigpen, Interview, 17 Sept. 1975. N.C. Director's Annual Report 1938, Halifax County Agent Report 1938, Extension Service Papers. AAA P.R. 1707–38, 1 May 1938, the AAA expected 40 million pounds to be sold in excess of quotas; in the end 80 million pounds were produced over the quota.

29. J. E. Thigpen, Interview, 17 Sept. 1975. Jones, Carteret, Craven County Agents' Reports 1938, Extension Service Papers. E. Y. Floyd to J. B. Hutson, 28 July 1938, J. E. Thigpen to H. D. Cooley, 28 July 1938, AAA (SC) Papers. AAA P.R. 1566–38, 8 April 1938; 198–39, 10 Aug. 1938.

30. Greenville *Daily Reflector*, 25 Aug. 1938. Lumberton *Robesonian*, 24 Aug. 1938. Craven, Wake, Carteret, Columbus County Agents' Reports 1938, Extension Service Papers.

31. Interview with J. E. Thigpen, 17 Sept. 1975. Interview with F. G. Bond, Jr., 24 Sept. 1975.

32. J. D. LeCron to J. C. Lanier, 10 Nov. 1938. Lanier to H. A. Wallace, 26 Oct. 1938, AAA (SC) Papers.

33. Lumberton *Robesonian*, 19, 22, 31 Aug. 1938. Greenville *Daily Reflector*, 25, 26 Aug. 1938. Smithfield *Herald*, 2 Sept. 1938. Greensboro *Daily News*, 13 Sept. 1938.

34. L. T. Weeks and E. Y. Floyd, *Producing and Marketing Flue-Cured Tobacco*, p. 73. Russell W. Bierman, *Flue-cured Tobacco*, p. 163.

35. Goldsboro *News Argus*, 5 Sept. 1938. Raleigh *News and Observer*, 7 Sept. 1938. Greensboro *Daily News*, 4 Sept. 1938.

36. Raleigh *News and Observer*, 3, 9 Sept. 1938. Greensboro *Daily News*, 10, 17 Sept. 1938. Rocky Mount *Herald*, 9 Sept. 1938.

37. Raleigh *News and Observer*, 5 Nov. 1938. Greensboro *Daily News*, 13 Nov. 1938.

38. Raleigh *News and Observer*, 11, 16 Nov. 1938. Greensboro *Daily News*, 15, 16, 19 Nov. 1938.

39. E. Y. Floyd to R. L. Pope, 7 Nov. 1938, Floyd to W. G. Finn, 8 Nov. 1938, AAA (AC) Papers.

40. Raleigh *News and Observer*, 26, 30 Nov., 1, 2 Dec. 1938. Greensboro *Daily News*, 2 Dec. 1938.

41. Raleigh *News and Observer*, 6 Dec. 1938. Speech, 7 Dec. 1938, Poe Papers. Corbitt, ed., *Addresses of Hoey*, pp. 468–69.

42. For Lanier see J. C. Lanier to L. C. Warren, 7 June, 16 Dec. 1938, E. G. Flanagan to Warren, 30 April 1938, Warren Papers.

43. J. B. Hutson to L. C. Warren, 23 Dec. 1938, AAA (SC) Papers. Vance County Agent Report 1939, Extension Service Papers.

44. Smithfield *Herald*, 29 Nov. 1938. Raleigh *News and Observer*, 1, 2 Dec. 1938.

45. Raleigh *News and Observer*, 3, 6 Nov., 2 Dec. 1938. Greensboro *Daily News*, 6

Nov., 5 Dec. 1938. John L. Shover, *Cornbelt Rebellion*, pp. 168–216. James C. Carey, "William Allen White and Dan D. Casement on Government Regulation," pp. 16–21. James C. Carey, "The Farmers' Independence Council of America," pp. 70–77. Sarah McCulloh Lemmon, "The Agricultural Policies of Eugene Talmadge," pp. 21–29. Michael S. Holmes, *The New Deal in Georgia*, pp. 224, 229, 232–33, 235–36. William Anderson, *The Wild Man of Sugar Creek*, pp. 111, 138, 140, 157.

46. AAA P.R. 1078–39, 30 Dec. 1938. Overall, 132,460 growers voted for control, 100,933 against. In North Carolina 88,222 voted for, 65,853 against.

47. Kinston *Daily Free Press*, 12 Dec. 1938. Greenville *Daily Reflector*, 12 Dec. 1938. Goldsboro *News Argus*, 12 Dec. 1938. Greensboro *Daily News*, 12 Dec. 1938. *Progressive Farmer*, Jan. 1939.

48. Don F. Hadwiger and Ross B. Talbot, *Pressure and Protest*, pp. 245–314.

49. Interviews, North Carolina, Joe Bean, Vernon Moore, The Johnsons, Federal Writers' Project Papers. J. B. Hutson, COHRC, p. 232.

50. W. Collins to J. D. Allman, 27 Dec. 1938, AAA (SC) Papers. J. C. Lanier to L. C. Warren, 16 Dec. 1938, Warren Papers. AAA P.R. 2081–38, 1 July 1938.

51. See maps 5 and 6. The Craven County agent, however, in his report for 1938, argued that it was the tenants who voted against control in defiance of their landlords, Extension Service Papers.

52. Edwin G. Nourse, John D. Black, and Joseph S. Davis, *Three Years of the Agricultural Adjustment Administration*, pp. 146–50.

Chapter 7. War Reaches North Carolina

1. Greensboro *Daily News*, 22 Dec. 1938, 4, 15, 26 Jan. 1939. Raleigh *News and Observer*, 29 Dec. 1938, 7, 15, 26 Jan. 1939.

2. Raleigh *News and Observer*, 26, 27 Jan. 1939. Greensboro *Daily News*, 26, 27 Jan. 1939. L. C. Warren to J. H. Blount, 15 Dec. 1938, Warren to E. F. Arnold, 21 Jan. 1939, Warren Papers.

3. Raleigh *News and Observer*, 27 April, 3 May 1939. Greensboro *Daily News*, 3 May 1939.

4. Raleigh *News and Observer*, 4, 11 May 1939. L. C. Warren to C. F. Cowell, 6 May 1939, Warren Papers. Greensboro *Daily News*, 11, 25 May 1939. The minimum limit for types of tobacco other than flue-cured was 2,400 pounds.

5. *CR*, vol. 84, 76th Cong., 1st sess. (1939), p. 8719.

6. J. W. Bailey to C. Goerch, 23 Jan. 1939, Bailey to S. H. Hobbs, Sr., 6 July 1939, Bailey to E. F. Arnold, 20 July 1939, 5, 16 Aug. 1939, Bailey Papers. *CR*, vol. 84, 76th Cong., 1st sess. (1939), p. 10294. Raleigh *News and Observer*, 2 Aug. 1939.

7. Raleigh *News and Observer*, 31 July 1939. *Progressive Farmer*, Sept. 1939.

8. E. W. Stone to J. W. Bailey, 31 July 1939, Bailey Papers. Greensboro *Daily News*, 3 April, 13, 15 July 1939.

9. Greensboro *Daily News*, 28 July 1939. Raleigh *News and Observer*, 1 Aug. 1939. Kinston *Daily Free Press*, 2 Aug. 1939.

10. Raleigh *News and Observer*, 5, 10 Aug. 1939. Greenville *Daily Reflector*, 5 Aug. 1939.
11. Kinston *Daily Free Press*, 31 Aug. 1939. Raleigh *News and Observer*, 1 Sept. 1939.
12. Raleigh *News and Observer*, 2 Sept. 1939. Kinston *Daily Free Press*, 6 Sept. 1939.
13. Raleigh *News and Observer*, 8, 9 Sept. 1939. L. T. Weeks and E. Y. Floyd, *Producing and Marketing Flue-Cured Tobacco*, pp. 69, 71.
14. Weeks and Floyd, *Producing and Marketing*, pp. 69, 71. *Progressive Farmer*, Nov. 1939.
15. Raleigh *News and Observer*, 9, 10 Sept. 1939.
16. Raleigh *News and Observer*, 10 Sept. 1939. J. B. Hutson, COHRC, pp. 249–52.
17. Raleigh *News and Observer*, 12, 13, 14 Sept. 1939. Greensboro *Daily News*, 14 Sept. 1939.
18. Josephus Daniels to Jonathan Daniels, 15 Sept. 1939, Jonathan Daniels Papers.
19. Raleigh *News and Observer*, 15, 29 Sept. 1939. J. W. Bailey to Editor, Raleigh *News and Observer*, 18 Sept. 1939, Bailey to F. D. Roosevelt, 18 Sept. 1939, Bailey to Lord Lothian, 25 Sept. 1939, Bailey to H. Hopkins, 25 Sept. 1939, F. D. Roosevelt to Bailey, 30 Sept. 1939, Bailey Papers. Greensboro *Daily News*, 19 Sept. 1939. For the general problems facing the British in financing supplies from the United States see H. Duncan Hall, *History of the Second World War: North American Supply*, pp. 55–59.
20. W. Kerr Scott to J. B. Hutson, 15 Sept. 1939, Hutson to Kerr Scott, 20 Sept. 1939, AAA (AC) Papers. Greenville *Daily Reflector*, 16 Sept. 1939. Greensboro *Daily News*, 25 Sept. 1939.
21. Raleigh *News and Observer*, 26 Sept. 1939. Greensboro *Daily News*, 26 Sept. 1939.
22. AAA P.R. 481–40, 13 Sept. 1939. Kinston *Daily Free Press*, 19 Sept. 1939. Greensboro *Daily News*, 26 Sept. 1939.
23. H. A. Wallace to growers, 16 Sept. 1939, Figures, Questions and Answers, enclosed by W. G. Finn to J. W. Bailey, 25 Sept. 1939, Bailey Papers. Raleigh *News and Observer*, 22, 23, 29 Sept. 1939.
24. Greensboro *Daily News*, 20, 28 Sept., 3 Oct. 1939.
25. Ibid., 26 Sept. 1939. Raleigh *News and Observer*, 26 Sept. 1939.
26. Raleigh *News and Observer*, 27, 30 Sept., 3 Oct. 1939. Greensboro *Daily News*, 28 Sept., 1, 2, 3, 4 Oct. 1939. "How Should Small Farmers Vote?," 1 Oct. 1939, Poe Papers.
27. David Leroy Corbitt, ed., *Addresses, Letters and Papers of Clyde Roark Hoey*, pp. 293–99.
28. Greensboro *Daily News*, 5 Oct. 1939. Wallace was reluctant to make this speech. He apparently had misgivings about appearing to dictate to the growers how they should vote. Interview with J. E. Thigpen, 22 Sept. 1976.
29. Raleigh *News and Observer*, 21, 22, 23, 27 Sept. 1939. Greensboro *Daily News*, 21, 22, 23, 27 Sept. 1939. Greenville *Daily Reflector*, 3 Oct. 1939. Jones, Stokes, Wake County Agents' Reports 1939, Extension Service Papers.
30. Greensboro *Daily News*, 26 Sept. 1939. Kinston *Daily Free Press*, 21, 27, 28

Sept. 1939. Greenville *Daily Reflector*, 26, 27, 28, 30 Sept., 2, 3 Oct. 1939. Wayne, Vance County Agents' Reports 1939, Extension Service Papers.

31. Raleigh *News and Observer*, 10, 21 Sept. 1939.

32. Ibid., 23 Sept. 1939. Greensboro *Daily News*, 27 Sept., 1 Oct. 1939.

33. Greensboro *Daily News*, 1 Oct. 1939. Raleigh *News and Observer*, 19 Sept. 1939.

34. Greenville *Daily Reflector*, 29 Sept. 1939. Raleigh *News and Observer*, 3, 5 Oct. 1939. Kinston *Daily Free Press*, 5 Oct. 1939.

35. Greensboro *Daily News*, 7 Oct. 1939. AAA P.R. 763–40, 2 Nov. 1939. Twenty thousand more growers voted in North Carolina than in December 1938. There was also an increase in participation in Virginia. This was not matched in the other states where most growers had already sold their tobacco. The North Carolina and Virginia growers had an immediate financial interest in the return of control. North Carolina growers voted 159,954 to 15,914 for control.

36. Greensboro *Daily News*, 10 Oct. 1939. Raleigh *News and Observer*, 12 Oct. 1939. Russell W. Bierman, *Flue-cured Tobacco*, p. 163.

37. Weeks and Floyd, *Producing and Marketing*, pp. 71–72. Joseph W. Hines, "Developments and Trends in the Export Trade in Flue-Cured Tobacco, 1939–50," pp. 87–88.

38. *CR*, vol. 86, 76th Cong., 3rd sess. (1940), p. 568. Greensboro *Daily News*, 20 Jan. 1940. C. Poe to L. C. Warren, 20 Jan. 1940, Warren Papers. Raleigh *News and Observer*, 11 Jan. 1940. *Progressive Farmer*, Feb. 1940.

39. Greensboro *Daily News*, 22 Feb. 1940. Raleigh *News and Observer*, 21, 28 Jan. 1940. For British awareness of the tobacco politicians' activities see Hall, *North American Supply*, pp. 83–84. Cordell Hull told the British Ambassador that senators from the tobacco states were crowding into his office to protest. As one British official wearily observed, "The farmers worry the representatives, the representatives worry the State Department, then the State Department worries us." See also William N. Medlicott, *History of the Second World War: The Economic Blockade*, 1: 351, 353, 375. *The State*, 3 Feb. 1940.

40. H. A. Wallace to L. C. Warren, 23 Jan. 1940, Warren Papers. Raleigh *News and Observer*, 25 Jan. 1940.

41. *Southern Tobacco Journal*, Nov. 1939. Greensboro *Daily News*, 10 Jan. 1940.

42. Greensboro *Daily News*, 10, 18, 21, 23 Feb. 1940. Raleigh *News and Observer*, 4 April 1940.

43. Raleigh *News and Observer*, 21 May 1940. L. C. Warren to H. D. Cooley, 20 May 1940, Warren Papers. J. W. Bailey to W. Woodruff, 6 April 1940, Bailey Papers. Cooley, who had been unopposed in 1936 and 1938, was fighting Major E. F. Griffin. Griffin was believed to be backed by the Pou family, seeking to avenge the defeat of George Ross Pou, who had been beaten by Cooley in the 1934 primary for the seat made vacant by the death of Pou's father. Tobacco congressmen, including Cooley, were unsuccessful later in the summer when they attempted to prevent a rise in the cigarette tax. Their efforts were thwarted by the government's need for additional revenue to meet defense appropriations.

44. Raleigh *News and Observer*, 19, 27 June 1940. Greensboro *Daily News*, 19 June, 11, 18, 19, 21 July 1940. Corbitt, ed., *Addresses of Hoey*, pp. 320, 326.

45. Wayne, Hertford, Moore County Agents' Reports 1940, Extension Service Papers.

46. Columbus County Agent Report 1940, Extension Service Papers. Raleigh *News and Observer*, 22 May 1940.
47. AAA P.R. 334–41, 27 Aug. 1940. Some 123,863 North Carolina growers voted for three-year control, 2,073 for one-year control, and 16,307 opposed any control.
48. AAA P.R. 251–41, 7 Aug. 1940. *Progressive Farmer*, Sept. 1940. Bierman, *Flue-cured Tobacco*, p. 163.
49. J. B. Hutson, COHRC, pp. 222–23.
50. Calvin B. Hoover and B. U. Ratchford, *Economic Resources and Policies of the South*, pp. 349–51.

Chapter 8. The Price of Prosperity

1. Interview with Selz Mayo, 26 Sept. 1975. Richard S. Kirkendall, "The New Deal and Agriculture," p. 106.
2. Russell W. Bierman, *Flue-cured Tobacco*, p. 163. United States Department of Agriculture, Agricultural Adjustment Administration, *Agricultural Adjustment, 1933–35*, p. 296.
3. Theodore Saloutos, "New Deal Agricultural Policy: An Evaluation," p. 398.
4. Ezra Taft Benson, *Cross Fire*, p. 416. L. T. Weeks and E. Y. Floyd, *Producing and Marketing Flue-Cured Tobacco*, pp. 74, 76. Joseph W. Hines, "Developments and Trends in the Export Trade," p. 74. Tobacco Associates, Incorporated, *Annual Report, 1964*, pp. 15, 17; *Annual Report, 1975*, pp. 12, 13.
5. A. Frank Bordeaux, Jr., and Russell H. Brannon, eds., *Social and Economic Issues Confronting the Tobacco Industry in the Seventies*, p. 264. Interview with Fred G. Bond, Jr., 24 Sept. 1975. Flue-Cured Tobacco Cooperative Stabilization Corporation, *Annual Report, 1975*, pp. 10–11.
6. Edwin G. Nourse, Joseph S. Davis, and John D. Black, *Three Years of the Agricultural Adjustment Administration*, p. 463. Interview with F. G. Bond, Jr., 24 Sept. 1975.
7. Bierman, *Flue-cured Tobacco*, p. 162. Charles M. Hardin, "The Tobacco Program: Exception or Portent," p. 920. Jonathan Daniels, *Tar Heels*, p. 87. In 1938 new farmers might be alloted 5 percent of the national quota. For 1939 the figure was reduced to 1 percent. By 1941 only 0.1 percent was available.
8. Calvin B. Hoover and B. U. Ratchford, *Economic Resources and Policies of the South*, p. 358. Frank Jeter, "New Way to Price Land." John E. Mason, "Acreage Allotments and Land Prices," pp. 176–81.
9. Donald H. Grubbs, *Cry from the Cotton*, pp. 19–26. David E. Conrad, *The Forgotten Farmers*, pp. 54–58, 66, 76–78.
10. J. A. Dickey to J. B. Hutson, 7 Nov. 1933, AAA (SC) Papers. Conrad, *Forgotten Farmers*, p. 199. Grubbs, *Cry from the Cotton*, p. 20, and Conrad, *Forgotten Farmers*, p. 60, mistakenly believed that the tobacco acreage-reduction contract for 1934–35 gave sharecroppers and tenants the right to share in all government payments including rental payments.
11. J. B. Hutson to C. C. Davis, 4 May 1934, AAA (SC) Papers. Pender, Stokes

County Agents' Reports 1935, Extension Service Papers. Robert E. Martin, "Negro-White Participation in the AAA Cotton and Tobacco Referenda in North and South Carolina," pp. 273–75. Interviews with F. S. Sloan and G. Capel, 2 Aug. 1974. C. Horace Hamilton, *Recent Changes in the Social and Economic Status of Farm Families in North Carolina*, pp. 104–107.

12. Raleigh *News and Observer*, 7 Feb. 1934, 18 Jan. 1935. Kinston *Daily Free Press*, 24 Feb. 1934. Paul E. Mertz, *New Deal Policy and Southern Rural Poverty*, p. 57. Gordon W. Blackwell, "The Displaced Tenant Farm Family in North Carolina," pp. 65–73. T. J. Woofter, Jr., *Landlord and Tenant on the Cotton Plantation*, pp. 155–56. Greensboro *Daily News*, 29 July 1935, 19 April 1938. Martin, "Negro-White Participation," p. 282.

13. J. W. Sanders to I. O. Schaub, 21 Feb. 1934, Schaub to C. W. Warburton, 26 Feb. 1934, Warburton to Schaub, 1 March 1934, Extension Service Papers. Raleigh *News and Observer*, 8 Feb. 1934, 18 Jan. 1935. Greensboro *Daily News*, 29 July 1935.

14. United States Department of Commerce, Bureau of the Census, *Statistical Abstract of the United States, 1934*, p. 551, *1941*, p. 682. Calvin B. Hoover, *Memoirs of Capitalism, Communism and Nazism*, pp. 156–57. Blackwell, "Displaced Tenant," p. 68. Hamilton, *Recent Changes*, pp. 98, 174. Mrs. J. Spicer to Mrs. A. O'Berry, 2 Nov. 1934, H. Spruill to Mrs. O'Berry, 6 Nov. 1934, North Carolina Emergency Relief Administration Papers. By 1937 C. Horace Hamilton was certain that the AAA "was definitely not to blame" for increased displacement of tenants and croppers. There were, he argued, considerable changes in tenure status in "normal" times, and in 1934 and 1935 most of that change was upward, with more laborers becoming croppers than croppers declining to laborers. It was in 1931 and 1932 that the changes in tenure status had been downward overall into the laborer class.

15. Hamilton, *Recent Changes*, p. 33. Blackwell, "Displaced Tenant," pp. 69–71. *Statistical Abstract, 1934*, p. 555, *1941*, p. 688.

16. *Progressive Farmer*, Feb. 1934, Feb. 1937. C. Poe to C. C. Davis and H. A. Wallace, 20 Jan. 1936, AAA (AC) Papers.

17. J. B. Hutson to C. Poe, 24 Jan. 1936, AAA (AC) Papers. J. B. Hutson, COHRC, pp. 142–43. Hamilton, *Recent Changes*, p. 98. The discrepancy between Hutson's figures, which demonstrated the large acreage cuts suffered by the large grower, and Hamilton's conclusions on the fate of the small owner-operator may be explained by the fact that 1934 acreage was compared by Hamilton to 1932 and by Hutson to 1933. In 1932 large farmers had abnormally small crops, since they found it difficult to finance their usual production. Small farmers could probably more easily maintain their customary acreage. Over the years, it has been shown that although the tobacco program disproportionately benefits the larger farmers, nevertheless small growers receive a greater share of the benefits of their program than producers of other commodities, J. T. Bonnen, "The Distribution of Benefits from Selected U.S. Farm Programs," pp. 488–97, 502–505.

18. Federal-State Crop Reporting Service, *North Carolina Farm Forecaster*, 1941.

19. Ibid. See Hamilton, *Recent Changes*, pp. 104–5, for increases in poultry, milk cows, and swine between 1932 and 1935 on the North Carolina farms he surveyed.

Richard S. Kirkendall, *Social Scientists and Farm Politics in the Age of Roosevelt*, pp. 164–92, provides an account of the development of the planning committees and a favorable assessment of their activities, but for doubts about their effectiveness at the local level and examples of lack of enthusiasm for organizing soil conservation districts in the Great Plains see Mary W. M. Hargraves, "Land-Use Planning in Response to Drought: The Experience of the Thirties," pp. 561–82. The demise of the planning committees during the war did prompt the Extension Service to develop the "neighborhood leader" program which in North Carolina attempted to involve 28,910 voluntary leaders in extension work, Program Planning Annual Report 1943, Extension Service Papers.

20. Leonard J. Arrington, "Western Agriculture and the New Deal," pp. 339, 341. U.S. House of Representatives, Committee on Agriculture, *Hearings on the Farm Security Administration*, 78th Cong., 1st sess. (1943), pp. 414–583, 610–11, 1086–91. Paul K. Conkin, *Tomorrow a New World: The New Deal Community Program*, pp. 277–93. Donald Holley, *Uncle Sam's Farmers*.

21. J. B. Hutson, COHRC, pp. 121–22.

22. Ibid., pp. 128–29. Hutson mistakenly placed the incident of the market opening in 1934. North Carolina Department of Agriculture, *North Carolina Tobacco Report, 1974–75*, p. 4.

23. J. B. Hutson, COHRC, p. 134. Interview with J. E. Thigpen, 22 Sept. 1976.

24. Hardin, "Exception or Portent," p. 925.

25. Ibid., pp. 926–32. Calvin B. Hoover and B. U. Ratchford, *Economic Resources*, pp. 351–56. Robert Charles Brooks, "Development of Flue-Cured Tobacco Programs, 1933–56," pp. 39–52. J. C. Williamson, Jr., and W. D. Toussaint, "Parity and Support Prices for Flue-Cured Tobacco," pp. 13–26.

26. Greensboro *Daily News*, 3 Aug. 1933. Jonathan Daniels, *Tar Heels*, p. 87.

27. Josephus Daniels to Jonathan Daniels, 15 Sept. 1939, Jonathan Daniels Papers.

28. J. H. Kerr to Democratic National Congressional Committee, 7 June 1935, Kerr Papers. For a fuller discussion of the relation of the North Carolina congressmen to the New Deal see Anthony J. Badger, "The New Deal and North Carolina: The Tobacco Program, 1933–1940," pp. 125–55.

29. Raleigh *News and Observer*, 3 Feb. 1938.

30. For Wallace on "economic democracy" see Henry A. Wallace, *New Frontiers*, pp. 263–68, Howard Zinn, ed., *New Deal Thought*, p. 237, and Donald C. Blaisdell, *Government and Agriculture*, p. 166. For criticisms of the grass roots approach see Roscoe C. Martin, *Grass Roots*, pp. 18–19, Philip Selznick, *TVA and the Grass Roots*, pp. 219–26, and R. G. Tugwell and E. C. Banfield, "Grass-Roots Democracy—Myth or Reality?," pp. 47–55.

31. Jonathan Daniels, *Tar Heels*, pp. 80–81. C. F. Cowell to J. C. B. Ehringhaus, 3 March 1936, Governors' Papers (E). *CR*, vol. 82, 75th Cong., 2nd sess. (1937), p. 1429. U.S. Senate, Committee on Agriculture, *Agricultural Adjustment Act of 1937: Hearings*, 75th Cong., 1st sess. (1937), p. 61.

32. J. B. Hutson, COHRC, p. 134.

33. Henry I. Richards, *Cotton under the AAA*, pp. 78–79. Chowan County Agent Report 1933, Extension Service Papers. On the rarity of black community committeemen even where blacks constituted an overwhelming majority of the

farmers see Ralph J. Bunche, *The Political Status of the Negro in the Age of FDR*, pp. 507–13.

34. Martin, ''Negro-White Participation,'' pp. 258–73.

35. Ibid., pp. 259–60. Louis Cantor, *A Prologue to the Protest Movement*, p. 22. Lists which enable comparisons to be made between committees for more than one year survive for sixteen counties.

36. Interview with J. E. Thigpen, 22 Sept. 1976. Raleigh *News and Observer*, 26 Nov. 1938.

37. AAA P.R. 1381–38, 7 March 1938. C. M. Hardin, ''Exception or Portent,'' p. 934.

38. Zinn, ed., *New Deal Thought*, pp. 237–38.

39. Martin, ''Negro-White Participation,'' pp. 229–41. For the generally high turnouts in tobacco referenda compared with votes in other commodities see L. V. Howard, ''The Agricultural Referendum,'' p. 22. For the particularly high turnout of North Carolina growers see Martin, ''Negro-White Participation,'' pp. 105–26.

40. Martin, ''Negro-White Participation,'' pp. 243–54, 289–90. For similar conclusions about indirect pressure, black participation, white acquiescence, and the hint of a change in racial attitudes see Bunche, *Political Status*, pp. 505–15. For an example of indirect pressure in the Bankhead Act referendum see Arthur F. Raper, *Preface to Peasantry*, p. 250. Not all North Carolina blacks were happy about the AAA, as Sam Hite complained, ''De committee in dis township cut de nigger and de pore white farmer down to where he didn't have nothing left. But de committee had more tobacco den dey ever had before. Dey wouldn't let niggers be on de acre committee, so we had no chance.'' North Carolina, Interview, Federal Writers' Project Papers.

41. Howard, ''The Agricultural Referendum,'' p. 24. AAA P.R. 1402–38, 11 March 1938. Greensboro *Daily News*, 4 March 1938.

42. Barton J. Bernstein, ''The New Deal: The Conservative Achievement of Liberal Reform,'' pp. 269–70.

43. Conrad, *Forgotten Farmers*, p. 206. See also Grubbs, *Cry from the Cotton*, pp. 60–61.

44. J. B. Hutson, COHRC, pp. 144–45.

45. Paul K. Conkin, *The New Deal*, p. 42. Van L. Perkins, *Crisis in Agriculture*, pp. 8–9.

46. Grubbs, *Cry from the Cotton*, p. 61. Cantor, *Prologue to Protest*, p. 154.

47. Sidney Baldwin, *Poverty and Politics*, p. 260.

48. James MacGregor Burns in *Deadlock of Democracy*, pp. 151–76, argues that the opportunity for party realignment existed in the 1930s. James T. Patterson effectively refutes this both in *Congressional Conservatism and the New Deal*, pp. 251–87, and in *The New Deal and the States*, pp. 168–93.

Bibliography

A Note on Sources

The Governors' Papers in Raleigh are a rich source for any student of the New Deal in North Carolina, and they throw considerable light on the development of the tobacco program. Governor O. Max Gardner's papers highlight the futility of the various attempts to form marketing cooperatives and to control acreage by individual state action before 1933. Those of his successor, J. C. B. Ehringhaus, fully document Ehringhaus's role as a leader in the fight for better tobacco prices. They are naturally fullest on the marketing crisis of 1933 and the controversy over an interstate compact in 1936, but they touch on all aspects of the tobacco program. This detail is typical of the wealth of material the collection contains on the state's relations with New Deal agencies and is conspicuously absent from the papers of Governor Clyde Hoey. Unlike his predecessor, Hoey had little political interest in the fortunes of the tobacco growers, and his whole style of government was more leisurely. He willingly delegated responsibility, and his papers reveal his lack of supervision and knowledge of the day-to-day running of the state government, as well as his overall opposition to the New Deal. The papers of the state agency that perhaps had the most contact with the federal government, the North Carolina Emergency Relief Administration, contain a good deal of material on the possibilities of the rehabilitation of rural relief clients. The survey of county relief directors in late 1934 is particularly helpful in assessing the extent of the problem of tenant displacement.

Of the twelve congressmen who represented North Carolina's flue-cured growing districts between 1933 and 1940, eight have left papers. Of these, those of Edward W. Pou and Carl T. Durham can safely be ignored. There are only a few miscellaneous items in the Pou collection and nothing of note for 1933 and 1934, while Durham's papers have very little on his first two years in Congress, 1939 and 1940, and nothing about tobacco. Despite the vast bulk of Robert Doughton's papers, their value is also minimal. His letters provide ample evidence of the close attention to constituency affairs that enabled him to stay so long in the House. Most of them deal with local patronage questions, particularly postmasterships, and they reveal next to nothing about the activities of the Ways and Means Committee and the development of the New Deal legislation that went through it. There is some material on tobacco taxation, and there is also a constant barrage of letters from S. Clay Williams giving the tobacco manufacturers' views of New Deal business policies in general.

Graham Barden's papers are more rewarding, if only for the collection of newspaper clippings that illustrate both the bizarre primary contests in the third district and Barden's attempts to fight wage-hour legislation and to curb the powers of the National Labor Relations Board. His correspondence is most useful for the reaction to tobacco grading legislation. The papers of the man he defeated, Charles L. Abernethy, reveal little more than the constant struggle against debt that was fought by both Abernethy and his son throughout the 1930s. Tobacco scarcely appears except for the evidence of dissatisfaction with control which C. L. Abernethy, Jr., attempted to exploit in 1938 in his second primary battle against Barden.

None of these congressmen played a prominent role in the drive for tobacco legislation. The papers of Harold Cooley, however, who held a key position in formulating legislation on the House Agriculture Committee, are a keen disappointment. The late Thomas A. Banks, a former political associate of Cooley's, expressed surprise to me that any of Cooley's papers survived, since he understood that they had all been burnt. All that remains in the Southern Historical Collection at Chapel Hill strongly suggests that the most important papers have indeed been destroyed. It is known, for example, that Cooley wrote to two hundred leading growers in his district to find out their views on the Flanagan grading bill, but neither his letter nor any of the replies survive. We are left with a few tantalizing glimpses of his political links in his constituency in 1935 and 1936 and some printed material from his 1940 primary campaign.

The most important therefore of the congressional papers are those of Lindsay Warren and John Kerr. Kerr's papers are particularly valuable for his role in the passage of the Kerr-Smith Act and the drive for the interstate compact in 1936. They are less interesting and full in those years when he was not fighting a primary campaign and in the years after 1936 as a whole. Warren's papers are even more valuable on purely tobacco matters, such as his efforts to protect small farmers, the controversy over grading legislation, and the development of the 1938 Farm Act. His correspondence throws light also on the activities and attitudes of Con Lanier and on the political background of the men in Pitt County who were so active in the formation of the Farm Bureau. Warren had written a history of his home town and seems to have been aware that historians would use his papers. He thus annotated a number of letters to place them in context and also dictated for the record a memorandum of a revealing private conversation with Speaker William Bankhead immediately after Roosevelt's announcement of the Court-packing plan.

Senator Bailey's papers match those of Robert Doughton in bulk but are much more informative. The senator could not resist the urge to explain his position on policy matters in lengthy, closely argued statements. His letters therefore contain many detailed expositions of his views on agricultural legislation, but they also reveal the constituency pressure that forced him to modify his anti-New Deal stance. At the same time, his opposition to compulsion attracted letters from articulate small farmers whose cause he championed, and his papers are particularly useful for the complaints and ideas of the opponents of control. The other North Carolina senator, Robert Reynolds, had no interest in tobacco and left no papers of any substance.

In addition to the state's politicians a number of North Carolina newspaper editors left useful manuscript collections. Jonathan Daniels of the Raleigh *News and Observer* did not merely comment on the tobacco program; he was an active participant in the mass meetings and policy discussions. His papers document this role, but they are less revealing in 1937 and 1938 when he was busy writing *A Southerner Discovers the South*. His father, Josephus Daniels, had played a similar role in the tobacco growers' struggle before 1933 and kept an anxious eye on their progress even after he went to Mexico City as ambassador. Although his correspondence reveals the tenacity of his suspicions of the tobacco manufacturers, particularly Clay Williams, they tell more about his wide political contacts throughout the United States and his enthusiastic support of Roosevelt than about the tobacco program and local state politics. The papers of Santford Martin, editor of the Winston-Salem *Journal*, are a valuable source for antimachine politics in the state but have nothing on tobacco. Of all the state's journalists, Clarence Poe of the *Progressive Farmer* ought to have left the most interesting papers. He was an inveterate correspondent on all matters relating to agriculture, but for evidence of that we have to rely on the letters that survive in the collections of their recipients. His own papers in Raleigh are extremely thin, containing only a few mimeographed items from the 1930s. There is a small amount of material on the tobacco politics of the 1930s in the East Carolina Manuscript Collection at Greenville. The papers of Richard T. Fountain, anti-organization candidate for governor in 1932, focus mainly on the period before 1933, but they do provide a little material on his 1936 race against Senator Bailey. Frank M. Wooten, Sr., a Greenville attorney, has left correspondence that emphasizes the breakdown of rural credit from 1929 onward. The papers of the Tapp-Jenkins Company, who were warehousemen and leaf dealers, cast some light on 1938–40 market conditions in a series of reports to one of their Danish customers. The J. Con Lanier Papers concentrate on the period after 1940.

The records of the farm organizations in North Carolina are scanty for this period. The records of the state Grange were destroyed in a fire, while those of the North Carolina Farm Bureau did not survive the various changes of headquarters made by the organization in its early years. There is no trace of any material of the North Carolina Tobacco Growers' Association. The situation is slightly better for the Extension Service. Official records have not survived at North Carolina State University, and there is nothing of value for the 1930s in the papers of Dean Schaub there. The Extension Service papers in the National Archives, however, do contain the annual reports of the county agents and other extension officials (available on microfilm at the North Carolina State University Library) and files of correspondence between the national director of extension and the Raleigh extension office. The agents' reports are often very limited formal statements that devote more attention to the results of their demonstration work than to their AAA activities. Nevertheless, valuable information can be gleaned from them on the difficulties the agents faced in implementing a control program and the attitude of the growers. The director's file of correspondence is particularly useful for Dean Schaub's awareness of the tensions between the traditional educational role of the Extension Service and its new regulatory function.

At the national level the basic source for the tobacco program is the Agricultural Adjustment Administration papers in the National Archives. These are arranged in part by subject, in part by the name of the correspondent. In the summer of 1933 most of the correspondence regarding the tobacco program found its way into the subject files, thereby giving a clear and coherent account of the development of the program up to and through the marketing crisis. After 1933, however, most of the material has to be found in the files arranged alphabetically by name of the correspondent. Finding such material is a matter of luck, looking for files of people who might have written to the AAA about tobacco. In addition, the central filing system did not necessarily catch all material relating to tobacco or specific individuals, and Hutson himself was little interested in keeping formal records. There are therefore no files or minutes for the meetings of the various growers' advisory committees which Hutson considered so important and which took up so much of his time. For information about these committee meetings we have to rely on occasional references in letters from Hutson and Claude Hall, accounts in the press, and the official press releases of the AAA. These last are also a convenient way of following the official policy decisions in the tobacco program from 1933 to 1940. There is a small amount of material on tobacco in the papers of the Secretary of Agriculture, and there is some reference to the question of tobacco taxes in the Roosevelt press conferences and the diary of Henry Morgenthau in the Roosevelt Library at Hyde Park.

The Oral History Research Center at Columbia University contains one essential source for the tobacco program: an interview with John B. Hutson, chief of the AAA's tobacco section. The interviews with L. J. Taber, M. Ezekiel, M. Jones, and H. R. Tolley are of general interest for New Deal agricultural policy, and all have some specific reference to tobacco. The interview with J. Con Lanier at the East Carolina Manuscript Collection is brief, but it does provide some colorful impressions of the personalities with whom Lanier worked in the short time he spent in the tobacco section.

My own interviews with James E. Thigpen were particularly useful for the technical problems that arose in administering the program in 1938. Thigpen was responsible for the detailed technical provisions then and also spent a considerable amount of time in the field helping local officials interpret the program. Interviews with officials of the Department of Agriculture, the Stabilization Corporation, and Tobacco Associates gave me a better understanding of the post-1940 tobacco program. Fred Sloan of the Extension Service provided an account of a county and district agent's work in the 1930s and recollections of Dean Schaub. Joseph G. Knapp recalled the abortive attempts to launch the tobacco cooperative in 1930–31, and Gladys Baker had some distinct memories of J. B. Hutson.

A student based permanently in the United States would have done more newspaper reading than I managed, but it is not clear that more newspaper consultation would have yielded much more significant information. The Raleigh *News and Observer* and the Greensboro *Daily News* were used for every day in the period and provided the basic information for the tobacco program. Given the geographical location of the Asheville *Citizen* and the Charlotte *Observer*, it is not surprising that they added nothing to an account of tobacco developments, but it is rather disappointing that the Winston-Salem *Journal* and the Durham *Morning Herald* provided nothing that could not be found in the Raleigh and Greensboro papers. The Kinston, Greenville, and Goldsboro papers covered the local operation of the program. Kinston and Greenville were two of the three major markets in the Eastern Belt; it was only possible to make substantial use of the newspaper of the third, the Wilson *Daily Times*, for 1938 because of the dilapidated condition of its files before that. Other local newspapers in the tobacco belt were consulted for the dramatic local events of 1938.

Of the magazines and periodicals, *The State* contributed colorful sidelights on the local politicians and miscellaneous aspects of North Carolina life. The *Southern Tobacco Journal* gave the viewpoint of the tobacco trade—the warehousemen and leaf dealers—while the Virginia-Carolinas edition of the *Progressive Farmer* served as Clarence Poe's mouthpiece and as a forum for the various farm organizations. The *Extension Farm News* was a "house journal" for the state Extension Service and occasionally unwittingly revealed the prejudices of extension officials.

The limitations of these various sources are obvious. Although the intention of this book has been to study a New Deal program in operation at both the national and local levels, it has reached down at the local level only to the grass tops not the grass roots. This is adequate for a study of policy making, but a number of questions, particularly about the impact of the tobacco program on small farmers, tenants, and croppers, cannot be satisfactorily answered at that level. These problems probably need the attention of a social historian. Case studies of two or three North Carolina counties might answer them. Such studies could take as their model Arthur Raper's examination of the impact of the depression and New Deal programs on the social and economic power structure of two Georgia counties in *Preface to Peasantry*. The evidence for such studies is likely now to prove elusive. Nevertheless, Robert E. Martin's Ph.D. dissertation, "Negro-White Participation in the AAA Cotton and Tobacco Referenda in North and South Carolina," based on six hundred interviews in 1945 and 1946, provides glimpses of the rich possible rewards, as do the transcripts on interviews of North Carolina farmers carried out by the Federal Writers' Project, some of which have been printed by Tom E. Terrill and Jerrold Hirsch in *Such as Us: Southern Voices of the Thirties*. Terrill and Hirsch have selected some excellent examples of paternalist landlord attitudes, of tenant farmer resentment, both black and white, and of the sheer unremitting toil that goes into tobacco growing. The transcripts of interviews in the Southern Historical Collection are particularly interesting, because they were carried out in 1938 and 1939 and thus reveal the whole gamut of complaints about the operation of control from small farmer doubts about the fairness of the local administration to Republican denunciations of the principle of control. It may well be that systematic oral history now represents the best chance of recapturing the tenant and sharecropper experience of the 1930s.

Manuscript Collections

Chapel Hill, N.C. Southern Historical Collection, University of North Carolina.
Papers of James O. Carr. Papers of Harold D. Cooley. Papers of Jonathan Daniels. Papers of Robert L. Doughton. Papers of Carl T. Durham. Papers of

the Federal Writers' Project. Papers of John H. Kerr. Papers of Lindsay C. Warren.

Durham, N.C. Duke University Library. Papers of Charles L. Abernethy. Papers of Josiah W. Bailey. Papers of Graham A. Barden. Papers of Santford Martin.

Greenville, N.C. East Carolina Manuscript Collection, East Carolina University. Papers of Richard T. Fountain. Papers of the Tapp-Jenkins Company. Papers of Frank M. Wooten, Sr.

Raleigh, N.C. North Carolina State Department of Archives and History. Papers of the Governors—O. Max Gardner, J. C. B. Ehringhaus, and Clyde R. Hoey. Papers of Clarence Poe. Papers of Edward W. Pou.

Raleigh, N.C. North Carolina State Records Center. Papers of the North Carolina Emergency Relief Administration.

Hyde Park, N.Y. Franklin D. Roosevelt Library. Papers of Henry Morgenthau. Papers of Franklin D. Roosevelt. Press Conferences of Franklin D. Roosevelt.

Washington, D.C. Library of Congress. Papers of Josephus Daniels.

Washington, D.C. National Archives. Papers of the Agricultural Adjustment Administration, Record Group 145. Papers of the Extension Service, Record Group 33. Papers of the Secretary of Agriculture, Record Group 16.

Interviews

Oral History Research Center, Columbia University, New York. Interviews of Mordecai Ezekiel, John B. Hutson, Marvin Jones, Louis J. Taber, Howard R. Tolley.

East Carolina Manuscript Collection, East Carolina University, Greenville, N.C. Interview of J. Con Lanier.

Interviews with the author: Gladys L. Baker, 17 Sept. 1975; Fred G. Bond, Jr., 24 Sept. 1975; George C. Capel, 2 Aug. 1974; E. Shelton Griffin, 22 Sept. 1975; Joseph G. Knapp, 17 Sept. 1975; Selz Mayo, 26 Sept. 1975; James E. Thigpen, 17 Sept. 1975, 22 Sept. 1976; Joseph P. Todd, 16 Sept. 1975; Fred Sloan, 2 Aug. 1974.

Newspapers and Periodicals

Extension Farm News, 1929–40
Franklin *Times*, 1938
Goldsboro *News Argus*, 1933–40
Greensboro *Daily News*, 1933–40
Greenville *Daily Reflector*, 1933–40
Kinston *Daily Free Press*, 1933–40
Lumberton *Robesonian*, 1938
New York Times, 1937–38
North Carolina Farm Forecaster, 1933–41
Progressive Farmer, 1930–40
Raleigh *News and Observer*, 1929–40

Reidsville *Review*, 1938
Rocky Mount *Herald*, 1938
Smithfield *Herald*, 1938
Southern Tobacco Journal, 1933–40
The State, 1933–40
Wilson *Daily Times*, 1938

Government Publications

North Carolina Department of Agriculture. *Biennial Report*. Raleigh, 1932–40.
_____. *North Carolina Tobacco Report, 1974–75*. Raleigh, 1975.
United States Congress. *Congressional Record*, vols. 77–86, 73rd to 76th Cong.,
    1933–40.
_____. House, Committee on Ways and Means, *Tobacco Taxes: Hearings*, 73rd
    Cong., 2nd sess., 1934.
_____. House, *Reports No. 1745 Kerr Tobacco Control Bill*, 73rd Cong., 2nd sess.,
    1934.
_____. House, Committee on Agriculture, *Hearings on the Farm Security Adminis-
    tration*, 78th Cong., 1st sess., 1943.
_____. Senate, Committee on Agriculture, *Agricultural Adjustment Act of 1937:
    Hearings*, 75th Cong., 1st sess., 1937.
United States Department of Agriculture. *Yearbook of Agriculture, 1930*. Washington,
    1930.
_____. *Yearbook of Agriculture, 1935*. Washington, 1935.
United States Department of Agriculture, Agricultural Adjustment Administration.
    *Agricultural Adjustment: A Report on the Agricultural Adjustment Administra-
    tion, May 1933 to Feb. 1934*. Washington, 1934.
_____. *Agricultural Adjustment in 1934: A Report of the Administration of the
    Agricultural Adjustment Act, 15 Feb. 1934 to 31 Dec. 1934*. Washington,
    1935.
_____. *Agricultural Adjustment, 1933–35. A Report of the Administration of the
    Agricultural Adjustment Act, 12 May 1933 to 31 Dec. 1935*. Washington,
    1936.
_____. *Agricultural Conservation, 1936. A Report of the Agricultural Adjustment
    Administration under the Provisions of the Agricultural Adjustment Act and the
    Soil Conservation and Domestic Allotment Act and Related Legislation from 1
    Jan. 1936 to 31 Dec. 1936*. Washington, 1937.
_____. *Agricultural Adjustment, 1937–38. A Report of the Activities Carried on by
    the Agricultural Adjustment Administration under the Provision of the Agricul-
    tural Adjustment Act of 1938, the Soil Conservation and Domestic Allotment
    Act, the Marketing Act of 1937, the Sugar Act of 1937, and Related
    Legislation, from 1 Jan. 1937 through 30 June 1938*. Washington, 1939.
_____. *Agricultural Adjustment, 1938–39. A Report of the Activities Carried on by
    the Agricultural Adjustment Administration, 1 July 1938 through 30 June 1939*.
    Washington, 1939.

————. *Agricultural Adjustment, 1939–40. A Report of the Activities of the Agricultural Adjustment Administration, 1 July 1939 through 30 June 1940.* Washington, 1940.
United States Department of Commerce, Bureau of the Census. *Fifteenth Census of the United States.* Washington, 1931.
————. *Sixteenth Census of the United States.* Washington, 1943.
————. *Statistical Abstract of the United States.* Washington, 1934–42.
United States Federal Farm Board. *Second Annual Report of the Federal Farm Board for the Year ending 30 June 1931.* Washington, 1931.

Secondary Works

Albertson, Dean. *Roosevelt's Farmer: Claude Wickard in the New Deal.* New York: Columbia University Press, 1961.
Anderson, William. *The Wild Man of Sugar Creek: The Political Career of Eugene Talmadge.* Baton Rouge: Louisiana State University Press, 1975.
Arrington, Leonard J. "Western Agriculture and the New Deal." *Agricultural History* 44 (1970): 337–53.
Badger, Anthony J. "The New Deal and North Carolina: The Tobacco Program, 1933–1940." Ph.D. dissertation, University of Hull, 1974.
Baker, Gladys L. *The County Agent.* Chicago: University of Chicago Press, 1939.
Baldwin, Sidney. *Poverty and Politics: The Rise and Decline of the Farm Security Administration.* Chapel Hill: University of North Carolina Press, 1968.
Benedict, Murray R. *Farm Policies of the United States, 1790–1950: A Study of Their Origins and Development.* New York: Twentieth Century Fund, 1953.
Benedict, Murray R.; and Stine, Oscar C. *The Agricultural Commodity Programs: Two Decades of Experience.* New York: Twentieth Century Fund, 1956.
Benson, Ezra Taft. *Cross-Fire: The Eight Years with Eisenhower.* New York: Doubleday, 1962.
Bernstein, Barton J. "The New Deal: The Conservative Achievements of Liberal Reform." In *Towards a New Past: Dissenting Essays in American History,* edited by Barton J. Bernstein, pp. 263–68. New York: Pantheon, 1967.
Bierman, Russell W. *Flue-cured Tobacco: An Economic Survey.* Richmond: Federal Reserve Bank of Richmond, 1952.
Blackwell, Gordon W. "The Displaced Tenant Farm Family in North Carolina." *Social Forces* 13 (1934): 65–73.
Blaisdell, Donald C. *Government and Agriculture: The Growth of Federal Farm Aid.* New York: Farrar and Rinehart, 1940.
Block, William J. *The Separation of the Farm Bureau and the Extension Service: Political Issue in a Federal System.* Urbana: University of Illinois Press, 1960.
Bonnen, James T. "The Distribution of Benefits from Selected U.S. Farm Programs." In National Advisory Commission on Rural Poverty, *Rural Poverty in the United States.* Washington, 1968.
Bordeaux, A. Frank., Jr.; and Brannon, Russell H., eds. *Social and Economic Issues Confronting the Tobacco Industry in the Seventies.* Lexington: University of Kentucky, 1972.

Brooks, Robert Charles. "The Development of Flue-cured Tobacco Programs, 1933–1956." M.Sc. thesis, North Carolina State College, 1958.

Bunche, Ralph J. *The Political Status of the Negro in the Age of FDR*. Chicago: University of Chicago Press, 1973.

Burns, James MacGregor. *The Deadlock of Democracy: Four-Party Politics in America*. Englewood Cliffs: Prentice-Hall, 1963.

Campbell, Christiana McFadyen. *The Farm Bureau and the New Deal: A Study in the Making of National Farm Policy, 1933–1940*. Urbana: University of Illinois, 1962.

Cantor, Louis. *Prologue to Protest: The Missouri Sharecroppers' Roadside Demonstration of 1939*. Durham: Duke University Press, 1969.

Carey, James C. "William Allen White and Dan D. Casement on Government Regulation." *Agricultural History* 33 (1959): 16–21.

_____. "The Farmers' Independence Council of America." *Agricultural History* 35 (1961): 70–77.

Conkin, Paul K. *The New Deal*. London: Routledge, Kegan and Paul, 1968.

_____. *Tomorrow a New World: The New Deal Community Program*. Ithaca: Cornell University Press, 1959.

Conrad, David E. *The Forgotten Farmers: The Story of Sharecroppers in the New Deal*. Urbana: University of Illinois Press, 1965.

Corbitt, David Leroy, ed. *Public Papers and Letters of Oliver Max Gardner, Governor of North Carolina, 1929–1933*. Raleigh: Council of State of North Carolina, 1937.

_____. *Addresses, Letters and Papers of Clyde Roark Hoey, Governor of North Carolina, 1937–41*. Raleigh: Council of State of North Carolina, 1944.

_____. *Addresses, Letters and Papers of John Christoph Blucher Ehringhaus, Governor of North Carolina, 1933–37*. Raleigh: Council of State of North Carolina, 1950.

Covington, R. Lee. *Banking and Tobacco in North Carolina*. New Brunswick: Rutgers University Press, 1944.

Cox, Reavis. *Competition in the American Tobacco Industry, 1911–1932: A Study of the Effects of the Partition of the American Tobacco Company by the United States Supreme Court*. New York: Columbia University Press, 1933.

Cronon, E. David. "Josephus Daniels as a Reluctant Candidate." *North Carolina Historical Review* 33 (1956): 457–82.

Cyrus, J. H.; and Hedrick, W. P. *The Tobacco Story*. Raleigh: North Carolina Department of Agriculture, n.d.

Daniel, James C. "The North Carolina Tobacco Marketing Crisis of 1933." *North Carolina Historical Review* 41 (1964): 370–82.

Daniels, Jonathan. *Tar Heels: A Portrait of North Carolina*. New York: Dodd, Mead, 1941.

Davis, Joseph S. *Wheat and the AAA*. Washington: Brookings Institution, 1935.

Durden, Robert F. *The Dukes of Durham, 1865–1929*. Durham: Duke University Press, 1975.

Emory, Samuel T. *Bright Tobacco in the Agriculture, Industry, and Foreign Trade of North Carolina*. Chicago: University of Chicago Press, 1939.

Fite, Gilbert C. *George N. Peek and the Fight for Farm Parity*. Norman: University of Oklahoma, 1954.

_____. "Farmer Opinion and the Agricultural Adjustment Act, 1933." *Mississippi Valley Historical Review* 48 (1962): 656–73.

Flue-Cured Tobacco Cooperative Stabilization Corporation. *Annual Report, 1974–1975*. Raleigh, 1975.

Garner, Wightman Wells. *The Production of Tobacco*. Philadelphia: Blakiston, 1951.

Grubbs, Donald H. *Cry from the Cotton: The Southern Tenant Farmers' Union and the New Deal*. Chapel Hill: University of North Carolina Press, 1971.

Hadwiger, Don F. *Federal Wheat Commodity Programs*. Ames: Iowa State University Press, 1970.

Hadwiger, Don F.; and Talbot, Ross B. *Pressure and Protest: The Kennedy Farm Program and the Wheat Referendum of 1963*. San Francisco: Chandler, 1965.

Hall, H. Duncan. *History of the Second World War: North American Supply*. London: Her Majesty's Stationery Office, 1955.

Hamilton, C. Horace. *Recent Changes in the Social and Economic Status of Farm Families in North Carolina*. Raleigh: North Carolina Agricultural Experiment Station Bulletin no. 309, 1937.

Hanna, John. "Agricultural Cooperation in Tobacco." *Law and Contemporary Problems* 1 (1934): 292–324.

Hardin, Charles M. "The Tobacco Program: Exception or Portent?" *Journal of Farm Economics* 28 (1946): 920–37.

Hargraves, Mary W. M. "Land-Use Planning in Response to Drought: The Experience of the Thirties." *Agricultural History* 50 (1976): 561–82.

Hawks, S. N., Jr. *Principles of Flue-Cured Tobacco Production*. Raleigh: North Carolina State University, 1978.

Hines, Joseph W. "Developments and Trends in the Export Trade in Flue-Cured Tobacco, 1939–50, with Special Emphasis on the Role of the United States Government in Grants and Loans." M.A. thesis, University of North Carolina, 1951.

Holley, Donald. *Uncle Sam's Farmers: The New Deal Communities in the Lower Mississippi Valley*. Urbana: University of Illinois Press, 1975.

Holmes, Michael S. *The New Deal in Georgia: An Administrative History*. Westport: Greenwood Press, 1975.

Hoover, Calvin B. *Memoirs of Capitalism, Communism, and Nazism*. Durham: Duke University Press, 1965.

Hoover, Calvin B.; and Ratchford, B. U. *Economic Resources and Policies of the South*. New York: Macmillan, 1951.

Howard, L. V. "The Agricultural Referendum." *Public Administration Review* 2 (1942): 9–26.

Hunter, Robert F. "The AAA between Neighbors: Virginia, North Carolina, and the New Deal Farm Program." *Journal of Southern History* 44 (1978): 537–70.

Jackson, Elmo L. *The Pricing of Cigarette Tobaccos: A Study of the Process of Price Developments in the Flue-Cured and Burley Auction Markets*. Gainesville: University of Florida Press, 1955.

Jeter, Frank. "New Way to Price Land." *Farm Journal*, Oct. 1945.

Key, V. O., Jr. *Southern Politics in State and Nation*. New York: Knopf, 1949.

Kirkendall, Richard S. *Social Scientists and Farm Politics in the Age of Roosevelt*. Columbia: University of Missouri Press, 1967.

————. "The New Deal and Agriculture." in *The New Deal*, edited by John Braeman, Robert Bremner, and David Brody, vol. 1, *The National Level*, pp. 83–109. Columbus: Ohio State University Press, 1975.

Knapp, Joseph G. *The Advance of American Cooperative Enterprise, 1920–1945*. Danville: Interstate Printers and Publishers, 1973.

————, and Paramore, L. R. "Flue-cured Tobacco Developments under the AAA." *Law and Contemporary Problems* 1 (1934): 325–48.

Lambert, Charles R. "New Deal Experiments in Production Control: The Livestock Program, 1933–1935." Ph.D. dissertation, University of Oklahoma, 1962.

Larson, Grace H; and Erdman, Henry E. "Aaron Sapiro: Genius of Farm Cooperative Promotion." *Mississippi Valley Historical Review* 49 (1962): 242–68.

Lefler, Hugh T.; and Newsome, Albert R. *North Carolina: The History of a Southern State*. Chapel Hill: University of North Carolina Press, 1963.

Lemert, Ben F. *The Tobacco Manufacturing Industry in North Carolina*. Raleigh: National Youth Administration of North Carolina, 1939.

Lemmon, Sarah McCulloh. "The Agricultural Policies of Eugene Talmadge." *Agricultural History* 28 (1954): 21–29.

Leuchtenburg, William E. *Flood Control Politics: The Connecticut River Valley Problem, 1927–50*. Cambridge: Harvard University Press, 1953.

Lord, Russell. *The Wallaces of Iowa*. Boston: Houghton Mifflin, 1947.

Marcello, Ronald Ely. "The North Carolina Works Progress Administration and the Politics of Relief." Ph.D. dissertation, Duke University, 1969.

Martin, Robert E. "Negro-White Participation in the AAA Cotton and Tobacco Referenda in North and South Carolina: A Study in Differential Voting and Attitudes in Selected Areas." Ph.D. dissertation, University of Chicago, 1947.

Martin, Roscoe C. *Grass Roots: Rural Democracy in America*. University: University of Alabama Press, 1957.

Mason, John E. "Acreage Allotments and Land Prices." *Journal of Land and Public Utility Economics* 22 (1946): 176–81.

May, Irvin, Jr. "Marvin Jones: Agrarian and Politician." *Agricultural History* 51 (1977): 421–40.

McConnell, Grant. *The Decline of Agrarian Democracy*. Berkeley: University of California Press, 1953.

Medlicott, William N. *History of the Second World War: The Economic Blockade*. Vol. 1. London: Her Majesty's Stationery Office, 1952.

Mertz, Paul E. *New Deal Policy and Southern Rural Poverty*. Baton Rouge: Louisiana State University Press, 1978.

Moore, John Robert. *Senator Josiah William Bailey of North Carolina*. Durham: Duke University Press, 1968.

Morgan, Thomas Sellers. "A Step towards Altruism: Relief and Welfare in North Carolina, 1930–1938." Ph.D. dissertation, University of North Carolina, 1968.

Morrison, Joseph L. *Josephus Daniels, the Small-d Democrat*. Chapel Hill: University of North Carolina Press, 1966.

————. *Governor O. Max Gardner: A Power in North Carolina and New Deal*

Washington. Chapel Hill: University of North Carolina Press, 1971.

Nicholls, William H. *Price Policies in the Cigarette Industry: A Study of "Concerted Action" and its Social Control*. Nashville: Vanderbilt University Press, 1951.

Noblin, Stuart. *The Grange in North Carolina, 1929–1954: A Story of Agricultural Progress*. Greensboro: North Carolina State Grange, 1954.

Nourse, Edwin G. *Marketing Agreements under the AAA*. Washington: Brookings Institution, 1935.

Nourse, Edwin G.; Davis, Joseph S.; and Black, John D. *Three Years of the Agricultural Adjustment Administration*. Washington: Brookings Institution, 1937.

Owen, Guy. *Journey for Joedel: A Novel*. New York: Crown, 1970.

Patterson, James T. *Congressional Conservatism and the New Deal: The Growth of the Conservative Coalition in Congress, 1933–1939*. Lexington: University of Kentucky Press, 1967.

_____. *The New Deal and the States: Federalism in Transition*. Princeton: Princeton University Press, 1969.

Peek, George N., with Crowther, Samuel. *Why Quit Our Own*. New York: Van Nostrand, 1936.

Perkins, Van L. *Crisis in Agriculture: The Agricultural Adjustment Administration and the New Deal, 1933*. Berkeley: University of California Press, 1969.

Pleasants, Julian McIver. "The Senatorial Career of Robert Rice Reynolds." Ph.D. dissertation, University of North Carolina, 1971.

Puryear, Elmer L. *Democratic Party Dissension in North Carolina, 1928–1936*. Chapel Hill: University of North Carolina Press, 1962.

Raper, Arthur F. *Preface to Peasantry: A Tale of Two Black Belt Counties*. Chapel Hill: University of North Carolina Press, 1936.

Richards, Henry I. *Cotton and the AAA*. Washington: Brookings Institution, 1936.

Robert, Joseph C. *The Story of Tobacco in America*. Chapel Hill: The University of North Carolina Press, 1967.

Rowe, Harold B. *Tobacco under the AAA*. Washington: Brookings Institution, 1935.

Rowley, William D. *M. L. Wilson and the Campaign for the Domestic Allotment*. Lincoln: University of Nebraska, 1970.

Saloutos, Theodore. *Farmer Movements in the South, 1865–1933*. Berkeley, University of California Press, 1960.

_____. "New Deal Agricultural Policy: An Evaluation." *Journal of American History* 61 (1974): 394–416.

Scanlon, John J.; and Tinley, J. M. *Business Analysis of the Tobacco Growers' Cooperative Association*. Washington: U.S. Government Printing Office, 1929.

Schuyler, Michael Wayne. "Agricultural Relief Activities of the Federal Government in the Middle West, 1933–1936." Ph.D. dissertation, University of Kansas, 1970.

Selznick, Philip. *TVA and the Grass Roots: A Study in the Sociology of Formal Organization*. Berkeley: University of California Press, 1949.

Shover, John L. *Cornbelt Rebellion: The Farmers' Holiday Association*. Urbana: University of Illinois Press, 1965.

Smith, Wilda M. "Reactions of Kansas Farmers to the New Deal Farm Program."
    Ph.D. dissertation, University of Illinois, 1960.
Snyder, Robert E. "Huey Long and the Cotton Holiday of 1931." *Louisiana History*
    18 (1977): 135–60.
Tennant, Richard B. *The American Cigarette Industry: A Study in Economic Analysis
    and Public Policy*. New Haven: Yale University Press, 1950.
Terrill, Tom E.; and Hirsch, Jerrold. *Such as Us: Southern Voices of the Thirties*.
    Chapel Hill: The University of North Carolina Press, 1978.
Tilley, Nannie May. *The Bright-Tobacco Industry, 1860–1929*. Chapel Hill: University
    of North Carolina Press, 1948.
Tobacco Associates, Inc. *Annual Report, 1964*. Raleigh: 1964.
———. *Annual Report, 1975*. Raleigh: 1975.
Tugwell, R. G.; and Banfield, E. C. "Grass-Roots Democracy—Myth or Reality?"
    Public Administration Review 10 (1950): 46–55.
Wallace, Henry A. *America Must Choose*. New York: Reynal and Hitchcock, 1934.
———. *New Frontiers*. New York: Foreign Policy Association, 1934.
Watson, Richard L., Jr. "A Southern Democratic Primary: Simmons vs Bailey in
    1930." *North Carolina Historical Review* 41 (1965): 21–46.
Weeks, L. T.; and Floyd, E. Y. *Producing and Marketing Flue-Cured Tobacco*.
    Raleigh: The Technical Press, 1941.
Whisehunt, Donald W. "Huey Long and the Texas Cotton Acreage Control Law of
    1931." *Louisiana Studies* 13 (1974): 142–53.
Wickens, David L.; and Forster, G. W. *Farm Credit in North Carolina: Its Cost, Risk
    and Management*. Raleigh: North Carolina Agricultural Experiment Station
    Bulletin no. 270, 1930.
Wilcox, Walter W. *The Farmer in the Second World War*. Ames: Iowa State College
    Press, 1947.
Williams, T. Harry. *Huey Long*. New York: Knopf, 1970.
Williamson, J. C., Jr.; and Toussaint, William D. "Parity and Support Prices for
    Flue-Cured Tobacco." *Journal of Farm Economics* 43 (1961): 13–26.
Wolters, Raymond. *Negroes and the Great Depression: The Problem of Economic
    Recovery*. Westport: Greenwood Press, 1970.
Woofter, T. J., Jr. *The Plight of Cigarette Tobacco*. Chapel Hill: The University of
    North Carolina Press, 1931.
———. *Landlord and Tenant on the Cotton Plantation*. Washington: Works Progress
    Administration, 1936.
Wooten, Hugh Hill. *Credit Problems of North Carolina Cropper Families*. Raleigh:
    North Carolina Agricultural Experiment Station Bulletin no. 271, 1930.
Zinn, Howard, ed. *New Deal Thought*. Indianapolis: Bobbs-Merrill, 1966.

Index